Do Arrests and Restraining Orders Work?

Editors

Eve S. Buzawa
Carl G. Buzawa

SAGE Publications
International Educational and Professional Publisher
Thousand Oaks   London   New Delhi

For information address:

 SAGE Publications, Inc.
2455 Teller Road
Thousand Oaks, California 91320
E-mail: order@sagepub.com

SAGE Publications Ltd.
6 Bonhill Street
London EC2A 4PU
United Kingdom

SAGE Publications India Pvt. Ltd.
M-32 Market
Greater Kailash I
New Delhi 110 048 India

Printed in the United States of America

Library of Congress Cataloging-in-Publication Data

Main entry under title:
Do arrests and restraining orders work? / editors, Eve S. Buzawa, Carl
  G. Buzawa.
    p. cm.
  Includes bibliographical references and index.
  ISBN 0-8039-7072-2 (acid-free paper). — ISBN 0-8039-7073-0
  (pbk. : acid-free paper)
    1. Conjugal violence—United States—Prevention. 2. Arrest—
United States. 3. Injunctions—United States. I. Buzawa, Eva
Schlesinger. II. Buzawa, Carl G.
  HV6626.2.D6 1996
  364.1'5553—dc20   95-41792

96 97 98 99 10 9 8 7 6 5 4 3 2 1

This book is printed on acid-free paper.

Sage Production Editor: Diana E. Axelsen
Sage Typesetter: Danielle Dillahunt

Contents

1

Introduction

EVE S. BUZAWA

CARL G. BUZAWA

EXTENT OF THE PROBLEM

Domestic violence is clearly a major problem in contemporary American society. Estimates of its extent are, of necessity, inexact, with "official" statistics not accepted as definitive. With the exception of cases resulting in homicides, no reliable criminal justice statistics document the rate of serious domestic violence incidents. This lack has made it difficult to develop a statistical base for estimating rates of victimization and therefore for evaluating whether any particular criminal justice agency is doing an adequate job at representing the needs of victims.

We believe that levels of "minor" domestic violence are staggeringly high. The National Criminal Victimization Survey (NCVS) estimated that during each year between 1987 and 1991, on average, women were the victims of more than 572,000 violent victimizations committed by an intimate, compared with approximately 49,000 incidents committed against men. About one in five females

1

victimized by her spouse or former spouse reported that, in the past 6 months, she had been a victim of a series of three or more assaults that were so similar that she could not distinguish them. For assaults in general, fewer than 1 in 10 victimization involved this type of serial victimization (Bureau of Justice Statistics, 1994). Such incidents were widespread, with 16% of married or cohabiting couples experiencing physical violence, and slightly more than 3% suffering severe abuse in any given year (Straus & Gelles, 1990).

The type of violence itself presents a challenge to agencies seeking to eradicate violence. The National Family Violence Resurvey (Straus & Gelles, 1986) found that 39% of all violence toward wives were serious incidents involving repeat punching with a fist, kicking, biting, beatings, and attacks with knives and guns, all types of incidents that could logically warrant a criminal justice response. And such violence is not wholly concentrated among a few families that police could actively monitor. One study estimated that approximately 16% of American couples have been involved in incidents of family violence that included punching, kicking, and attacks with an object or a weapon (Straus & Gelles, 1986).

Incidents of domestic violence are not merely a problem of one particular social class. Although most criminal justice involvement has been with the lower socioeconomic groups, numerous researchers have noted that the stress of being indigent, the relative lack of adaptive nonviolence skills, and increased rates of substance abuse may result in higher levels of domestic violence in lower socioeconomic groups but that acts of familial violence are by no means restricted to this group (Bassett, 1980; Coates & Leong, 1980; Ferraro, 1989; Hart et al., 1984; U.S. Department of Justice, 1984). In fact, even the American Medical Association, in 1992, noted that doctors simply did not recognize widespread signs of abuse in middle-class patients. It stated that because many doctors were white, middle- to upper-class males, they were particularly subject to denying abuse from men with whom they could identify.

THE TOLL OF VIOLENCE

The high number of assaults has resulted in massive numbers of dead and injured victims. According to the FBI (1992), about 15%

of the murders in 1992 for which the relationship between victim and assailant was known involved a victim described in police records as an intimate—that is, spouse, former spouse, boyfriend, or girlfriend of the killer (Bureau of Justice Statistics, 1994).

The rates are far higher if only female victims are considered. Unpublished data from the *Supplementary Homicide Report* collected as part of the Uniform Crime Reporting Program of the FBI show that, from 1980 to 1991, over 50% of women age 18 or older who were killed were killed by a husband, former husband, common-law husband, or boyfriend (Carmody & Williams, 1987).

It has been estimated that, each year, approximately 1.5 million women and 500,000 men require medical attention because of a domestic assault, more than half of which necessitate hospital visits or stays (Straus & Gelles, 1986).

The impact of domestic violence is far higher than the physical injury itself. Victims often become emotionally traumatized, with subsequent high rates of medical complaints, psychosocial problems, and disproportionate risks of rape, miscarriage, abortion, alcohol and drug abuse, general mental illness, and attempted suicide, the latter at a rate five times as high as in the general population. Furthermore, it appears that the evidence of mental illness starts after the abuse, not as a cluster of which abuse is merely one factor.

Children are almost as vulnerable as the original victim. One estimate is that approximately 3.3 million children witness acts of domestic violence each year. Despite the victim trying to hide acts of violence from the children, one study found that children were present in almost half of all battery incidents; thus, children of abusive families are the "hidden victims." It is noteworthy that this victimization may manifest itself in a later tendency to become either a victim or a victimizer. Thus, battered women were found to be 6 times as likely to have witnessed violence as a child than adult batterers; batterers originate largely in abusive homes, being 10 times as likely than other children to become abusers themselves (Kalmuss, 1984; Rosenbaum & O'Leary, 1981; Star, 1978). Children who witness violence also are lower in social competency and higher in depression, anxiety, aggression, shyness, and other school problems (Wolfe, Jaffe, Wilson, & Zak, 1985). In addition and in perhaps the most chilling prospect, witnessing parental violence is highly correlated with subsequent suicide attempts of children. One study found that 65% of children who had attempted suicide had previously witnessed family violence (Kosky, 1983).

Why have we restated the prevalence and toll of domestic violence? These figures are, after all, depressingly known to those who seek to cope with its aftermath and to those with a purely academic interest. It is because we recognize that any policy advocated must be prepared with full realization of the magnitude of the problem in the service community. Any shortcut to such understanding may invite policy nostrums or administrative fiats imposed without any real chance of success. This prospect results in a high probability of failure and subsequent bitterness and cynicism of both victims and service providers.

ROLE OF THE
CRIMINAL JUSTICE SYSTEM

Since empirical research on domestic violence began in the 1970s, it has become clear that, without societal intervention, significant percentages of domestic violence cases escalate into more serious incidents. Unfortunately, although virtually all observers acknowledged the importance of the police and prosecutors in the control of such crimes, by the early 1970s it was also widely observed that their practices had been of limited effectiveness. It was a truism that police used their discretion to avoid arresting domestic violence offenders whenever possible. The police as an institution were repeatedly criticized for neglecting opportunities to deter future acts of violence and for generally failing to respond to urgent requests for assistance by victims.

Prosecutors shared the same biases toward inaction as police. They perceived that discretion was an integral component of their job and applied this to filter out cases lacking sufficient public purpose to prosecute. In effect, prosecutorial discretion historically has been used to eliminate not only weak cases but also those considered unimportant. To the extent that misdemeanor domestic violence was judged to be an insignificant crime (yet dangerous to the safety and trivial to the career of responding officials), the strong bias to defer and minimize agency response is not surprising.

Although the criminal justice response to domestic violence was clearly not ideal, this did not mean it would be altered. Researchers and practitioners had long acknowledged performance failures, but traditional responses remained relatively unchanged for literally decades. Before the late 1970s, the statutory structure for handling domestic violence could charitably be described as "benevolent neglect" of a "family problem." State assistance, to the limited extent provided, went to traditional social welfare agencies handling a variety of family problems. Until relatively recently, the problem was never formulated as resulting from persistent neglect of governments to perform their responsibilities.

Agencies acted in concert with the statutory scheme. Police departments as institutions (and to a lesser extent, prosecutors) were known to be remarkably resistant to change and thus made street-level implementation of any directives problematic at best. Compounding this problem was the failure of key actors (practitioners, researchers, and feminist-activists) to agree on the goals and methods to be used to control violence.

CHANGE IN THE SYSTEM

Despite such problems, in the 1970s the criminal justice system commenced a series of reforms resulting in substantial structural and (to a somewhat lesser extent) operational changes. From the late 1970s to date, an almost unprecedented wave of statutory change sought to alter official reaction to domestic violence. During this time, all states have enacted legislation designed to modify official behavior. Such legislation, often the result of the interplay of pressure from feminist groups, actions of concerned legislators, and professionals in the criminal justice system, has markedly changed the underlying legal philosophy toward this problem.

Although differing greatly in their scope and limitations, the new statutes expressly sought profound structural change in the response of governmental agencies to domestic violence. Major improvements were enacted: removal of procedural barriers to official action, new substantive domestic violence laws, increased use of arrests of and prior restraints on known offenders, and development of court-sponsored mediation and counseling programs.

Not surprisingly, police were challenged to intervene more proactively and to use their new arrest powers to an extent not previously contemplated. District attorneys were told that "the policy of the state" was to intervene earlier and more effectively than in the past. Federally funded demonstration projects and training programs consistently emphasized the benefits of aggressive early intervention. Unfortunately, the process of institutionalizing change never received adequate attention from these "change agents." As a result, a pattern of mandating changes has been decoupled from the administrative detail sufficient to ensure actual change.

For those agencies still resistant (or when results did not demonstrate immediate change), pressure mounted to limit the discretion of "obviously" recalcitrant officers and bureaucracies. The result has been the proliferation of statutory and administrative restrictions on the autonomy of police officers—so-called mandatory arrest rules—and limits on the previously largely unbridled power of prosecutors to drop cases. Although this can be argued as being far superior to the alternative, the application of discretion by an unsympathetic bureaucracy and the failure to critically focus on implementation strategies may have led to inadequate, simplistic solutions that do not fix the problem and that may even lead to new problems. As a result, new crimes, such as stalking, may at worst be at least partially related to inadequate past attempts at control.

All of this effort is well intentioned and clearly superior to past practices of not so benign neglect. Our primary concern is that, to a large extent, we as criminal justice researchers cannot with authority tell decision makers the most effective method of responding to domestic violence. This is becoming a critically important gap in our knowledge. Arrest, the method most advocated by battered women's activists, imposes heavy costs to the agency as well as to the assailant and often, paradoxically, to the victim and her family. Another method, that of liberally granting restraining orders and then actively prosecuting their violation, has been proposed as being more cost effective for many offenders and as a means for protecting victims.

THE CHAPTERS

The chapters in this volume help fill in this gap by addressing several key policy issues: the proper role of arrest and to what degree the prosecution can rely on restraining orders as a relatively low-cost technique to prevent future violence.

A number of the chapters were originally derived from the May/June 1993 special edition of the *American Behavioral Scientist*, which was devoted to the impact of arrest on domestic assault. Since this journal was published, the publisher and the authors have received many requests for reprints and publication in a book format; the result is this project.

In addition to the police-focused articles, we have supplemented this research with several key contributions to the study of specific actions taken by officers of the courts: prosecutors, the judiciary, and probation officers. Not only does this research have intrinsic merit, but there is also a growing recognition that it may be too simplistic to focus on the impact of any particular criminal justice response on domestic violence. Although in the past, research did legitimately focus on the impact of a particular intervention strategy, we now realize that such strategies may achieve markedly different results, depending on the actions taken by other key players in the criminal justice system. The new contributions present a wide variety of research methods and analyses and, befitting an area of much dispute, often reach markedly different conclusions.

Murray A. Straus presents a brief theoretical analysis of the various potential criminal justice interventions in cases of spousal assault. His suggestion for the use of the empirically based Conflict Tactics Scales (CTS) to classify cases of domestic violence may prove a valuable alternative to what has been an imperfect practice—that of typologizing violence. The integration of the CTS or similar vehicles into criminal justice agency policies may prove important to both criminal justice agencies and policy researchers who are confronted with a bewildering variety of nonstandardized and often highly subjective official forms and reports and the need to try to standardize treatments based on such typologies.

Four chapters focus on the ongoing discussion of whether arrest practices can deter future violence. Richard J. Gelles discusses the seminal work in this area, the Minneapolis Domestic Violence Experiment. He explores the methodological limitations of that study and casts considerable doubt on the speedy implementation of mandatory arrest policies that swept the country thereafter. In doing so, he brings a highly effective critical perspective on the effect of social science research studies and how these may prematurely influence policy.

Janell D. Schmidt and Lawrence W. Sherman, in a major reversal of past positions, suggest that the role of arrest as a deterrent to domestic violence is deeply flawed. Their critique of the 1981 Minneapolis experiment (coauthored by Sherman) and analysis of the "replication" studies are informative, as well as provocative.

In a new chapter written specifically for this volume, J. David Hirschel and Ira W. Hutchison cover the Charlotte experiment, one of the six replication studies conducted for the National Institute of Justice in response to the Minneapolis experiment. They found that the offender's prior criminal activity accounted for much of the variance in rates of recidivism, whereas other sociodemographic variables, such as race, age, marital status, and employment, were not significant. After analyzing prevalence, incidence, and time to failure data, they conclude that arrest may not be an effective deterrent to future abuse. In a particularly well-reasoned analysis, however, they explain why they disagree with Sherman's conclusion that their data demonstrate clear escalation after arrest.

In a final chapter on deterrence, Peter K. Manning expresses consternation over its current emphasis on judging the proper role of arrest. He finds this misplaced and questions the frequent assumption that the criminal justice system is responsible for and capable of ensuring deterrence for criminal offenses. Furthermore, he properly critiques the use of official data as a measure of the concept of deterrence.

Using a different orientation, Barbara Hart provides an overview of issues from the perspective of the battered women entering the criminal justice system. She emphasizes the need for a more flexible and responsive system because domestic violence victims, like those of other violent crimes, do not all have the same needs or desire the same outcomes.

Evan Stark presents a continuation and elaboration of his earlier critiques of the arrest-related chapters. His well-reasoned analysis presents a spirited rejoinder to the basic orientation of many, if not all, of the foregoing chapters questioning new aggressive arrest policies. His analysis typologizes and responds to the various critiques of such policies.

In addition to disputes over the proper role of arrests, another controversy has arisen over whether police act neutrally when deciding whether to make an arrest. Thus, acknowledged differences in the rate of arrest between cases involving stranger assaults and domestic cases have been claimed by Elliott, Sherman, and others to merely reflect situational differences; for example, the police act in the same manner when confronted with the same type of domestic or nondomestic assault. In this volume, Thomas L. Austin and we present a study examining differential arrest practices for victims of domestic and stranger assaults. Using police reports (considered by many to be intrinsically "biased" toward the police version of facts), we found that arrests were between 1.5 and 3.5 times as likely to occur in stranger assaults than in domestic cases even when controlling for victim preferences and several other key variables.

In this volume, we also supplement our earlier discussion of the role of arrests with studies about various initiatives being undertaken by prosecutors, the judiciary, and probation departments. The first of these chapters, written by Donald J. Rebovich, presents the results of data generated from 142 prosecutors' offices in a national mail survey conducted by the American Prosecutors Research Institute. His survey describes existing domestic violence programs, the prosecutorial perception of obstacles to their successful functioning, and what is necessary to address these shortcomings. He reports that victims' attitudes toward criminal justice intervention often complicated the task of subsequent effective prosecution (in only 12% of cases did the victim, rather than the police, initiate the case, and a high percentage of victims did not want to serve as witnesses). In addition to presenting findings about victim interactions with the system, Rebovich presents a survey of prosecutors' opinions on the effect of various remedies available to these court officers. For example, many prosecutors he surveyed relied on protective orders, yet only 11% found them highly effective.

To determine whether Rebovich's observation of the perceived utility of restraining orders is a universal phenomenon or, instead, the result of a prosecutorial system in flux, we include a chapter by Andrew R. Klein that focuses on the effect of restraining orders on new acts of abuse in Quincy, Massachusetts. This court's domestic violence program has served as a national model program of a mandatory integrated response.

Unlike the cases Rebovich found that were brought to the prosecutors' attention, police were involved in just over 10% of cases in Quincy wherein victims obtained restraining orders. Despite this and other differences, it is clear that restraining orders often do not work to deter future violence; in the Quincy case, almost half of the victims were re-abused within 2 years of the restraining order, and 34% of the batterers were arrested for abuse. Klein also raises the interesting point that the criminal justice system may be trying to cope with a distinct, far more dangerous subset of batterers for whom other, less punitive measures may not be effective. Although most batterers in general may not have criminal records, the majority of batterers brought to court by their victims for restraining orders did. Although almost half of the women dropped their restraining orders prior to the 1-year termination, no differences were found in the rate of re-abuse from those victims who maintained their orders for the full period. Therefore, Klein concludes, restraining orders are not adequate protection for women and children from future abuse.

Adele Harrell and Barbara E. Smith report on a survey of 335 women who filed petitions for temporary restraining orders (TROs). Like Klein, they examined the impact of TROs on future acts of abuse against victims who earlier had been the target of severe acts of abuse. Of policy interest is their finding that the severity of the incident causing the request for an order did not predict the victims' subsequent risk; however, the profile of their victimization during the previous year did. In addition, the authors report that victims who sought to obtain permanent restraining orders experienced a great deal of difficulty in doing so.

A major thrust of reform for responding to domestic violence has been to more aggressively involve the criminal justice system. This assumes that informal social norms are themselves failures. The focus of attention has been on forcing the criminal justice system to recognize and take responsibility for responding to acts of domestic violence.

David A. Ford, Ruth Reichard, Stephen Goldsmith, and Mary Jean Regoli close this volume with their chapter on future directions for criminal justice policy on domestic violence.

RESEARCH AND POLICY IMPLICATIONS

Although it is far too early to draw any definitive conclusions from individual studies, the chapters in this volume raise the disturbing possibility that the goals and methods of having the criminal justice system respond to domestic violence may not be adequate. Studies on arrest collectively tend to show that deterrence, to the extent that it is the relevant variable and has been the focus of many advocates, may be greatly increased by arrest. Similarly, Klein (Chapter 11) and Harrell and Smith (Chapter 12) suggest that one of the primary new tools of prosecutors, that of aggressive use of restraining orders, may not be effective.

Perhaps a new orientation needs to be developed. Agency personnel should be aware that certain batterers disproportionately tend to become involved in the criminal justice system and are not deterred from future violence by "normal" methods of achieving deterrence." For these people, the act of being arrested may be of no consequence because they, as a group, have been arrested many times in the past. At the same time, even in the very disciplined environment of a model court, for a high percentage of offenders the imposition of a restraining order simply does not deter violent behavior. The criminal justice system must develop the capabilities to identify those batterers for whom normal deterrence can be effective, perhaps the majority in terms of number of incidents. It should also be able to differentiate, segregate, and incapacitate batterers who must be deterred by special approaches.

Perhaps we should also become more cognizant that the concept of deterrence has not been fully measured to date and perhaps can never be measured through the impact of one variable, such as arrest or a restraining order. What is needed is an assessment of how many potential batterers are deterred through other means—for example, public education in conflict avoidance, legislation making domestic violence a criminal offense, publicizing a proarrest policy by the police force, and availability and enforcement of restraining orders. It is, after all, only for that subpopulation that we are now studying the actual impact of the criminal justice system on rate of future criminal activity.

Given the pressure for cost-effective use of limited resources, further research must be conducted on determining what percentage of potential offenders is deterred from abusive behavior at each point before and after intervention of the police, the courts, and the probation system. From such analysis, we can come much closer to assessing the proper application and mix of resources to be applied.

It may also be incumbent on advocates of an aggressive domestic violence response to realize the limitations of the criminal justice system as most probably exist. In other words, although some advocates might prefer to see social work type police officers adroitly respond to every assault in a compassionate and resolute manner, the reality may be that the system cannot cope as well as they might like. We must be aware that because of the population of assailants the criminal justice system encounters—those not yet deterred by increasingly well publicized proarrest policies—a high percentage will not be dissuaded from future violence. Similarly, restraining orders may only have a modest impact on hard-core offenders. We would ask that advocates of mandatory arrest and no-drop policies, policies designed to limit the discretion of both the criminal justice system and victims, should reconsider whether this policy is in the victims' best interests and whether the victims' preferences should be given more preference. The possible fundamental conflict of interest between society's interests and those of the victims should be acknowledged.

Mandatory processing of an offender who may find a new victim may be justified to prevent victimization of others. We look forward to essays acknowledging the existence and resolution of this dilemma.

REFERENCES

Bassett, S. (1980). *Battered rich.* Port Washington, NY: Ashley.

Bureau of Justice Statistics. (1994). *Violence between intimates.* Washington, DC: U.S. Department of Justice.

Carmody, D. C., & Williams, K. R. (1987). Wife assault and perceptions of sanctions. *Violence and Victims, 2*(1), 25-38.

Coates, C. J., & Leong, D. J. (1980). *Conflict and communication for women and men in battering relationships* (Report for the Denver Anti-Crime Council). Washington, DC: U.S. Department of Justice.

Federal Bureau of Investigation (FBI). (1992, December). *Crime in the U.S.: 1991.* Washington, DC: U.S. Department of Justice.

Ferraro, K. (1989). The legal response to women battering in the United States. In J. Hamner, J. Radford, & E. Stanko (Eds.), *Women, policing, and male violence* (pp. 155-184). London: Routledge & Kegan Paul.

Hart, W., Ashcroft, J., Burgess, A., Flanagan, N., Meese, C., Milton, C., Narramores, C., Ortega, R., & Steward, F. (1984). *Attorney General's Task Force on Family Violence.* Washington, DC: Government Printing Office.

Kalmuss, D. (1984). The intergenerational transmission of marital aggression. *Journal of Marriage and the Family, 46,* 11-19.

Kosky, R. (1983). Childhood suicidal behavior. *Journal of Child Psychology and Psychiatry and Allied Disciplines, 24,* 457-468.

Rosenbaum, A., & O'Leary, K. D. (1981). Marital violence: Characteristics of abusive couples. *Journal of Consulting and Clinical Psychology, 49,* 63-71.

Star, B. (1978). Comparing battered and nonbattered women. *Victimology, 3*(1-2), 32-44.

Straus, M. A., & Gelles, R. J. (1986). Societal change and change in family violence from 1975 to 1985 as revealed by two national surveys. *Journal of Marriage and the Family, 48,* 465-479.

Straus, M. A., & Gelles, R. J. (1990). How violent are American families? Estimates from the National Family Violence Resurvey and other studies. In M. A. Straus & R. J. Gelles (Eds.), *Physical violence in American families: Risk factors and adaptation in 8,145 families* (pp. 95-112). New Brunswick, NJ: Transaction Books.

U.S. Department of Justice. (1984). *Attorney General's Task Force on Family Violence: Final report.* Washington, DC: Author.

Wolfe, D. A., Jaffe, P., Wilson, S. K., & Zak, I. (1985). Children of battered women: The relation of child behavior to family violence and maternal stress. *Journal of Consulting and Clinical Psychology, 53,* 657-665.

2

Identifying Offenders in Criminal Justice Research on Domestic Assault

MURRAY A. STRAUS

In this chapter, I identify sampling and measurement problems that need to be addressed if research on domestic assault from a criminal justice perspective is to take into account differences in severity and chronicity. Such differences are important to consider because they affect the appropriateness of various criminal justice system inter-ventions. I describe ways in which some of these measurement problems can be dealt with by use of the Conflict Tactics Scales (CTS; Straus, 1979, 1990a) in conjunction with a checklist (pre-sented in this chapter) to help identify relevant cases.

CRITERIA FOR
CRIMINAL JUSTICE INTERVENTION

I have advocated involving the criminal justice system in cases of domestic assault since the mid 1970s (Straus, 1976). I also recognized, however, that incarceration is not likely to end spousal assault any more than it ends other crime. Nevertheless, at some point in the continuum ranging from occasional slaps and shoves to beatings or even to murder, a decision must be made whether to seek criminal penalties.

The 1975 and 1985 National Family Violence Surveys found that about one third of the 8,145 couples studied experienced one or more physical assaults on a spouse in the course of the marriage (Straus & Gelles, 1990). These are lower-bound estimates. The true figure may be as high as two out of three American couples (Straus, Gelles, & Steinmetz, 1980, pp. 35-36). In most cases, however, the assaults were minor, such as slapping and plate throwing, and such incidents tended to occur relatively infrequently over the course of the marriage.

Both moral and practical considerations require condemnation of even the most minor assaults and intervention to end such behavior. However, that does not necessarily mean criminal penalties. If even half of domestic assaults came to the attention of the police, the courts would have to deal with literally millions of such incidents and would be overwhelmed. In addition, there are grounds for questioning the appropriateness of applying criminal penalties in all cases of spousal assault.

As Straus and Lincoln (1985) noted, it is not at all certain that families and society would be better off if the same standards were used to control crime within the family as well as outside the family. For one thing, in the case of the family, society has conflicting interests. In addition to the interest in maintaining a "civil" society in which citizens can live without fear of victimization, society has an interest in encouraging and protecting the family as a social institution and for the well-being of the entire family group. Consequently, there is a reluctance to take punitive actions that, however justified on other grounds, might break up a family or punish other members of the family as much as or more than the offender.

A related question about applying the same criminal justice system procedures to intrafamily crime as to strangers arises because families are different from individuals and other groups in many ways, including legal status. Crime is only one of many types of behavior for which there are different rules and expectations for the family as compared with other groups or situations. These differences are part of what makes the family a unique and important institution. For example, the family is concerned with "the whole person," not just some specific aspect of the person. A university department chair will be concerned about things related to the faculty members' teaching and scholarship, whereas the family will be concerned not only with job performance but also with religion, politics, and friends.

Even if the same norms about assault and other crimes are applied within the family, there may be good reason for not involving the legal system in enforcing those norms. The police and the courts cannot be expected to understand the unique circumstances of each family, and they cannot be depended on to take actions that are in the best interest of the victim, the offender, or the family as a whole.

Finally, the issue of assaults by women on male partners is difficult and controversial. More than 20 investigations have shown that women carry out such assaults at about the same rate as men (summarized in Straus & Gelles, 1990) and that, in about half the cases, women are the first to physically assault (Straus, in press). If criminal penalties are to be applied to men who "only" slap their wives a few times, should they also be applied to the equally great number of women who do this?

CONFLICT TACTICS SCALES

The above discussion suggests the need for standardized methods of classifying cases of spousal assault that correspond to the legal distinctions between simple and aggravated assault. Consequently, I outline here[1] ways of using the Conflict Tactics Scales (CTS; Straus, 1979, 1990a; Straus, Hamby, Boney-McCoy, & Sugerman, 1996) and a supplemental checklist to identify cases involving chronic and severe assaults for which there would be little question concerning the need for criminal penalties.

The CTS takes only a few minutes to administer, either within an interview or as a self-administered questionnaire, and is presented in the chapter appendix. It has been used in two national surveys (Straus & Gelles, 1990; Straus et al., 1980) and in more than 100 studies, including those within the criminal justice system (e.g., Dutton, 1988; Ford, 1991). A test manual containing more than 300 references to the CTS and documentation of validity and reliability is available (Straus, 1989). The assessment needs of the criminal justice system, however, are often different. I therefore here describe ways of using the CTS to classify cases into what are believed to be categories helpful for research on such issues as whether diversion to treatment programs is advisable and the level of surveillance that may be needed.

The CTS has three scales: Reasoning, Verbal Aggression, and Physical Aggression or Violence. The Violence items are further subdivided into "minor" and "severe" violence (see appendix). The minor violence items are K, L, and M. The severe violence items, N through S, are believed to have a greater danger of causing an injury that needs medical treatment. I describe here a checklist that can be used in conjunction with the CTS to identify a level of violence for which criminal justice intervention is most urgently needed. This third level of violence is labeled *high risk*.

CRIMINAL JUSTICE'S
SYSTEM-RELEVANT MEASUREMENT

Although large areas overlap, the measurement needs of basic research and of criminal justice system researchers and practitioners tend to be different, sometimes in surprising ways. Space constraints permit discussion of only four of these.

Level of Measurement

Every course in statistics and research methods stresses the superiority of interval or ratio measurement over nominal-level measurement. This follows from the emphasis on the mean and measures of covariance because those techniques work best with interval or ratio-level measurement. Criminal justice system research, however, often needs to classify cases into groups that correspond to case-processing categories. Consequently, nominal-level measurement will usually be the most appropriate.[2]

Noncomparability of Criminal Justice
and Community Populations

The characteristics of a "clinical" population, in this case an apprehended offender population, often differ from the characteristics of those in the general population who manifest the same problematic behavior. Following are some examples.

The characteristics associated with abuse of the elderly among a representative sample of persons 65 years of age and older in the Boston metropolitan area studied by Pillemer and Finkelhor (1988) differ in important ways from the characteristics associated with abuse cases known to the adult protective services departments of the states as reported by Steinmetz (1988). Pillemer and Finkelhor found that the victims tend to be men in their 70s who are assaulted by their wives, whereas Steinmetz found that the victims tend to be older, widowed women. She suggested that the difference arises because the minor assaults of elderly women on their husbands rarely produce the type of injury that will bring a case to the attention of adult protective services.

Discrepancies have been found between alcoholics identified among the general population and alcoholism in treatment samples (Room, 1980). For example, alcoholics in the general population tend to be young, whereas alcoholics in treatment tend to be middle-aged or older.

In the case of drug abuse, 85% to 90% of cocaine users do not become addicted (Gawin, 1992), and it is likely that those who do become addicted differ from those who do not in a number of important social and psychological characteristics.

Psychologists distinguish between people suffering from major depression and those suffering from so-called subclinical depression found by epidemiological surveys of the general population.

In research on crime, data from studies of incarcerated persons may be misleading because they are analogous to studies on business using samples of businesses that have failed. The findings may not apply to the large number of persons who commit a certain type of crime and are not apprehended and incarcerated.

The discrepancy between the characteristics of survey populations and clinical populations in research on alcoholism, depression, and elder abuse illustrates what has been termed the "clinical fallacy" or "the clinician's illusion" (Cohen & Cohen, 1984). The coin has two sides, however; there is also a "researcher's fallacy" or a "representative sample fallacy" (Straus, 1990b). That is, there is an equal hazard in generalizing from a representative sample of a community to a clinical population (an identified offender population). The findings from community samples may represent the community, but they do not represent a population of identified offenders. They tend to be low-rate or single-instance offenders, whereas identified offender populations usually consist mainly of long-duration offenders because the probability that a case will appear in the sample is proportional to the duration of offending behavior (Cohen & Cohen, 1984). Because single-instance or low-rate offenders tend to differ from repeat offenders in many other ways, findings based on community samples may not apply to cases processed through the criminal justice system. To the extent that is correct, it is necessary to identify the differences in the characteristics of domestic assault offenders identified by these two processes; they are likely to have important implications for criminal justice system practice.

Antecedents and Consequences

It follows from the above discussion that the antecedents and consequences of violence determined in a general population sample of violent persons may not apply to apprehended violent offenders. Therefore, to extrapolate from a community sample to a criminal justice sample runs the risk of the "representative sample fallacy" noted above. Consequently, studies of nationally representative population samples, such as the National Family Violence Surveys (Straus & Gelles, 1990), may not be an appropriate guide for procedures to be used by the police and other elements of the criminal justice system. For example, findings on the perceived deterrent effect of various sanctions (Carmody & Williams, 1987) may not apply to an identified offender population.

Test Norms

Another implication of the difference between offenders identified by epidemiological surveys and apprehended offenders is that norms for tests, such as the CTS, based on community samples may not be appropriate for evaluating cases already known to be violent. In that situation, the question is not the presence or absence of violence, but how serious it is. The distribution of scores for known offenders may start about where the community case distribution ends (Straus, 1990b). Norms based on community samples may have too limited a range of scores to be useful. Thus, the appropriate normative reference point for classifying cases may not be a large and representative sample of the population, but rather a sample of apprehended cases.

IDENTIFICATION OF
HIGH-RISK VIOLENCE

When the issue is one of identifying offenders who pose an ongoing risk of future severe assaults on a spouse, the CTS distinction between severe and minor violence is not by itself adequate to identify the extreme and often life-threatening level of violence that characterizes these men. Factor analyses of the CTS have repeatedly shown that Items R and S, both of which refer to use of weapons, form a separate factor from the other Violence items (Straus, 1979, 1990a). Use of these two items by themselves is not adequate to identify high-risk cases, however, because although the use of a weapon is a definitive indicator, it is only one of many indicators and therefore will fail to detect many cases. Fortunately, a number of studies of extreme marital violence provide information that can be used to identify high-risk cases. These include studies of abusers murdered by their victims (Browne, 1987), partners of battered women in shelters (Giles-Sims, 1983; Okun, 1986), court-referred male offenders (Gondolf, 1988; Hamberger & Hastings, 1991; Saunders, 1992), and convicted homicide offenders (Goetting, 1989, 1991).

The ability to identify the presence of this third level of violence is important because such cases require immediate and decisive intervention. It is difficult to find an appropriate term for such extreme violence. Because a distinguishing characteristic of this level of violence is the risk of serious bodily harm or death, I identify it as high-risk violence.

Criteria for High-Risk Violence

As explained above, the Violence Index of the CTS is not sufficient to identify cases posing a high risk. The checklist in Table 2.1 therefore was developed to identify cases posing such a risk. The checklist is based on studies of cases of extreme violence, including studies of partners of battered women in shelters (Giles-Sims, 1983; Okun, 1986), of abusers murdered by their victims (Browne, 1987),

TABLE 2.1 Checklist for Identifying "High-Risk" Cases

Criterion A
   Initiated three or more instances of violence in previous year

Criterion B
   Threatened partner with a weapon in hand or threatened to kill partner
   Medical treatment needed by victim (regardless of whether it was obtained)
   Physical abuse of a child
   Physical abuse when a child
   Severe violence between parents
   Drunk five or more times in past year
   Drug abuse in past year
   Extreme dominance or attempts to achieve such dominance
   Thinks there are some situations when it is OK for a man to hit his wife
   Physically forced sex on partner
   Extensive or repeated destruction of property
   Threats or actual killing or injuring a pet
   History of psychological problems
   Assault of a nonfamily person or other violent crime
   Extreme jealousy and surveillance or restriction of partner
   Police involved in domestic assault incident in previous 12 months

SOURCE: Adapted from Aldarondo and Straus, 1992.

and of court-referred cases (Gondolf, 1988; Hamberger & Hastings, 1991; Saunders, 1992; Tolman & Bennett, 1990), and the Danger Assessment Checklist of Stuart and Campbell (1989). It must be emphasized that the checklist, though based on published studies of serious offenders, has not been validated by empirical research. With this caution in mind, men who meet both Criteria A and B as listed in Table 2.1 are suggested as cases that pose a high risk.

Criterion A

The criterion of three or more assaults during the previous 12 months was selected on the assumption that once or perhaps even twice might reflect a transient condition but that a third time would indicate an ongoing problem. The importance of chronicity was confirmed by analyses of covariance computed for the 645 violent men in the 1985 National Family Violence Survey.

These analyses indicated that chronicity of assaults accounted for more of the variance in the dependent variable than did the severity of assaults.

Criterion B

Criterion B is the presence of a certain number of the characteristics listed. Research is needed on whether that should be one or two of the characteristics, three of them, or possibly even four. In the absence of such research, researchers using the checklist will need to experiment with analyzing their data by using one, two, three, and four characteristics to determine which seems to be the most appropriate.

It is important to note that the number of cases meeting the high-risk criteria is a small fraction of the total number, probably less than 10% of all violent couples. The appropriate role of criminal justice intervention may be quite different for the 90% of wife assaulters who do not fit into the high-risk category. Diversion to family therapy, for example, may be appropriate for that group, but for the high-risk group, family therapy may have little effect and might put the spouse at increased risk of further and more serious assaults.

HIGH-RISK VIOLENCE AND
THE DISPUTE OVER FEMINIST VERSUS
FAMILY THERAPY INTERVENTION MODELS

A major reason for differentiating cases of high-risk violence from other patterns of marital violence is the assumption that high-risk cases require a different intervention. If this is correct, it can help in dealing with the often bitter controversy between advocates of the feminist and family therapy models of appropriate interventions.

The *feminist model* emerged from the battered women's shelter movement. It assumes that the fundamental cause of marital violence is the patriarchal social order, including a patriarchal family structure, and that men are the offenders and women the victims. It therefore stresses empowering women, the criminal prosecution of assaultive men, and the necessity of separate programs for men and women. From this perspective, couples therapy not only is inappropriate but also exposes women victims to further exploitation and violence.

The *family therapy model* assumes that a fundamental cause of marital violence is lack of interpersonal skills and a dysfunctional relationship. This cause results in an escalating pattern of frustration and anger that eventually leads to violence. The family therapy model therefore emphasizes improving interpersonal skills, including negotiating skills, and correcting dysfunctional relationships, only one of which is inequality in power.

I suggest that part of the difference between the two approaches occurs because the empirical basis of the feminist perspective is men who assaulted their partners so severely and chronically that the partner was driven to the extreme step of seeking the protection of a shelter for battered women. These men tend to have many of the characteristics in Criterion B and assault their partners an average of about 60 times per year, whereas the partners of battered women in the general population engaged in an average of about 5 assaults per year (Straus, 1990a). Consequently, the feminist image of marital violence is that of what I have called the *high-risk offender*.

The empirical basis of the family therapy model is the characteristics of the clientele, which rarely include violence at the high-risk level, except for a few therapists who treat court-mandated cases. In Colorado, state law prohibits couples therapy in court-mandated cases of marital violence. This legislation was passed in response to the efforts of the shelter movement. In effect, it assumes that all cases of marital violence are in the high-risk category.

Part of the controversy between family therapists and the shelter movement can be mitigated by distinguishing between high-risk violence and more "usual" types of marital violence. Therapists can diagnose and refer high-risk cases to programs designed for male batterers, and feminist activists may be able to accept the fact that the majority of cases of marital violence, including some that are severe enough to attract the attention of the police, are appropriately treated by family therapy.

The preceding discussion suggests that although the controversy over the appropriateness of family therapy intervention for marital violence is grounded in the differences in theoretical approaches and objectives, differences in the clientele of the two groups also play a role. Shelter cases and police cases tend to be at the high-risk level, whereas such cases are rare in family therapy or community surveys. It is important that both family therapists and the criminal justice system be able to differentiate cases involving high risk so that each uses procedures suited to the level of violence and risk.

CONCLUSION

Research on domestic assaults from a criminal justice perspective requires standardized procedures for identifying relevant cases. These procedures need to provide much more information than the basic fact of whether an assault occurred. The additional information includes the chronicity of the assaultive behavior and the criminal record and other characteristics of the offender in order to identify high-risk offenders. In this chapter, I described use of the Conflict Tactics Scales and a checklist for that purpose. These assessment tools enable identification of high-risk offenders on the basis of whether the assaults are chronic and severe and the presence of other risk factors, such as alcohol or drug abuse or prior arrest or conviction for violent crime.

Research on the effectiveness of various interventions needs to distinguish between high-risk offenders and others because a given mode of intervention may work for one but not the other. It is ironic that what are here called high-risk offenders may be those for whom criminal justice sanctions have little or no deterrent effect (Sherman, 1992). Although criminal justice penalties for this group may have little specific deterrent effect, they may nonetheless be important for general deterrence. For cases that do not cross the line to the high-risk category, the cost of prosecution to society and to the victim and the offender may outweigh the benefits. Arrest without necessarily subsequent prosecution, especially if the victim is given the option of not proceeding with prosecution, can serve to empower victims (Ford, 1991); symbolizes the fact that society regards such assaults as "real" crime, not just a "family fight"; and is by itself a severe sanction (Carmody & Williams, 1987). Investigation of these issues requires assessment tools such as those described in this chapter.

APPENDIX

Clinical Setting Administration
of the Conflict Tactics Scales (CTS)

The CTS is flexible and easily administered. It takes only about 5 minutes to administer, and one can do a rough scoring of the violence scale in about 2 minutes. As a result of its flexibility and brevity, the CTS can be administered to the same subjects in a variety of ways without undue burden. It can be used in questionnaire format by replacing such phrases as "I'm going to read some things that you . . ." with "Here is a list of things that you . . ."

FORMS

Form RC (Table 2.2) is a version of Form R for clinical use. The format has been modified in two minor ways to facilitate hand scoring: (a) It uses 0 to 25 as the response categories instead of 0 to 6, and (b) there are places in the right margin to enter the chronicity scores and to enter the sum of the items for each scale. There is now a revised version—the CTS2 (Straus et al., 1996).

REFERENT PERIOD

The CTS most often has been used to obtain information on violence in the previous 12 months. However, it is not restricted to

TABLE 2.2 Conflict Tactics Scales, Couple Form RC

No matter how well a couple gets along, there are times when they disagree, get annoyed with the other person, or just have spats or fights because they're in a bad mood or tired or for some other reason. They also use many different ways of trying to settle their differences. I'm going to read some things that you and your (spouse/partner) might do when you have an argument. I would like you to tell me how many times (once, twice, 3-5 times, 6-10 times, or more than 20 times) in the past 12 months you:

How the argument was settled[a]   *Score:*

	You[b]	Spouse[b]	If "never" for both[c]	You	Spouse
A. Discussed an issue calmly	1 2 4 8 15 25 0	1 2 4 8 15 25 0	1 0	___	___
B. Got information to back up your/his/her side of things	1 2 4 8 15 25 0	1 2 4 8 15 25 0	1 0	___	___
C. Brought in, or tried to bring in, someone to help settle things	1 2 4 8 15 25 0	1 2 4 8 15 25 0	1 0	___	___
D. Insulted or swore at him/her/you	1 2 4 8 15 25 0	1 2 4 8 15 25 0	1 0	___	___
E. Sulked or refused to talk about an issue	1 2 4 8 15 25 0	1 2 4 8 15 25 0	1 0	___	___
F. Stomped out of the room or house or yard	1 2 4 8 15 25 0	1 2 4 8 15 25 0	1 0	___	___
G. Cried	1 2 4 8 15 25 0	1 2 4 8 15 25 0	1 0	___	___
H. Did or said something to spite him/her/you	1 2 4 8 15 25 0	1 2 4 8 15 25 0	1 0	___	___
I. Threatened to hit or throw something at him/her/you	1 2 4 8 15 25 0	1 2 4 8 15 25 0	1 0	___	___
J. Threw or smashed or hit or kicked something	1 2 4 8 15 25 0	1 2 4 8 15 25 0	1 0	___	___
K. Threw something *at* him/her/you	1 2 4 8 15 25 0	1 2 4 8 15 25 0	1 0	___	___
L. Pushed, grabbed, or shoved him/her/you	1 2 4 8 15 25 0	1 2 4 8 15 25 0	1 0	___	___
M. Slapped him/her/you	1 2 4 8 15 25 0	1 2 4 8 15 25 0	1 0	___	___
N. Kicked, bit, or hit him/her/you with a fist	1 2 4 8 15 25 0	1 2 4 8 15 25 0	1 0	___	___
O. Hit or tried to hit him/her/you with something	1 2 4 8 15 25 0	1 2 4 8 15 25 0	1 0	___	___
P. Beat him/her/you up	1 2 4 8 15 25 0	1 2 4 8 15 25 0	1 0	___	___
Q. Choked him/her/you	1 2 4 8 15 25 0	1 2 4 8 15 25 0	1 0	___	___
R. *Threatened* him/her/you with a knife or gun	1 2 4 8 15 25 0	1 2 4 8 15 25 0	1 0	___	___
S. Used a knife or fired a gun	1 2 4 8 15 25 0	1 2 4 8 15 25 0	1 0	___	___

NOTE: a. Each item is asked first of the respondent and then of the spouse. See note 3 in the Notes section.[3]
b. Scoring is as follows: 1 = once, 2 = twice, 4 = 3-5 times, 8 = 6-10 times, 15 = 11-20 times, 25 = more than 20 times, and 0 = never.
c. If "never" is listed for both, the researcher should ask "Has it ever happened?" (scored 1 = yes, 0 = no).

this or any other period. The subjects may be asked to report on the previous month, the first year of the relationship, the year when violence first occurred (if it did not occur during the first year), the middle year, and for the previous 12 months, previous 6 months, and so on. Because of its brevity, the CTS can be given at the beginning of a session and scored immediately. This ease makes it practical to administer the CTS to assess change in violence at several points. When used in this way, it is important to administer the entire CTS, not just the Violence Scale, because the Reasoning and Verbal Aggression Scales provide an opportunity for subjects to show they have made a variety of changes and therefore may be less defensive in responding to the violence items.

OTHER FAMILY ROLES

By changing the instructions from "your partner" to "your father," "your mother," a specific child, and so on, the CTS can also provide information on violence by and toward (a) the parents of the subject to obtain data on whether the subject was physically abused and (b) the subject's children to obtain data on use of physical punishment and physical abuse of children and violence by children toward their parents and their siblings (see the CTS manual).

MODE OF ADMINISTRATION

The CTS has been used successfully in different formats with little difference in the results, including face-to-face interview, telephone interview, and self-administered questionnaire.

NOTES

1. In this section, I can only summarize the most salient characteristics of the CTS. Further information is in the CTS manual. Substantial parts of this manual are also in Straus and Gelles (1990, chaps. 3-8 and Appendix B).

2. This can often involve use of interval-, ratio-, or ordinal-level test scores as a step in the process of classification, as in the use of "clinical cutting points" to classify a case as above or below a "clinical threshold."

3. Because of space restrictions, an exact duplicate of the Couple Form RC could not be printed here. The main thing left out was the researcher's introduction to the form: "No matter how well a couple gets along, there are times when they disagree, get annoyed with the other person, or just have spats or fights because they're in a bad mood or tired or for some other reason. They also use many different ways of trying to settle their differences. I'm going to read some things that you and your (spouse/partner) might do when you have an argument. I would like you to tell me how many times, (once, twice, 3-5 times, 6-10 times, 11-20 times, or more than 20 times) in the past 12 months you:"

REFERENCES

Aldarondo, E., & Straus, M. A. (1994). Screening for physical violence in couple therapy: Methodological, practical, and ethical considerations. *Family Process, 33*, 425-439.

Browne, A. (1987). *When battered women kill.* New York: Free Press.

Carmody, D. C., & Williams, K. R. (1987). Wife assault and perceptions of sanctions. *Violence and Victims, 2*(1), 25-38.

Cohen, P., & Cohen, J. (1984). The clinician's illusion. *Archives of General Psychiatry, 41*, 1178-1182.

Dutton, D. G. (1988). *The domestic assault of women: Psychological and criminal justice perspective.* Boston: Allyn & Bacon.

Ford, D. A. (1991). Preventing and provoking wife battery through criminal sanctions: A look at the risks. In D. D. Knudsen & J. L. Miller (Eds.), *Abused and battered: Social and legal responses to family violence.* Hawthorne, NY: Aldine.

Gawin, F. H. (1992). Cocaine addiction: Psychology and neurophysiology. *Science, 251*, 1580-1586.

Giles-Sims, J. (1983). *Wife battering: A systems theory approach.* New York: Guilford.

Goetting, A. (1989). Men who kill their mates: A profile. *Journal of Family Violence, 4*(3), 285-296.

Goetting, A. (1991). Female victims of homicide: A portrait of their killers and the circumstances of their death. *Violence and Victims, 6*(2), 159-168.

Gondolf, E. W. (1988). Who are those guys? Toward a behavioral typology of batterers. *Violence and Victims, 3*, 187-203.

Hamberger, L. K., & Hastings, J. E. (1991). Personality correlates of men who abuse their partners: A cross-validation study. *Journal of Family Violence, 1*, 323-341.

Okun, L. (1986). *Woman abuse: Facts replacing myths.* Albany: State University of New York Press.

Pillemer, K., & Finkelhor, D. (1988). The prevalence of elder abuse: A random sample survey. *Gerontologist, 28*, 51-57.

Room, R. (1980). Treatment, sampling populations, and larger realities. In G. Edwards & M. Grant (Eds.), *Alcoholism treatment and transition.* London: Croom Helm.

Saunders, D. G. (1992). Woman battering. In R. T. Ammerman & M. Herson (Eds.), *Assessment of family violence* (pp. 208-235). New York: John Wiley.

Sherman, L. (1992). *Policing domestic violence: Experiments and dilemmas.* New York: Free Press.

Steinmetz, S. K. (1988). *Duty bound: Elder abuse and family care.* Newbury Park, CA: Sage.

Straus, M. A. (1976). Sexual inequality, cultural norms, and wife-beating. *Victimology, 1,* 54-76.

Straus, M. A. (1979). Measuring intrafamily conflict and violence: The Conflict Tactics Scales. *Journal of Marriage and the Family, 41,* 75-88.

Straus, M. A. (1989). *Manual for the Conflict Tactics Scales.* Durham: University of New Hampshire, Family Research Laboratory.

Straus, M. A. (1990a). The Conflict Tactics Scale and its critics: An evaluation and new data on validity and reliability. In M. A. Straus & R. J. Gelles, (Eds.) *Physical violence in American families: Risk factors and adaptations to violence in 8,145 families.* New Brunswick, NJ: Transaction Books.

Straus, M. A. (1990b). Injury and frequency of assault and the "representative sample fallacy" in measuring wife beating and child abuse. In M. A. Straus & R. J. Gelles (Eds.), *Physical violence in American families: Risk factors and adaptations to violence in 8,145 families.* New Brunswick, NJ: Transaction Books.

Straus, M. A. (1993). Physical assaults by wives: A major social problem. In R. J. Gelles & D. Loseke (Eds.), *Current controversies on family violence.* Newbury Park, CA: Sage.

Straus, M. A., & Gelles, R. J. (Eds.) (1990). *Physical violence in American families: Risk factors and adaptations to violence in 8,145 families.* New Brunswick, NJ: Transaction Books.

Straus, M. A., Gelles, R. J., & Steinmetz, S. K. (1980). *Behind closed doors: Violence in the American family.* New York: Anchor.

Straus, M. A., Hamby, S. L., Boney-McCoy, S. & Sugerman, D. B. (1996). The revised Conflict Tactics Scales (CTS2): Development and preliminary pyschometric data. *Journal of Family Issues, 17*(3).

Straus, M. A., & Lincoln, A. J. (1985). A conceptual framework for understanding crime and the family. In A. J. Lincoln & M. A. Straus (Eds.), *Crime and the family.* Springfield, IL: Charles C Thomas.

Stuart, E. P., & Campbell, J. C. (1989). Assessment of dangerousness with battered women: The danger assessment. *Issues in Mental Health Nursing, 10*(3), 245-260.

Tolman, R. M., & Bennett, L. W. (1990). A review of quantitative research on men who batter. *Journal of Interpersonal Violence, 5*(1), 87-118.

3

Constraints Against Family Violence
How Well Do They Work?

RICHARD J. GELLES

It is unusual, if not unprecedented in the social sciences, when empirical research results combine with social advocacy, popular political agendas, public support, and conventional wisdom to bring about a change in social policy and social action. Yet, this is exactly what occurred with regard to the implementation of mandatory arrest procedures in instances of domestic assault. Within a matter of months after the public release of the results of the Minneapolis Domestic Violence Experiment (Sherman & Berk, 1984), police departments across the nation began to adopt either mandatory or presumptive arrest policies for cases of marital assault. The U.S. Attorney General's Task Force on Family Violence (U.S. Department of Justice, 1984) drew heavily on the results of the Minneapolis study in framing its final report and recommendations, which began with recommending that family violence be recognized and responded to as criminal activity. A number of individual states revised or established laws pertaining to domestic violence and established mandatory or presumptive arrest laws for violent offenders (see Buzawa & Buzawa, 1990). The quick and widespread adoption of mandatory or presumptive arrest policies was cheered by feminists and battered women's advocacy groups, who had often criticized the police and sometimes taken legal action against police departments for either being indifferent about domestic violence or using inappropriate intervention strategies. Social scientists, too, were approving of the change in police attitudes and actions because the new control approach to domestic assault was seen as one possible means of canceling the hitting license that was thought to be a causal factor in domestic violence (e.g., see Straus, Gelles, & Steinmetz, 1980).

The speed with which arrest policies were adopted can be best illustrated in the following brief timetable. The first public notice of the results of the Minneapolis Domestic Violence Experiment may have been an article that appeared in the April 5, 1983 issue of the *New York Times*. The article reported the preliminary results of the Minneapolis study and included comments from other social scientists, including Peter Rossi, past president of the American Sociological Association and a noted evaluation researcher. The article concluded by noting that the New York City Police Department had a policy of making arrests in domestic assault cases but that the order was widely disregarded. Ten days later, on Sunday, April 15, 1983, the *New York Times* reported that Police Commissioner Benjamin Ward had issued new orders requiring police officers to make arrests. The article noted that the results of the Minneapolis Domestic Violence Experiment were among the reasons for the new rules. By January 1987, 176 cities across the United States were using some form of arrest policy.

To fully appreciate the unprecedented nature of the widespread acceptance of the study results, the willingness to put the results into action, and the speed with which social policy about the role of the police in domestic violence changed, one needs to consider the many other areas in which social scientists have conducted policy-related research. For example, consider the likelihood that the social science research on the effects of segregated education would have led school districts in the South to voluntarily desegregate within weeks following either the release of the research report or the Supreme Court's *Brown v. Board of Education* ruling. Or, consider the likelihood of social science research on the death penalty leading states to abolish the death penalty weeks after the study results were released on a television news show. Or, imagine research on the effects of television violence on children or the effects of spanking leading states and the federal government to ban violent television programs and to outlaw spanking. In few, if any, examples in social science research in general, or criminological research specifically, have research results led to swift and wide-spread changes in social policy.

How and why did the Minneapolis Domestic Violence Experiment have such an enormous impact? The study's principal investigator might argue that it was because of the scientific rigor of the study. The study, funded by the National Institute of Justice (NIJ) and conducted by the Police Foundation, called for the police in two precincts in Minneapolis to randomly assign violent family offenders to one of three experimental conditions: arrest, separation, or advice/mediation. Eligible households were those in which both offender and victim were present when police arrived and in which the nature of the incident was classified as "misdemeanor assault." During a 6-month period following the experimental condition, interviews were conducted with victims and offenders. Official records of subsequent incidents of family violence were also collected. An analysis of the follow-up data indicated that those receiving the arrest intervention had the lowest rate of recidivism (10%) and that those who were separated had the highest (24%). The fact that the Minneapolis Domestic Violence Experiment was a field experiment with random assignment certainly made the study results far more compelling than the results of either uncontrolled experiments or social surveys that attempt to make causal inferences from cross-sectional data. Clearly, the apparent strength of the study design made the Minneapolis Domestic Violence Experiment a strong piece of research. Yet, the apparent internal validity of one study is not sufficient explanation for the rapid change in police practice.

Other forces at work established fertile ground for the results of Sherman and Berk's study. One important factor was the feminist and women's movement argument that the criminal justice system was indifferent to wife abuse. Those advancing this argument claimed the criminal justice system, and most especially the police, treated intimate violence differently from instances of stranger assault. Critics claimed the police assign domestic disturbance calls a low priority, do not respond or delay response to these categories of calls, and avoid arrest or use of other control strategies in favor of simply restoring order or calming down the violent parties (Bowker, 1982; Dobash & Dobash, 1979; Eisenberg & Micklow, 1977; Field & Field, 1973; Fields, 1978; Gelles, 1976; Lerman, 1986; Roy, 1977; Straus et al., 1980). A number of class action suits were filed in the 1970s on behalf of battered women in an attempt to force local police departments, prosecutors, and other criminal justice agencies to apply the same standards of protection and law enforcement to intimate violence that were assumed to be applied to stranger assaults.[1]

Another factor that led to the adoption of arrest strategies was the publication of the U.S. Attorney General's Task Force on Family Violence report in 1984. Drawing heavily from the results of the Minneapolis Domestic Violence Experiment, this report called for police departments and criminal justice agencies to recognize family violence as criminal activity and to respond accordingly. The report recommended arrest as the preferred strategy for responding to cases of family violence.

Another factor may have been the case of *Thurman v. City of Torrington* (Connecticut). Tracy Thurman was a battered wife who had frequently sought help from the Torrington police to protect her from the violent attacks of her estranged husband. Thurman was badly battered and left permanently injured in June 1983, and she subsequently filed a civil suit against the city of Torrington and 29 police officers (*Thurman v. City of Torrington*, 1985). Thurman was awarded $2.3 million and later settled out of court for $1.9 million. The threat of similar suits motivated a number of eastern U.S. municipalities to adopt the policy of mandatory arrest for cases of family violence.[2]

A final but by no means minimal factor that may have influenced police departments to adopt more control interventions in cases of family violence is the general "control" criminal justice atmosphere that had arisen in society in the past decade and that was especially vibrant during the Reagan years. The advocacy of a control model of intervention flourished during the period of political conservatism, and repeated calls have been made for strict and severe controls to punish all violent crime, not just family violence.

Although not a major factor in the adoption of mandatory arrest policies, research on family violence supported the claims that the police appeared indifferent to domestic violence and that a more active approach to domestic violence was necessary. Parnas's (1967, 1971) examination of the police suggested that police response to domestic violence was perfunctory. Wilt and Bannon (1977) noted that, in cases of domestic homicide, the police generally had been called to the home on many occasions prior to the homicide because of instances of domestic violence. Thus, it appeared that an appropriate police response could prevent domestic homicides.

DO CONTROL STRATEGIES WORK?

As someone who advocated for more aggressive and effective police intervention, I should have found the sweeping changes in police practices gratifying. Rather than being gratified by the changes, however, I became skeptical. Police departments were adopting mandatory arrest policies before most social scientists had a chance to fully examine the design of and data from the Minneapolis Domestic Violence Experiment. The study may have had solid internal validity, of course, but the external validity was still unproven—a fact that led the funding agency, the NIJ, to call for proposals to replicate the study. Although the empirical results were indeed impressive at first glance, there was little in the way of theoretical justification for why mandatory arrest would actually work to deter abusive men (or women). Delbert Elliott (personal communication, 1991) noted the scant empirical or theoretical support in the juvenile delinquency literature and the general criminology literature for the view that arrest deters juvenile or adult offenders.

A more complete and sobering look at the Minneapolis Domestic Violence Experiment and the results of the subsequent replications indicates that the initial claim of the deterrent value of mandatory arrest policies may well be the social science equivalent of cold fusion. A number of significant problems concerned the internal and external validity of the Minneapolis Domestic Violence Experiment. The internal validity problems include questions about the degree to which the treatment was truly based on random assignment (for a more complete discussion, see Berk & Sherman, 1988). Officers could have violated the assumptions of random assignment either by avoiding a domestic disturbance call or by "upgrading" a call to "felony assault" or "nonmisdemeanor violence." Another problem of internal validity arises because the vast majority of the cases in the study were the results of the work of only a few police officers in the two precincts. Also, the investigators had significant problems with missing data. Without sophisticated statistical procedures to deal with the problems of missing data, the investigators would have had too few cases for valid analysis. Despite problems of what Berk and Sherman (1988) called "when random assignment fails," the investigators thought their data supported the conclusion that arrest deters wife beaters. A reanalysis of the Minneapolis data that modeled the violations of random assignment actually found larger treatment effects than were previously reported (Berk & Sherman, 1988).

Partly because of the internal validity problems of the Minneapolis Domestic Violence Experiment and partly because of problems of external validity, the NIJ funded six replications of the Minneapolis experiment. The results of three of the replications are available in either published or report form. Dunford, Huizinga, and Elliott (1990) replicated the Minneapolis Domestic Violence Experiment in Omaha, Nebraska. The design, like the other replications, attempted to correct for the threats to the internal validity of the Minneapolis study. The major finding was, on the one hand, contrary to the evidence from Minneapolis, that arrest and the immediate period of custody associated with arrest were not a deterrent to continued domestic violence. On the other hand, arrest did not appear to place victims in greater danger of increased conflict or violence than did separation or mediation. What the police did when responding to cases of misdemeanor violence in Omaha neither helped nor hurt victims. Dunford et al. expanded the Minneapolis design to include an experimental trial of issuing arrest warrants in cases in which suspected abusive men were not present when the police arrived. The researchers found that men who had warrants issued against them scored lower on prevalence and frequency of repeat offending.

Hirschel, Hutchison, Dean, Kelley, and Pesackis (1990) replicated the police experiment in Charlotte, North Carolina. The Charlotte experiment shared common experimental design and features with the other replications. The only differences were that the Charlotte project used police-issued citations as one treatment option (in addition to arrest, separation, and mediation) and employed the entire patrol division in round-the-clock and citywide sampling for the full duration of the project. The investigators concluded their analysis of the experimental results by stating, "The results of the Charlotte experiment are decisive and unambiguous, clearly indicating that arrest of spouse abusers is neither substantially nor statistically a more effective deterrent to repeat abuse than either of the other two police responses examined in this study" (p. 154).

The third replication for which reports are available was conducted in Milwaukee by Lawrence Sherman and his colleagues (Sherman et al., 1990; Sherman & Smith, 1990). The Milwaukee replication was, as Sherman and his colleagues noted, the only study among the seven domestic violence arrest studies to be conducted in a Northern industrial-urban black ghetto. The Milwaukee study involved three treatments: (a) standard arrest, in which suspects were held until morning unless they could post bail (mean of 11 hours in custody); (b) a short arrest (mean of 3 hours in custody), after which all suspects were released on recognizance; and (c) no arrest, but a standard police warning. The results of the Milwaukee study indicated that arrest was not associated with the prevalence or monthly rate of future violence. Arrest did, however, delay the average time until the next incident of violence. Thus, arrest did not have any direct effect on the likelihood of future violence. Arrest did interact with employment status, however, such that persons who were randomly assigned to be arrested and who were employed were less likely to recidivate than unemployed offenders (Sherman & Smith, 1990). A second analysis of the Milwaukee data (Sherman et al., 1990) produced more controversial results. Short arrest appeared to decrease the chances of repeat violence and was a greater deterrent to violence than no arrest. Over the long term, however, short arrest increased the offender's violence rate. Full arrest did not have the long-term violence consequences for victims. These results are based on the assumption that the differences found did not occur by chance—a possibility because a large number of significance tests yielded only a few significant results. Even with the specific findings of some apparent benefits, the Sherman et al. study joined with the two other published replications in concluding that arrest for misdemeanor violence does not have a long-term deterrent value.

Richard Berk (personal communication, 1991) drew different conclusions from the results of the replications sponsored by the

NIJ. He stated that three of the five replications do show that arrest works (he had access to the results of the Colorado Springs replication and one other that he did not identify) but only for offenders who have something to lose, especially people who have jobs (the Milwaukee replication) or are in the military (the Colorado Springs replication). The results that Berk cited are not yet publicly available. The NIJ, the funding agency for the six replications, requires that all study findings be carefully reviewed before release. The review is designed to ensure that the studies actually replicated the Minneapolis experiment. Until the findings are publicly available, there is no assurance that any of the studies met the criteria of a true replication.

Williams and Hawkins's (1989) analysis of survey data collected as part of the Second National Family Violence Survey tends to support the notion that arrest would work—but only for abusers with something to lose. Williams and Hawkins found that arrest appears to be meaningful to men in terms of the indirect cost it poses to them in their social environment. The personal humiliation of arrest appears to be the central factor in the meaning of arrest for wife assault and the possible deterrent effect of arrest. Of course, these results may indicate a more cultural than specific deterrent effect, in that the threat of arrest may deter men from even beginning to hit their wives, rather than deter them once they have initiated violent behavior.

The results of empirical research on the deterrent value of one control strategy—arrest—are not nearly as clear and convincing as the results of the Minneapolis Domestic Violence Experiment indicated. As Sherman and others noted, the most recent empirical data fail to support the notion that arrest in and of itself deters violent husbands from future violence.

Other Control Strategies

Arrest alone is not the only control strategy that can be brought to bear to deter wife assault. Arrest can be part of what is referred to as more global *community intervention projects* (CPIs). CPIs are system-level interventions designed to change the overall criminal justice system approach to wife assault. CPIs are often staffed by battered women's advocates and include arrest in the total approach. Also included in the total approach are efforts to ensure the prompt prosecution of perpetrators and the inclusion of the battered woman in the process of investigation and sentencing. A number of CPIs defer stayed jail time in return for mandated enrollment in batterers' treatment programs.

The evaluation of CPIs is considerably less rigorous than assessments of mandatory arrest. Gamache, Edleson, and Schock (1988) examined system-level activity changes in three communities that established CPIs. They found that the CPIs increased the number of arrests, convictions, and court-mandated treatments. No assessment of later violence was obtained, however. Pence and Shepard (1988) assessed the "Duluth model," which was a system-level approach to domestic violence. Six months after men completed their involvement in the city's Domestic Abuse Intervention Program, 51% of the victims reported no subsequent violence, compared with 41% of a comparison group. It is impossible to determine, however, whether any specific part of the program (arrest, court action, treatment) was responsible for the outcome. Steinman (1988, 1989) evaluated components of a CPI in Lincoln, Nebraska. He reported that postarrest sanctions had little to do with lower rates of recidivism (violence). His second study (Steinman, 1989) found that arrest without coordination with other sanctions produced greater subsequent violence. Arrests in coordination with other criminal justice efforts were a significant deterrent.

LATENT EFFECTS OF
CONTROL INTERVENTIONS

Most of the attention on control interventions has focused on the manifest effects of arrest strategies. A number of investigators have also discussed the latent effects of arrest interventions. One significant latent effect that has been examined is the likelihood of increased violence as a result of arrest. Dunford et al. (1990) specifically addressed this issue in the Omaha study and found no greater risk of violence in the arrest condition. As noted above, Sherman et al. (1990) also looked at the latent effects of arrest for both the short term and the long term. Ford (1991) also found that arrest interventions and prosecution outcomes did not place women at increased risk of violence.

A second latent outcome is what battered women's advocates refer to as "empowerment of victims." Ford (1991) noted that mandatory arrest and prosecution strategies may actually work *against* empowering women. Many women who call the police may not want to have their husbands arrested. They may use the call and the police visit as a means of controlling their violent husbands even if the police do not make an arrest. Mandatory arrest removes the power from the woman victim. On the one hand, it is argued, mandatory arrest reduces the chances that victims will be intimidated or injured by partners. On the other hand, mandatory arrest may deter women from calling the police because they may not want their husbands arrested.

Another latent effect of mandatory arrest is the subversion of the policy by police. Ferraro (1989) noted that police often subvert the policy of mandatory arrest because they believe that such a policy interferes with the appropriate use of discretion. Buzawa and Buzawa (1990) stated that the latent effect of mandatory arrest policies is that there is now even *less* consistency and predictability in officer actions. Officers have become adept at circumventing rules, laws, and policies that do not conform to their underlying beliefs.

Some anecdotal evidence suggests that mandatory arrest policies may produce undesirable results for both victim and offender. In a newspaper article, Kerr (1991) described the case of a woman and her husband who had to sneak into their apartment because the husband had been arrested twice under the provisions of the Rhode Island Domestic Violence Law. Both times, the police had been called by neighbors who overheard loud fights and arguments. Both times, the husband had been arrested. Neither the wife nor the husband had wanted the arrest, and now the wife has to "smuggle" her husband into their apartment; she fears that if the neighbors or the police see him with her, he will be arrested again.

A final form of latent effect was discussed by Burton Weinstein (personal communication, 1991), the attorney for Tracy Thurman. Weinstein argued that mandatory arrest statutes are necessary because there is an increased likelihood that the current Supreme Court will refuse to apply the equal protection under the law provision of the Fourteenth Amendment of the Constitution to any group other than racial minorities.

PRACTICAL AND POLICY IMPLICATIONS
OF RESEARCH ON ARREST

The first study that failed to support the proposition that arrest deters violent husbands appeared in the journal *Criminology* in the spring of 1990 (Dunford et al., 1990). No press conference was held, the investigators were not invited to appear on the *MacNeil Lehrer Newshour* as Lawrence Sherman had been, and the Commissioner of Police in New York did not reverse or soften his rules on arrest in cases of domestic violence 10 days after the report was published. In fact, there appears to have been no impact on public policy of the findings of the studies in Omaha, Charlotte, and Milwaukee. Whereas researchers were embraced for the findings from the Minneapolis study, those involved in subsequent studies are largely ignored now or are criticized for the methodological flaws—both real and imagined—in their studies. The vast majority of public speakers on domestic violence and wife abuse continue to point to the Minneapolis study or the Duluth model as convincing evidence that police should continue to use and expand arrest as a means of preventing wife abuse and domestic violence.

What should the police policy and practice be, in the light of the available evidence on the effects of arrest interventions? Arrest in and of itself appears not to be the deterrent it was espoused to be in the original Minneapolis study. When combined with other criminal justice sanctions, however, and in combination with particular attributes of the offender, arrest may be a deterrent. Arrest might also be a general deterrent that, though not reducing violence among offenders, may reduce the likelihood of an initial battering because of the perceived likelihood that battering will result in arrest (Mederer & Gelles, 1989).

Dunford et al. (1990) noted the difficult dilemma posed by the results of current research on the deterrent value of arrest:

> The failure to replicate the Minneapolis findings will undoubtedly cast some doubt on the deterrent power of a mandatory or even a presumptive arrest policy for cases of misdemeanor domestic assault. At this point, researchers and policy makers are in the awkward position of having conflicting results from two experiments and no clear, unambiguous direction from the research on this issue. . . . For those who are directly involved in responding to domestic assaults, it might be profitable to begin thinking about new or additional strategies for dealing with this problem. (p. 204)

It appears, however, that both the results of the Omaha study and the suggestions from the investigators have fallen on deaf ears. Arrest policies are still in place, and few states or localities have given serious thought to other strategies. The control approach to this social problem and many others, including substance abuse and nonintimate violence, appears to have a firm grasp.

NOTES

1. Elliott (1989) reviewed the data that compare the rates of arrest for family and nonfamily assaults and found that the arrest rate for stranger violence is not significantly higher than the arrest rate for family violence.

2. The story of Tracy Thurman was subsequently told in a made-for-television movie broadcast in the autumn of 1990. Although the movie likely did not play a role in the spread of the control intervention strategy for domestic violence, it did support the notion that police were indifferent to wife abuse and that arrest was the most appropriate way to deal with violent men.

REFERENCES

Berk, R. A., & Sherman, L. W. (1988). Police responses to family violence incidents: An analysis of an experimental design with incomplete randomization. *Journal of the American Statistical Association, 83*(401), 70-76.

Bowker, L. H. (1982). Police services to battered women. *Criminal Justice and Behavior, 9*(4), 476-494.

Brown v. Board of Education, 347 U.S. 483 (1954).

Buzawa, E. S., & Buzawa, C. G. (1990). *Domestic violence: The criminal justice response.* Newbury Park, CA: Sage.

Dobash, R. E., & Dobash, R. (1979). *Violence against wives.* New York: Free Press.

Dunford, F. W., Huizinga, D., & Elliott, D. S. (1990). The role of arrest in domestic assault: The Omaha Police Experiment. *Criminology, 28*(2), 183-206.

Eisenberg, S., & Micklow, P. (1977). The assaultive wife: "Catch 22" revisited. *Women's Rights Law Reporter, 3,* 138-161.

Elliott, D. S. (1989). Criminal justice procedures in family violence crimes. In L. Ohlin & M. Tonry (Eds.), *Family violence* (pp. 427-480). Chicago: University of Chicago Press.

Ferraro, K. (1989). Policing domestic violence. *Social Problems, 36*(1), 61-74.

Field, M. H., & Field, H. F. (1973). Marital violence and the criminal process: Neither justice nor peace. *Social Services Review, 47,* 221-240.

Fields, M. D. (1978). Wife beating: Government intervention policies and practices. In U.S. Commission on Civil Rights (Ed.), *Battered women: Issues of public policy* (pp. 20-27). Washington, DC: U.S. Commission on Civil Rights.

Ford, D. A. (1991). Preventing and provoking wife battery through criminal sanctions: A look at the risks. In D. D. Knudson & J. L. Miller (Eds.), *Abused and battered: Social and legal responses to family violence* (pp. 191-209). Hawthorne, NY: Aldine.

Gamache, D. J., Edleson, J. L., & Schock, M. D. (1988). Coordinated police, judicial, and social service response to woman battering: A multi-baseline evaluation across three communities. In G. R. Hotaling, D. Finkelhor, J. T. Kirkpatrick, & M. A. Straus (Eds.), *Coping with family violence: Research and policy perspectives* (pp. 193-209). Newbury Park, CA: Sage.

Gelles, R. (1976). Abused wives: Why do they stay? *Journal of Marriage and the Family, 38*, 659-668.

Hirschel, J. D., Hutchison, I. W., III, Dean, C. W., Kelley, J. J., & Pesackis, C. E. (1990). *Charlotte Spouse Assault Replication Project: Final report.* Unpublished manuscript.

Kerr, R. (1991, November 4). Domestic violence law is clear. *Providence Journal Bulletin*, pp. C1-C2.

Lerman, L. G. (1986). Prosecution of wife beaters: Institutional obstacles and innovations. In M. Lystad (Ed.), *Violence in the home: Interdisciplinary perspectives* (pp. 250-295). New York: Brunner/Mazel.

Mederer, H. J., & Gelles, R. J. (1989). Compassion or control: Intervention in cases of wife abuse. *Journal of Interpersonal Violence, 4*(1), 25-43.

Parnas, R. (1967). The police response to domestic disturbance. *Wisconsin Law Review, 2*, 914-960.

Parnas, R. (1971). Police discretion and diversion of incidents of intra-family violence. *Law and Contemporary Social Problems, 36*, 539-565.

Pence, E., & Shepard, M. (1988). Integrating feminist theory and practice: The challenge of the battered woman's movement. In K. Yllö & M. Bograd (Eds.), *Feminist perspectives on wife abuse* (pp. 282-298). Newbury Park, CA: Sage.

Roy, M. (1977). Some thoughts regarding the criminal justice system and wifebeating. In M. Roy (Ed.), *Battered women: A psychosociological study of domestic violence* (pp. 138-139). New York: Van Nostrand Reinhold.

Sherman, L., & Berk, R. (1984). The specific deterrent effects of arrest for domestic assault. *American Sociological Review, 49*, 261-272.

Sherman, L. W., Schmidt, J. D., Rogan, D. R., Gartin, P. R., Cohn, E. G., Collins, D., & Bacich, A. (1990). *From initial deterrence to long-term escalation: Short-custody arrest for underclass domestic violence.* Unpublished manuscript.

Sherman, L. W., & Smith, D. A. (1990). *Ghetto poverty, crime, and punishment: Legal and informal control of domestic violence.* Unpublished manuscript.

Steinman, M. (1988). Evaluating a system-wide response to domestic violence: Some initial findings. *Journal of Contemporary Criminal Justice, 4*, 172-186.

Steinman, M. (1989). Lowering recidivism among men who batter women. *Journal of Police Science and Administration, 17*, 124-132.

Straus, M., Gelles, R., & Steinmetz, S. (1980). *Behind closed doors: Violence in the American family.* Garden City, NY: Doubleday.

Thurman v. City of Torrington, 595 F. Supp. 1521 (1985).

U.S. Department of Justice. (1984). *Attorney General's Task Force on Family Violence: Final report.* Washington, DC: Author.

Williams, K. R., & Hawkins, R. (1989). The meaning of arrest for wife assault. *Criminology, 27*, 163-181.

Wilt, M., & Bannon, J. (1977). *Domestic violence and the police: Studies in Detroit and Kansas City.* Washington, DC: Police Foundation.

4

Does Arrest Deter
Domestic Violence?

JANELL D. SCHMIDT
LAWRENCE W. SHERMAN

During the mid-1980s, widespread concern about the incidence and prevalence of domestic violence led many big-city police departments to change radically the way they policed a crime that affects millions of women each year. The often-maligned "arrest as a last resort" tradition was replaced with written policies and state laws requiring arrest as the sole police recourse. Nationally, this enthusiastic shift generated, from 1984 to 1989, a 70% increase in arrests for minor assaults, including domestic. Yet, the movement to arrest batterers may be doing more harm than good. Research in six cities testing the "arrest works best" premise in deterring future assaults has produced complex and conflicting results. Police and policymakers are now faced with the dilemma that arrest may help some victims at the expense of others and that arrest may assist the victim in the short term but facilitate further violence in the long term.

The revolution in policing misdemeanor cases of domestic violence can be attributed, in part, to the 1984 publication of the

43

Minneapolis Domestic Violence Experiment, the first controlled, randomized test of the effectiveness of arrest for any offense. Results from this endeavor were that arresting abusers cut in half the risk of future assaults against the same victim during a 6-month follow-up period. Alternative police responses tested were the traditional "send the suspect away for 8 hours" and "advise the couple to get help for their problems." The efficacy of each treatment was measured by interviews with victims and official records tracking the offense and arrest history of each suspect. Because arrest worked better than separating or advising couples, the authors recommended that states change laws prohibiting police from making warrantless arrests in misdemeanor domestic violence cases. They also advocated that replication studies be conducted to test the generalizability of the results in other cities with varying economic conditions and demographic complexions. But absent further research results, their recommendation to law enforcement was "to adopt arrest as the preferred policy for dealing with such cases, unless there were clearly stated reasons to do something else" (Sherman, Schmidt, & Rogan, 1992, p. 3).

Although the study authors opposed mandating arrest until further studies were completed, within 8 years legislatures in 15 states (including 1 in which a replication was being conducted) and the District of Columbia moved to enact laws requiring police to arrest in all probable cause incidents of domestic violence. This dramatic expansion of arrest practices has also been attributed to successful litigation against police departments who failed to arrest, to the recommendations of the 1984 Attorney General's Task Force on Domestic Violence, and to political pressure applied by women's advocacy groups.

It is not clear, however, how well these policies and laws have been followed or whether they have controlled repetitive acts of domestic assault. Observations of compliance of the Phoenix, Minneapolis, and Milwaukee police departments found that only Milwaukee officers consistently adhered to the policy. More important, the lack of labeling cases as domestic prior to policy changes renders attempts at before/after measures difficult. Further complicating evaluation or comparison efforts is the variable threshold for probable cause to arrest in incidents of domestic assault. In Wisconsin, only a complaint of pain is needed for police to effect an arrest; in

Nebraska, visible injuries are required. Until 4 years ago, Florida law required the parties to be married or formerly married in order for the incident to be considered domestic.

What is known about the impact of police arrest policies relative to domestic assault is that the vast bulk of cases brought to police attention involve lower-income and minority-group households. One reason may be a higher rate of domestic disputes among these groups; another reason may be a lack of alternatives short of police intervention that offer immediate relief. Although arresting thousands of unemployed minority males each year may assist the goals of victim advocates and provide a brief respite for the victims, the skepticism of many police and criminologists relative to the deterrent power of arrest still remains. The key question of whether other police alternatives could prove more powerful or whether the police could be effective at all led the National Institute of Justice (NIJ) to fund replication studies in six major urban cities.

Beginning in 1986 and early 1987, police in Omaha (Nebraska), Milwaukee (Wisconsin), Charlotte (North Carolina), Metro-Dade County (Miami, Florida), Colorado Springs (Colorado), and Atlanta (Georgia) began controlled experiments to replicate the Minneapolis findings. Each site was afforded leeway to improve the methodology of the Minneapolis study and to design alternative nonarrest treatments to build on its theoretical foundation. Researchers in all the cities sought to obtain a sample size larger than the 314 cases analyzed in Minneapolis in order to test for interaction effects among the various treatments. In Metro-Dade, for example, a sample of 907 cases was obtained so that researchers could compare arrest to no arrest, both with and without follow-up counseling by a specially trained police unit. In Colorado Springs, more than 1,600 cases were used to contrast arrest and nonarrest with immediate professional counseling at police headquarters or the issuance of an emergency protection order. In Milwaukee, police provided 1,200 cases for the researchers to test the length of time in custody—a short 2-hour arrest versus arrest with an overnight stay in jail, compared to no arrest. The experimental team in Charlotte included a citation response along with arrest, mediation, or separation treatments in its 686-case sample. Only Omaha followed the Minneapolis design with 330 cases but added an offender-absent window of cases to test the effect of having police pursue an arrest warrant.

The results from five of these six later studies (results from Atlanta are not forthcoming) have clouded the issue for police and policymakers, although some victim advocates remain strident in their view that arrest works best. Perhaps most striking is that none of the innovative treatments—namely, counseling or protective orders—produced any improvement over arrest versus no arrest. The citation used to notify offenders to appear at a future court date in Charlotte caused more violence than an arrest. Only Omaha broke ground and found an effective innovation in its offender-absent experiment. Offenders who left the scene before police arrived and whose cases were randomly assigned to the warrant group produced less repeat violence than did similarly absent offenders assigned to the nonwarrant group. The issuance of a warrant may have acted as a "sword of Damocles" hanging over an offender's head.

In short, the new experiments reported both deterrent and backfiring effects of arrest. Arrest cured some abusers but made others worse; arrest eased the pain for victims of employed abusers but increased it for those intimate with unemployed partners; arrest assisted white and Hispanic victims but fell short of deterring further violence among black victims. To understand these diverse findings and move toward a policy resolution, it is necessary first to focus on the effects of arrest compared to nonarrest, because that is the central issue for police and policymakers concerned with determining the most effective or appropriate police response (see Table 4.1).

One central finding is that arrest increased domestic violence recidivism among suspects in Omaha, Charlotte, and Milwaukee. Although these three cities produced some evidence of a deterrent effect of arrest within the first 30 days, victims found that this protective shield quickly evaporated and that they suffered an escalation of violence over a longer period of time. None of the follow-up measures produced the 6-month deterrent effect reported in Minneapolis. Some measures showed no difference in the recidivism of offenders arrested, compared with those whom police did not arrest.

Researchers in Colorado Springs and Metro-Dade found some support for the Minneapolis findings but only with limited measures. A narrow window of victim interview data (a 58% response rate in Colorado and 42% in Metro-Dade) confirms the deterrent

TABLE 4.1 Summary of Results of Six Arrest Experiments for Repeat Violence Against the Same Victim

Finding	Minneapolis	Omaha	Charlotte	Milwaukee	Colorado Springs	Miami
6-month deterrence, official measures	Yes	No	No	No	No	1 of 2
6-month deterrence, victim interviews	Yes	Border	No	No	Yes	Yes
6- to 12-month escalation, official measures	No	Yes	Yes	Yes	No	No
6- to 12-month escalation, victim interviews	*	No	No	No	No	No
30- to 60-day deterrence, official measures (any or same victim)	Yes	No	Border	Yes	No	1 of 2
Escalation effect for unemployed	*	Yes	*	Yes	Yes	*
Deterrence for employed	*	Yes	*	Yes	Yes	*

SOURCE: From Sherman, Schmidt, and Rogan, 1992, p. 129.
NOTE: * = relationship not reported.

power of arrest. But the less than ideal response rate might mean that victims who were interviewed were different from those who were not interviewed. Official records tracking recidivism in Colorado Springs did not uncover a deterrent effect of arrest, as some records did in Metro-Dade. Confounding the interpretation of the Colorado results was the fact that the vast majority of experimental cases (58%) were based on the offender's nonviolent harassing or menacing behavior toward the victim, perhaps distinct from the physical attack required to arrest for battery in the other cities.

The different results from different measures in these cities suggests, then, that arrest has a different effect on suspects from different kinds of households. This finding is best summarized by the following statement:

Evidence that the effects of arrest vary by suspect comes from Milwaukee, Colorado Springs, and Omaha. In each of those cities, nonexperimental analyses of the official records data suggest that unemployed suspects become more violent if arrested, but that employed suspects do not. This consistent pattern supports a hypothesis that the effects of criminal punishment depend upon the suspect's "stakes in conformity," or how much he has to lose from the social consequences of arrest. Similar effects were found in Milwaukee for unmarried versus married suspects; unemployed, unmarried suspects experienced the greatest escalation of violence after arrest. The unemployment result is the single most consistent finding from the domestic violence experiments, and has not been contradicted in any of the analyses reported to date. (Sherman et al., 1992, p. 17)

Could other factors explain this varying effect of arrest on different suspects in different cities? A comparison of the data on prosecution rates, level of victim injury, number of married couples, unemployment rate, and ages of the suspects across all studies showed no consistent variation between the two groups of cities finding a deterrent or escalating effect of arrest. The only major difference was that a larger proportion of black suspects was found in the "arrest backfires" cities (Omaha, Charlotte, and Milwaukee), compared to the "arrest deters" cities (Colorado Springs, Minneapolis, and Metro-Dade). But this pattern is not consistent: One deterrent city (Metro-Dade) shared a similar rate of black suspects with a backfiring city (Omaha)—42% and 43%, respectively.

How carefully should policymakers and advocates tread through this maze of diverse findings? Applying these results to crime control strategies is complicated by the dilemmas and choices they present. Urban legislators and police chiefs in at least 35 states can choose between continuing the status quo and not mandating arrest, a choice that will continue to harm some victims. They can also legislate arrest, a choice that may harm victims currently served by a lack of policy. Choosing between the lesser of two evils is best guided by the following summary of the facts and dilemmas gleaned from the domestic violence research published to date (see Sherman et al., 1992, pp. 19-20):

1. *Arrest reduces domestic violence in some cities but increases it in others.* It is not clear from current research how officials in any city can know which effect arrest is likely to have in their city. Cities that do not adopt an arrest policy may pass up an opportunity to help victims of domestic violence. But cities that do adopt arrest

policies—or have them imposed by state law—may catalyze more domestic violence than would otherwise occur. Either choice entails a possible moral wrong.

2. *Arrest reduces domestic violence among employed people but increases it among unemployed people.* Mandatory arrest policies may thus protect working-class women but cause greater harm to those who are poor. Conversely, not making arrests may hurt working women but reduce violence against economically poor women. Similar trade-offs may exist on the basis of race, marriage, education, and neighborhood. Thus, even in cities where arrest reduces domestic violence overall, as an unintended side effect it may increase violence against the poorest victims.

3. *Arrest reduces domestic violence in the short run but may increase it in the long run.* Three-hour arrests in Milwaukee reduced the 7% chance that a victim would be battered as soon as the police left to a 2% chance of being battered when the spouse returned from jail. But over the course of 1 year, those arrests doubled the rate of violence by the same suspects. No arrest means more danger to the victim now, whereas making an arrest may mean more danger of violence later for the same victim or for someone else.

4. *Police can predict which couples are most likely to suffer future violence, but our society values privacy too highly to encourage preventive action.* Largely because of the value our society attaches to privacy, especially marital and sexual privacy, no one has developed a recognized method, or even advice, for police to use in preventing domestic violence. A small group of chronically violent couples and incidents reported in apartment buildings produce most of the cases of domestic violence that police learn about, but the only policies now available react to the *incidents*, rather than to the *patterns*. Ignoring those patterns allows violence to continue; addressing them requires methods that many Americans would call invasions of family privacy.

Concomitant with these dilemmas is an even tougher question for officials charged with implementing effective policing strategies: Just how much research is enough to inform policy? The authors of the Minneapolis results were the target of much second-guessing and criticism from their colleagues over the reported findings and influence that the study enjoyed. Criminologists sought a more rigorous testing of the initial conclusions, perhaps foreseeing the risk of policy changes later proving to be unwise. Advocates, whose beliefs were validated by the results, and police policymakers, at least in Milwaukee, used the study to adopt arrest as the mandatory police response. In 1988, the Wisconsin legislature, perhaps less cautious than criminologists and motivated by ideological or politically pragmatic grounds, passed a law mandating arrest as the statewide response. This action occurred despite their awareness of the ongoing replication in Milwaukee testing the specific deterrent power of arrest. If a little medicine was good, a lot was even better.

The dilemma between limited research results and the need to do something about today's problems is also clearly illustrated by the Omaha offender-absent experiment. These findings may be far more compelling and relevant than the Minneapolis results because the offender is gone by the time police arrive in about half the cases brought to police attention. Yet, the study has had no observable influence on policy since its publication in an obscure journal. Modestly presented as a pilot study, no replications are being planned. Thus, there is little risk that the findings will inform policy and later be contradicted. In the meantime, assaults on thousands of victims could conceivably be thwarted if prosecutors heeded the policy implications.

Sherman et al. (1992) posited that

> the replication dilemma thus also poses a choice between two wrongs. Both using and burying research results entail risks of harm. But as Americans become more sophisticated about the scientific process, they may come to expect revisions of policy based on new scientific evidence in this realm of knowledge as in others. Americans are accustomed to constant revisions of findings about diet and disease. Cholesterol, sugar, caffeine, alcohol, jogging . . . the "latest" evidence about their relations to health and longevity has changed significantly and repeatedly over the last twenty years, and many people and businesses have changed their behavior in response. (p. 21)

To some, the choice between two wrongs invokes despair and inaction. Yet, policing domestic violence may not be hopeless. Careful review of the policy implications, combined with the freedom to test alternative policies, can lead to more effective solutions.

Use of the best information that Sherman et al. (1992, pp. 23-24) have to date guides the following five policy recommendations:

1. *Repeal mandatory arrest laws.* The most compelling implication of these findings is to challenge the wisdom of mandatory arrest. States and cities that have enacted such laws should repeal them, especially if they have substantial ghetto poverty populations with high unemployment rates. These are the settings in which mandatory arrest policies are most likely to backfire. It remains possible but unlikely that mandatory arrest creates a general deterrent effect among the wider public not arrested. Even if it does, however, increased violence among unemployed persons who are arrested is a serious moral stain on the benefits of general deterrence. The argument that arrest expresses the moral outrage of the state also appears weak if the price of that outrage is increased violence against some victims.

2. *Substitute structured police discretion.* Instead of mandating arrest in cases of misdemeanor domestic violence, state legislatures should mandate that each police agency develop its own list of approved options to be exercised at the discretion of the officer. Legislatures might also mandate 1 day of training each year to ensure that discretion is fully informed by the latest research available. The options could include allowing victims to decide whether their assailants should be arrested, transporting victims to shelters, or taking the suspects to an alcohol detoxification center.

3. *Allow warrantless arrests.* Whereas mandatory arrest has become the major issue in some states, warrantless arrest remains an issue in others. Sixteen jurisdictions have adopted mandatory arrest laws, but at last report 9 others have still not given officers full arrest powers in misdemeanor domestic violence cases that they did not witness: Alabama, California, Michigan, Mississippi, Montana, Nebraska, New York, Vermont, and West Virginia. The success of arrest in some cities suggests that every state should add this option to the police tool kit. Deciding when to use it can then become a matter of police policy based on continuing research and clinical experience, rather than on the massive effort required to change state law.

4. *Encourage issuance of arrest warrants for absent offenders.* The landmark Omaha experiment suggests that more domestic violence could be prevented by this policy than by any offender-present policy. The kinds of people who flee the scene might be more deterrable than those who stay. A prosecutor willing to issue warrants and a police agency willing to serve them can capitalize on that greater deterrability. If the Omaha warrant experiment can be replicated in other cities—a very big if—then the warrant policy might actually deter more violence than do arrests of suspects who are still present. Because it will likely be years before more research on the question is done, such policies should be adopted now. They can easily be discarded later if they are found to be harmful or ineffective.

5. *Special units and policies should focus on chronically violent couples.* Because a limited number of couples produce most of the domestic violence incidents in any city, it makes little sense for police to treat all violent couples alike. It makes even less sense to frame the whole policy debate around responses to *incidents* when most of the problem is those chronic *couples*. The challenge is to develop procedures for violent couples that do not invade family privacy. Trial and error through research and development is required for any major breakthroughs. But an effective policy for dealing with chronic couples would have more impact than any other breakthrough. It deserves the highest priority in policing domestic violence.

The opposition to mandatory arrest laws presented here may frustrate or even anger many tireless advocates who have relentlessly grasped arrest as the preferred police response to incidents of domestic violence. To them, the suggestion that other institutions, such as shelters for battered women, treatment programs for victims and offenders, schools, and welfare agencies, may better serve victims is perhaps blasphemy. But they need not become too alarmed. However sensible that approach may be, the climate in many communities today is for law enforcement officials to get tough on crime. Regardless of the results of any scientific studies, the police will remain the primary institution coping with domestic violence among the poor and unemployed. This country's current fiscal crisis dooms any substantial investment in developing new programs in both the law enforcement and social service fields. The troublesome fact remains, however, that the punishment sought by advocates and community policymakers may encourage more crime.

REFERENCE

Sherman, L. W., Schmidt, J. D., & Rogan, D. P. (1992). *Policing domestic violence: Experiments and dilemmas.* New York: Free Press.

5

Realities and Implications of the Charlotte Spousal Abuse Experiment

J. DAVID HIRSCHEL

IRA W. HUTCHISON

It is widely recognized that domestic violence is a major problem facing the United States. As policymakers struggle to devise and implement the optimum strategies for combatting this problem, we encounter fierce debate over the role that should be played by both the law and law enforcement agencies. Contributing to this debate has been the research conducted on the deterrent effect of arrest and the results of the Minneapolis experiment (Sherman & Berk, 1984a, 1984b) and its progeny (Berk, Campbell, Klap, & Western,

AUTHORS' NOTE: Research conducted under Grant No. 87-IJ-CX-K004 from the National Institute of Justice, Office of Justice Programs, U.S. Department of Justice. Points of view or opinions in this chapter are those of the authors and do not necessarily represent the official position or policies of the U.S. Department of Justice.

1992; Dunford, 1990; Dunford, Huizinga, & Elliot, 1989, 1990; Hirschel & Hutchison, 1992; Hirschel, Hutchison, & Dean, 1992; Hirschel, Hutchison, Dean, Kelley, & Pesackis, 1991; Pate & Hamilton, 1992; Pate, Hamilton, & Annan, 1992; Sherman et al., 1991; Sherman et al., 1992).

Although those who have reviewed the experimental studies have raised many valid issues, some concerns appear to be based on either a misreading or a misinterpretation of what the researchers have said or done. In this chapter, we take another look at one of the experimental studies—that conducted in Charlotte, North Carolina. After reviewing the objectives, design, and reported results of the Charlotte experiment, we examine issues that have been raised about the study and delineate the realities and implications of the experiment.

The Charlotte Experiment in Context

We have described in detail elsewhere (Hirschel, Hutchison, Dean, & Mills, 1992) the evolving attitudes toward spousal abuse, the extent of the problem of spousal abuse, and the role played by both the law and law enforcement in responding to and seeking to combat spousal abuse. We have also traced the development of preferred arrest policies and the contributions of the Minneapolis experiment to the preferred arrest movement. Showing as it did that arrest was more effective at deterring subsequent abuse than advising or separating the couple, the Minneapolis experiment blended in well with the current political climate and received an extraordinary degree of national attention. Concerns did arise, however, about basing policy on the results of a single site study that had a number of methodological problems (e.g., see Binder & Meeker, 1988; Elliot, 1989, pp. 453-454; Lempert, 1989, pp. 152-154). As a consequence, the National Institute of Justice (NIJ) funded six additional experimental studies, first in Omaha, and then later in Atlanta, Colorado Springs, Dade County (Florida), Milwaukee, and Charlotte (North Carolina).

Objectives of the Charlotte Experiment

This study of police response to spousal abuse in Charlotte was initiated in response to the NIJ request for proposals to replicate and extend the Minneapolis experiment. The suggestion to apply for the grant came from the chief of police, and from its inception the experiment was a collaborative venture between the Charlotte Police Department and researchers from the University of North Carolina at Charlotte.

The scope of the research was dictated by the original NIJ request for proposals: Its focus was on the rather narrow research issue of whether arrest was more effective than other police responses at deterring subsequent abuse. Although arrest had to be one of the response options employed in the research design, research teams were free to propose whatever other responses they wished to test. In addition to arrest, Charlotte decided to examine the deterrent effect of advising (and possibly separating) the couple and issuing a citation (an order requiring the offender to appear in court to face specific criminal charges).

Certain additional core elements were required of all the replication studies: All employed an experimental design in which cases that met predefined eligibility requirements were assigned randomly to treatment responses; all focused on the misdemeanor range of cases, in which the police were empowered but not required to make an arrest; and a 6-month follow-up was conducted on all eligible cases through the use of police records and interviews with victims.

In recognition of the importance of these studies, NIJ took the unusual step of retaining the proposal review team as an advisory board to help guide and coordinate the activities of the different research teams. At meetings, the core elements, which had been described in each of the proposals, were more fully developed. Each phase of the projects—design, implementation, and data analysis— was scrutinized by the NIJ advisory board. This occurred at quarterly meetings and through site visits and other communications. Data tapes were presented to the board on an ongoing basis, and all core analyses were subjected to independent verification.

The research teams were permitted, within budgetary constraints, to build around the core elements and to develop ancillary issues for investigation. As we describe the design of the Charlotte experiment, we highlight its unique features and outline some of the additional issues explored.

DESIGN

Location

Charlotte is the largest urban area between Washington, D.C., and Atlanta, Georgia. At the time the study was initiated in 1986, the city had a population of 352,070 (U.S. Bureau of the Census, 1988, p. 690). Economically, the city remains diversified; unemployment rates are generally lower than in other parts of the state or nation and have seldom exceeded 5% in the past decade. At the midpoint of the study in 1988, the average household income was $34,000, and per capita income was $13,463 (Charlotte Chamber of Commerce, telephone interview, May 1990).

Police Department

At the time of the study, the Charlotte Police Department had more than 1,000 employees, of whom approximately 20% were civilians. The sworn officers were categorized into patrol, investigative, and administrative divisions, with the patrol division constituting 75% of the sworn personnel. Approximately two thirds (66%) of the patrol officers were white males; 17% were black males; 12% were white females; and 5% were black females. More than 50% of the patrol officers had been on the force for fewer than 3 years.

Research Design

The Charlotte project investigated the effectiveness of three police responses to spousal abuse: (a) advising and possibly separating the couple, (b) issuing a citation to the offender, and (c) arresting the offender. The citation was unique to the Charlotte experiment and was initiated to provide a contrast with the less formal advise/separate treatment and the more formal arrest treatment. Additionally, the Charlotte experiment was the only one of the NIJ replication experiments to use the entire patrol force and to operate citywide 24 hours a day.

Eligibility

We anticipated at the outset of the project that the eligibility requirements would result in only a small proportion of spousal abuse calls received by the police qualifying for the experiment. This is an important issue to recognize because some criticisms of the replication projects have been directed at the small numbers of eligible cases as compared with the total population of domestic calls received by the police (e.g., see Zorza, 1992, who exaggerates this ratio considerably by erroneously attributing Charlotte with receiving "591,664 calls for domestic disturbance help," [p. 69], when in actuality that number was the total calls for assistance *for all purposes* during the 99-week experiment). The eligibility criteria were a combination of legal requirements, policy judgments, and issues of research design.

The primary legal criterion was that eligible cases must have been *misdemeanor* offenses. The necessity for this criterion was that an abusive incident must have been such that any of the three assigned treatments could have been assigned but none was required. If an arrest were mandatory (e.g., if the offender were subject to an outstanding warrant), then neither of the other two treatments would have been an option. Conversely, if the responding officers concluded that no offense had been committed, then arrest would not have been an option. The requirement that eligible cases fall within the misdemeanor range ensured the selection of cases in which *police were empowered but not required to make a warrant-less arrest.*

Unlike some of the other NIJ replication experiments, the Charlotte project included *only* (a) female victims (b) of male offenders (c) who were or had been in spouse or spouse-like relationships. This project focused on couples who were married, separated, divorced, cohabitants, or former cohabitants. Although certainly deserving of support and legal protection, we excluded same-sex relationships, sibling relationships, parent-child relationships, and noncohabiting boyfriend-girlfriend relationships as falling outside the purview of spousal abuse research. This exclusion makes the Charlotte project less vulnerable to the criticism that "numerous cases that may have far different dynamics . . . were lumped together" (Zorza, 1992, p. 67). As noted by Garner, Fagan, and Maxwell (in press), the inclusion of different types of relationships in such spousal abuse studies funded by NIJ does muddy the potential comparisons across projects.

Other policy decisions were to exclude cases in which either the victim or the offender was under age 18 (because special parental approval would have been required) and cases in which safety required case exclusion. The research was designed so that the project should not pose any additional danger to either the victims or the responding officers. Victim safety is a concern that has been raised appropriately by some commentators (e.g., see Bowman, 1992) and is a rationale for exclusion that apparently has been missed by others (e.g., see Zorza, 1992, p. 70) despite its clear articulation in previously published reports of the Charlotte experiment (e.g., see Hirschel, Hutchinson, Dean, Kelley, & Pesackis, 1991, pp. 14-15; Hirschel & Hutchison, 1992, p. 90; Hirschel, Hutchison, & Dean, 1992, p. 14). Officers could make an arrest if the victim insisted on arrest, if the offender threatened or assaulted the officers, and if the officers thought the offender posed imminent danger to the victim. It should be noted that if an offender were randomly assigned to the arrest treatment, the officers were not free to cancel the arrest at the victim's request. In short, officers could implement a *more* serious response (e.g., arrest) if safety warranted, but not a less serious treatment (e.g., advise/separate) at the request of the victim.

The final eligibility criterion arose directly from the research design. Because it was not possible for responding officers to deliver all treatments if either the victim or the offender was not present at the scene, the absence of either made the case ineligible for inclusion in the experiment. This criterion proved to be a major exclusionary factor because approximately half of the offenders left the scene prior to the arrival of the police. Among the NIJ replication experiments, only Omaha (Dunford et al., 1989) included an offender-absent component in the research.

Cases selected for this experiment clearly do not represent all spousal abuse calls that the police receive; however, they do represent cases in which police have the discretionary power to make warrantless arrests, and it is to this population that the results of the experiment may be applied.

Random Assignment of Treatments

The purpose of employing random assignment procedures in an experiment is to obtain equivalence among the cases in different experimental groups. Such equivalence, established prior to the delivery of the treatments, ensures that (a) any differences observed prior to treatments occur by chance and that (b) any differences observed subsequent to the treatments are then attributable to treatment effect.

As described in more detail elsewhere (Hirschel & Hutchison, 1992, pp. 90-91; Hirschel, Hutchison, Dean, Kelley, & Pesackis, 1991, pp. 32-40), the Charlotte experiment used the police department's computer-assisted dispatch system to generate codes for random treatment assignment. The procedure was based on the time a call was received and was not subject to manipulation because the time stamp used to generate the response code occurred automatically before the telecommunication operator was informed of the reason for the call. To prevent knowledge of the code influencing determination of case eligibility, the computer program was structured so that the randomized number appeared on the dispatcher's screen only when requested by the dispatcher and after an officer had arrived on the scene and determined case eligibility. By removing the assignment process from human decision making (and despite considerable initial resistance from many patrol officers during training sessions), this aspect of the experiment was implemented as designed.

Comparisons made on 29 victim, offender, and offense characteristics that might have been responsible for an unknown bias in the random assignment process gave reason for a high level of confidence in the integrity of the randomization process. In only 1 of the 29 comparisons (whether the victim and offender lived together) was a statistically significant difference found between the three groups at the .05 level (Hirschel, Hutchison, Dean, Kelley, & Pesackis, 1991, pp. 35-39).

Police Treatments

The Charlotte research was designed to measure the impact of three police treatments (responses) on spousal abuse recidivism. The three treatments had both common and distinctive elements; each had prescribed police actions, optional actions, and proscribed actions (cf. Hirschel, Hutchison, Dean, Kelley, & Pesackis, 1991, pp. 61-77, for additional detail). Two features were common to all three treatments. First, the responding officers (almost always two) were to attempt to calm matters down and restore order. Second, each victim was to be given an information card that provided basic details about the availability of local resources that could be of assistance—namely, the Victim Assistance Program and the battered women's shelter. Additionally, general police procedures allowed officers to transport a person to another location.

Other features differentiated the three treatments. The advise/ separate response required that officers attempt to help the couple solve their immediate problem; this might involve referring them to a social service agency. The citation response required that the officers issue the offender a standard citation and explain the required court appearance to both the victim and the offender. The arrest treatment required that the offender be arrested, handcuffed, and transported to the local jail for an appearance before a magistrate. Both citation and arrest were typically carried out in the presence of the victim. According to police data, one tenth of the victims in the citation response category and almost one fourth of those in the arrest response category argued against the mandated treatment.

Treatment Integrity

Treatment integrity, the degree to which treatments were consistently delivered as designed, is highly desirable in experimental research. Unfortunately, it is far simpler in controlled experimental conditions (as in much medical research) than in field experiments to duplicate the identical "treatment" from one case to another. The dilemma, then, is the opportunity for considerable variation in how police "deliver" a particular treatment. For example, one officer might be handcuffing an offender and be apologizing for the need to do so while another is taking the same action but is curt and unfriendly. Technically, the two treatments are the same because both offenders are handcuffed, but the contexts are quite different. Such variation in delivery exists both across police officers and within the pattern of a single officer. Human interaction is far too variable and complex for anyone to claim that treatment delivery is constant. That said, comparisons of police report data and victim interview data do show more congruence than incongruence between officer and victim reports; both agree that a specific procedure was done or not done. Data from both police and victims confirm that the core of each treatment was usually carried out as designed—for example, arrested offenders were handcuffed the majority of the time; offenders who received a citation did have it explained to them; and officers almost always "calmed things down and restored order."

Although our data show numerous departures from the designed treatment, our analysis of treatment integrity (cf. Hirschel, Hutchison, Dean, Kelley, & Pesackis, 1991, pp. 71-77) suggests two conclusions. First, police implemented the treatments as designed most of the time. Second, although there is built-in commonality on some treatment actions, there is sufficient distinction between them to have confidence in the uniqueness of each treatment.

Caseflow and Officer Participation

Between the inception of the field test on August 8, 1987, and its conclusion on June 30, 1989, the project received 686 eligible cases at the rate of almost 1 case per day. During this research, approximately 550 patrol officers were involved at one time or another in patrol duties. Because of normal attrition (e.g., internal transfers, injuries, illnesses, retirement), some officers had little or no opportunity to produce an eligible case. Moreover, the majority of calls (96.2%) were answered by two or more officers, only one of whom completed the paperwork and received "credit" for participation. It is thus impossible to state precisely which officers and how many simply did not participate, but we can estimate—contrary to allegations made by Sherman (1992b, p. 144)—that the number of nonparticipants was small. A total of 252 officers were officially credited with producing the 686 eligible cases, with 116 officers contributing 1 case; 48 officers, 2 cases; 21 officers, 3 cases; 21 officers, 4 cases; and 46 officers, 5 or more cases. The top three contributors produced 54 eligible cases, 7.8% of the total.

Assigned and Delivered Treatments

As noted above, eligible calls were randomly assigned one of the three treatments. Occasionally, the assigned treatment was not followed and another treatment was actually delivered. A high rate of treatments not delivered as assigned would undermine the integrity of the experiment, so every effort was made to minimize the nondelivery of assigned treatments. Because the Charlotte project alone used the entire patrol force, we expected that a higher rate of misdelivery of treatment would occur than if an elite (and highly trained) squad had been employed. The actual misdelivery rate was higher than we would have liked but within acceptable limits for a field experiment of this nature.[1] We reiterate that the design "permitted" movement from less severe to more severe treatments on the basis of officer judgment; however, no comparable permission was given to move from a more severe to less severe treatment, although there was sometimes a logical reason for doing so.[2]

Data Sources

Two data sources were used to reveal acts of abuse perpetrated by the offender on the victim subsequent to the presenting incident (the abusive incident that brought the couple into the research): official police records and victim interviews.

Police Records

Re-arrest provides a conservative measure of abuse subsequent to the presenting incident. As we have noted elsewhere (e.g., see Hirschel, Hutchison, & Dean, 1992, p. 9), only half of abused women *ever* call the police to report an abusive incident, and of those who do call, most do not call to report every abusive incident. Moreover, even if every abusive incident were reported to the police by the women in this experiment, most incidents would not produce a re-arrest of the offender. Dutton (1987) calculates that the probability is approximately 1% that an abusive incident will eventually result in the arrest of the offender. Nonetheless, arrest is accepted as a standard measure of recidivism in criminological studies and is used here as a counterpart measure to victim interviews.

Victim Interviews

The research design called for the victims to be interviewed twice by female interviewers: first, shortly after the presenting incident, and again 6 months after the presenting incident. A total of 686 eligible cases were obtained during the experiment; 40 of these were excluded from the interview process because they involved repeat victims who had already been assigned interviews ($N = 36$) or were cases for which it was discovered, after the officers had carried out the assigned treatment, that either the victim or the offender was under age 18 ($N = 4$). Initial interviews were obtained in 419 of the 646 cases assigned for interview, an assigned interview completion rate of 65%. In over half the cases for which we failed to obtain an initial interview, the victim refused to be interviewed primarily because she feared retaliation by the offender if he found out about the interview. In line with our concern for victim safety, we had decided early in the project to be cautious about pressuring women for interviews. It is possible that we adopted an overly cautious approach, and it is uncertain what impact this had on interview completion rates.

Six-month interviews were obtained from 324 victims, an assigned 6-month victim interview rate of 83%. The completion of 324 6-month interviews produced an overall assigned interview completion rate (both initial and 6-month) of 50.2%. Although this rate is lower than desired, the generalizability of the results to the larger pool of eligible cases is still sound. Interview completion for victims in the different treatment categories did not vary at statistically significant levels for either initial or 6-month interviews (cf. Hirschel, Hutchison, Dean, Kelley, & Pesackis, 1991, pp. 84, 91). If cases that produced interviews were significantly different from those that did not produce interviews, then the results might be suspect. Analysis of these two groups on 26 relevant victim, offender, and offense characteristics, however, produced no significant differences in 24 of the 26 comparisons. The hypothesis that "less socially bonded couples (were) harder to interview" (Sherman, 1992a, p. 31) is not supported by these data. Indeed, on one of the only two variables that showed a significant difference between the two groups (possession of a prior state felony record), the interviewed cases had the higher percentage of offenders with prior records (34.8% vs. 25.1%, $\chi^2 = 5.95$, $p = .02$).[3] In addition, victims who were not interviewed were more likely than those who were interviewed to have offenders who were employed at the time of the presenting incident (71.4% vs. 67.1%, $\chi^2 = 1.10$, $p = .30$).

FINDINGS

Analysis of Calls Received

During the 99 weeks (August 8, 1987, through June 30, 1989) the experiment was in operation, the police department received

591,664 calls for assistance for all purposes (e.g., traffic, burglary, domestic). Most of these calls (537,053; 90.8%) resulted in an officer being dispatched to the scene. Of those calls in which an officer was dispatched to the scene, 47,687 (8.9%) were received under the domestic violence (10-91) code. Naturally, not all of these calls turned out to involve domestic situations. Conversely, a number of calls dispatched on other codes (in particular, 10-90, the assault code) turned out to involve domestic situations. Altogether 18,963 cases were determined at the scene to constitute spouse-like situations; this represents 3.2% of all calls received and 3.5% of all calls dispatched. Of the 18,963 spouse-like cases, 15,583 (82.2%) were determined to involve situations with no probable cause to believe that a crime had been committed, and 3,380 (17.8%) cases had a determination of probable cause. Of the 3,380 probable cause cases, 882 (26.1%) were cases in which an on-the-scene arrest was deemed to be mandatory, generally because the victim insisted on arrest (603; 68.4% of the cases) or because the officers thought that arrest was necessary to ensure the victim's safety (182; 20.6% of the cases). A total of 1,646 (48.7%) were cases for which an on-the-scene arrest was not feasible, primarily because the offender had already left the scene (1,437; 87.3% of the cases). Finally, 852 (25.2%) were cases for which an on-the-scene arrest was discretionary. Cases in which arrest was discretionary differed from the other two categories in that they were most likely to involve male victims and female offenders (categories excluded from the experimental study). This finding perhaps indicates that female offenders were less likely than their male counterparts either to pose further danger to their victims or to leave the scene.

Profile of Experimental Cases

In the Charlotte experiment, 686 eligible cases were produced. Most were dispatched as domestics to a residence and were responded to by two or more officers. Almost 50% of the cases involved married couples, and over 40% involved cohabitants; in over 80% of the cases, the victim and offender were currently living together. Victims tended to be in their late 20s, offenders in their early 30s. In approximately 50% of the cases, at least one child under the age of 18 was at the residence when police arrived. Approximately two thirds of the victims and offenders were black, and similar proportions were currently employed. Roughly half of the offenders and a quarter of the victims were judged by the responding officers to be impaired by or under the influence of alcohol and/or drugs. The majority of the victims were reported to have bruises, but relatively few required medical care. Approximately two thirds of the offenders had local arrest records.

Measuring Treatment Effects

The 686 eligible cases involved 650 different offenders. In each of the 36 cases in which an offender reentered the experiment with a new offense, the incident was processed as a repeat offense and the second incident was not counted as a new case.

Of concern in all the experiments was the question of how deterrence was to be conceptualized and measured. The general focus was on the concept of "failure": If a treatment for a specific case did not deter subsequent abuse, this would be a case of treatment failure, or recidivism. Although this conceptualization may appear relatively clear and unambiguous, the reality is far more complicated.

What exactly would be considered "subsequent abuse"? How would it be measured? All projects used both official police records (primarily arrest data) and unofficial records (the victim interviews). All projects had three measures of recidivism at their disposal: prevalence, incidence, and time to failure. Finally, all projects had the potential to conduct analyses and report findings based on either treatment as assigned or treatment as delivered. Thus, the *simplest* explication has a minimum of 12 possible bases for research conclusions (2 data sources × 3 measures of recidivism × 2 approaches to reporting treatment). It is little wonder there has been so much confusion over inconsistent results (cf. Garner et al., in press).

We begin with (a) arrest (b) prevalence (c) based on treatment as assigned. This measure has been the most widely reported (though not necessarily accurately or consistently) measure by the different spousal abuse projects.

Prevalence of Treatment Failure

Arrest as a Measure of Treatment Failure

In this study, primary arrest recidivism was operationalized as "Any arrest for any subsequent offense by the same offender against the same victim committed within six months of the presenting incident" (Hirschel, Hutchison, Dean, Kelley, & Pesackis, 1991, p. 94). Although most (76.4%) of the offenses committed by offenders constituted assaults against the person, this operational definition is not so limited and includes a variety of other offenses, such as criminal trespass and damage to property. This operationalization does not include a subsequent arrest made on the basis of an offense committed during the presenting incident. Likewise, arrests for procedural matters (e.g., an arrest for failure to appear in a citation case) are not included as arrest recidivism.

The prevalence of arrest recidivism (percentage of cases with at least one failure) for the three treatments during the 6 months after the presenting incidents is reported in Table 5.1. Examination of the data in Table 5.1 indicates an overall prevalence rate of 16.5; this means that, overall, one offender in six was re-arrested for another offense against the victim within 6 months following the presenting incident. The overall rate encompasses a prevalence rate of 18.2 for the arrest, 11.8 for the advise/separate, and 19.2 for the citation treatment. The differences among the three treatments are not statistically significant at the .05 level. On the basis of this measure of prevalence, arrest is no better at deterring failure than the other two treatments; nor is it *statistically* worse—that is, there is no statistically significant escalation effect.

Alternative Measures of Arrest and Treatment Failure

The preceding data focus on recidivism results based on arrest of the same offender for an offense against the same victim, a somewhat narrow definition of recidivism. However, different definitions of the dependent measure are possible. To assess treatment effects on spousal abuse recidivism more thoroughly, we investigate additional operational definitions of arrest recidivism.

Four operational definitions are examined. All use the 6-month follow-up period and incorporate an arrest or re-arrest of the same offender involved in the presenting incident. The first of these four definitions of secondary arrest recidivism is similar to primary arrest recidivism except that we include arrests related to the presenting incident; for example, the couple receives the advise treatment at the presenting incident but the victim secures a warrant for the offender's arrest for that same incident the following

TABLE 5.1 Prevalence and Incidence of Arrest Recidivism, by Treatment[a]

| | Treatment Assigned | | | |
	Arrest	Citation	Advise/Separate	Total
Number of subsequent arrests				
0	175	181	187	543
1	36	33	24	93
2	2	7	1	10
3	1	1	0	2
4	0	2	0	2
Total failures	39	43	25	107
Total cases	214	224	212	650
Prevalence[b]	18.2	19.2	11.8	16.5
Incidence[c]	.201	.259	.123	.195

NOTE: a. As measured 6 months subsequent to presenting incident.
b. $\chi^2 = 5.063$, d.f. = 2, $p = .080$
c. F ratio = 4.211, d.f.(1) = 2, d.f.(2) = 647, $p = .015$.

day. The second operational definition allows a subsequent arrest of the offender for any crime of violence against any person. The third operational definition is to include crimes against property in addition to the crimes of violence. The fourth operational definition is all-encompassing: any subsequent arrest of the offender for any offense (spousal abuse, assaults against others, property damage, drug-related crimes; in short, any crime for which a person may be arrested).

The analyses of these data, which are reported in detail elsewhere (Hirschel & Hutchison, 1992, pp. 106-109; Hirschel, Hutchison, Dean, Kelley, & Pesackis, 1991, pp. 113-117), provide some important insights. First, these analyses produced no statistically significant differences for any of the four definitions. Different operational definitions of arrest, however, did generate strikingly different p values. The p values vary considerably, ranging from .080 for our measure of primary arrest recidivism (the only one approaching statistical significance at the .05 level; the next lowest p value was .30) to .67 for our broadest definition of secondary arrest recidivism. In general, the narrower the definition of arrest recidivism, the lower the p value. Second, the different operationalizations of arrest recidivism lead to markedly different conclusions about the amount of recidivism. The recidivism rate using the most generic definition is twice the rate using the primary and more specific definition (32.6% vs. 16.5%). Third, these analyses produce some change in the rank ordering of the treatments in terms of their effectiveness. When, for example, the broadest definition of arrest recidivism (any subsequent arrest whatsoever) is used, the citation treatment produces the lowest rate of recidivism; when the narrowest definition of arrest recidivism (same couple excluding presenting incident) is used, the citation treatment produces the highest rate of recidivism. However, none of these treatment differences is statistically significant at the .05 level.

The importance of selecting a suitable operational definition of arrest cannot be overemphasized. The theoretical framework of this study resulted in the choice of the narrow definition of arrest recidivism presented above. The choice of a different definition would have produced a different rank ordering of the treatments. Likewise, the importance of thoroughly investigating the details of each arrest even against the same victim cannot be overly stressed. Simply taking a rap sheet at face value without examining case reports may lead to the erroneous inclusion of arrests on procedural matters as arrests for subsequent offenses.

Arrest Prevalence Reexamined

The primary analyses of official recidivism were conducted by using treatment as assigned as the independent variable and by performing the analyses on the 650 couples that produced eligible cases. As clearly demonstrated in the preceding analyses, the three treatments are not different in producing either a deterrent or an escalation effect at statistically significant levels.

In this subsection, we examine the results obtained by (a) taking into account race, prior criminal record, and other such variables, (b) conducting the analyses on sample sizes that are theoretically important but different from the basic sample of 650, and (c) using treatment as delivered as the independent variable.

Analyses on Treatment as Assigned, Taking Other Variables Into Account. These analyses take into account such offender-related variables as race, age, employment status, and prior record; such victim-related variables as race, age, employment status, and victim-suspect relationship; and such incident-related variables as location of the offense and infliction of injury and property damage. Initial examination of the association between these variables and arrest recidivism indicated that the strongest predictors of recidivism were measures of the offender's prior criminal activity. Further analysis led to the conclusion that although prior criminal activity was significantly associated with recidivism, other offender-related variables (e.g., race, age, marital and employment status) were not. Analyses of prevalence controlling for these variables yielded no significant interactions with treatment effects (for more details, see Hirschel & Hutchison, 1992, p. 104; Hirschel, Hutchison, Dean, Kelley, & Pesackis, 1991, pp. 104-105).

Analyses Based on Sample Sizes Other Than That of the Basic Sample. As noted above, all primary analyses on arrest recidivism were conducted on a sample size of 650. Although we consider this sample size to be the most appropriate for the analyses undertaken, we acknowledge that arguments may be raised in favor of other sample sizes.

First, it may be argued that, instead of treating repeat cases as treatment failures, they should be counted as new cases, although this inclusion violates the assumption of independence. Because this study had 36 repeat cases, the sample size rises to 686. Second, it may be argued that cases that entered the experiment during the final 6 months of operation should be excluded from analysis because operational procedures changed on June 30, 1989, when eligible cases were no longer randomly assigned one of the three treatments. Excluding these cases reduces the sample size to 513. Third, it may be argued that analysis should be conducted solely on cases that were assigned and delivered the same treatment. Of the 650 eligible cases, 545 were delivered the treatment they had been assigned.

All three analyses produced results insignificant at the .05 level. The analyses of repeat cases treated as new cases ($N = 686$) and all cases except those that entered the experiment during the final 6 months ($N = 513$) yielded statistically insignificant results similar to those obtained by the primary analysis of arrest recidivism. Analysis of the delivered-as-assigned cases ($N = 545$), however, showed the arrest treatment to have the highest recidivism rate, but still not at a statistically significant level (17.0, as compared with 15.7 for the citation and 12.4 for the advise/separate treatment: $\chi^2 = 1.62, p = .44$).

Analyses Based on Treatment as Delivered. Primary analyses were conducted on treatments as assigned. This yielded the most unambiguous results relative to statistical standards. Because not all of the treatments were delivered as assigned, we considered it worthwhile to examine the results obtained by using treatment as delivered as the independent variable. This approach yielded results insignificant at the .05 level. In this analysis, however, the arrest treatment produced the highest failure rate (18.9, compared with 15.3 for citation and 14.5 for advise/separate; $\chi^2 = 1.94, p = .38$).

Prevalence of Failure as Reported in Victim Interviews

The research design called for victims to be interviewed twice: first, shortly after the presenting incident, and again 6 months after the presenting incident. The initial interview focused on episodes of abuse that occurred between the time of the presenting incident and the first interview. The 6-month interview included only incidents that occurred after the first interview. Each victim was asked about six types of victimization—namely, whether the offender had (a) threatened to hurt her, (b) actually hurt or tried to hurt her, (c) threatened to hurt any member of the family, (d) actually hurt or tried to hurt any member of the family, (e) threatened to damage property, and (f) actually damaged any property. Victims were asked to estimate how often each type of victimization had occurred and were posed more detailed questions on the first and most recent occurrence of victimization.

As noted earlier, the Charlotte project produced a completed interview rate of 50% for *both* first and second interviews. This result has led some (e.g., Sherman, 1992b, p. 197) to suggest that the victim-based information is suspect because data were not obtained from a larger proportion of the experimental cases and that the arrest data are inherently better. We think that victim-based data are highly important and that, although it is certainly true a higher completion rate would have been desirable, it is important to keep the following in mind. First, as reported earlier, extensive comparisons conducted on interviewed versus noninterviewed cases showed the two groups to be very similar. Thus, it is reasonable to conclude that the interviewed women are representative of all the women who entered the experiment. Second, although Sherman (1992b, p. 197) has suggested that the interviewed constitute a "special pool" of the larger sample, the fact is that the special pool concept is as applicable to those arrested as to those interviewed. Misdemeanants are not uniformly arrested. As other research has shown (e.g., see Berk & Newton, 1985, p. 260), police are most likely to arrest those they would have arrested anyhow. Thus, there is no reason to conclude that *arrest* is a highly accurate barometer of repeat abuse. Third, because even women who are inclined to call the police do not call them for every abusive incident, the arrest measure can be faulted because it is contingent on someone, the victim or another, initiating the sequence. Fourth, as Lerman (1992) points out, it is possible that an interrelationship exists between the treatments and the likelihood of calling the police for subsequent abuse, with victims assigned nonarrest interventions less likely to report because of "disappointment with the police response" (p. 228).

The bottom line is that we know half the cases in the Charlotte experiment produced two interviews and that cases that produced interviews were very similar to those that did not. We do not know exactly what percentage of cases with subsequent abuse was reported to the police, but we can gauge that it was less than 50%. Moreover, we do not know how these cases differed from those that were not reported to the police. Thus, it is problematic to conclude that the arrest data are either more complete or inherently more reliable than the victim-based data.

Analysis of the victim interview data produced no statistically significant differences among the three treatments for any of the six measures of recidivism examined in either the initial or the 6-month interviews. A composite measure of recidivism obtained by summing the responses to the screen questions for the six types of victimization also showed no significant differences among the three treatments for either the initial or the 6-month interviews (for more details, see Hirschel & Hutchison, 1992, pp. 110-112; Hirschel, Hutchison, Dean, Kelley, & Pesackis, 1991, pp. 120-129).

To obtain a complete accounting for all acts of recidivism for the full follow-up period, data obtained from the initial interviews were combined with data from the 6-month interviews. Table 5.2 indi-

TABLE 5.2 Victim-Reported Recidivism, by Treatment[a]

Treatment Assigned	Arrest	Citation	Advise/Separate	Total
Number of incidents of recidivism				
0	46	43	41	130
1	14	18	10	42
2	2	12	8	22
3	12	6	13	31
4	3	9	3	15
5 or more	35	36	27	98
Total failures	66	81	61	208
Total N interviewed	112	124	102	338
Prevalence[b]	58.9	65.3	59.8	61.5
Incidence[c]	2.152	2.226	2.078	2.157

NOTE: a. Based on initial and 6-month interviews combined.
b. $\chi^2 = 1.202$, d.f. $= 2$, $p = .548$.
c. F ratio $= .132$, d.f.$(1) = 2$, d.f.$(2) = 335$, $p = .875$.

cates a prevalence rate of 65.3 for the citation, 59.8 for the advise/separate, and 58.9 for the arrest treatment. Consistent with all the findings on the prevalence of victim-reported recidivism, no significant differences were found among the three treatments in subsequent victim-reported incidents.

Thus, although neither a deterrent nor escalation effect is shown in the victim interview data, these data do show far higher rates of recidivism than the arrest data. At the time of the initial interview, generally within 2 weeks of the presenting incident, almost one third (31.0%) of the women had already experienced another abusive incident. At the time of the 6-month interview, that proportion had increased to almost two thirds (61.5%). This prevalence rate of recidivism reported by the victims is almost four times greater than that indicated by the arrest data (16.5%).

Prevalence of Failure Using Both Arrest and Victim Data

The respective strengths and weaknesses of the two measures of recidivism have been discussed in detail elsewhere (e.g., see Hirschel,

Hutchison, Dean, Kelley, & Pesackis, 1991, pp. 137-138). Cross-tabulation of the prevalence of arrest recidivism with the prevalence of victim-reported recidivism revealed a high degree of congruence between the two data sources, with statistical association significant beyond the .001 level. When this analysis was repeated, controlling for treatment as assigned, similar results were obtained. The absence of treatment effect for the combined arrest and victimization data was confirmed by a log-linear analysis (cf. Hirschel & Hutchison, 1992, pp. 113-114; Hirschel, Hutchison, Dean, Kelley, & Pesackis, 1991, pp. 139-145).

Incidence of Treatment Failure

The analyses in the preceding section focused on the prevalence of certain occurrences as measures of failure. In this section, we use *incidence of failure* to provide an alternative viewpoint. *Incidence* is defined as the average number of failures per case within a given treatment group.

Incidence of Failure as Measured by Arrest

As shown in Table 5.1, the incidence rate of arrest recidivism for the total sample was .195. The rate was .201 for those in the arrest treatment, .123 for offenders in the advise/separate treatment, and .259 for those in the citation treatment. Analysis of variance based on the number of subsequent arrests produced an overall F ratio significant at the .05 level. Scheffé multiple range comparisons and chi square analyses, however, yielded significance at the .05 level only for the advise/separate-citation comparison (Hirschel & Hutchison, 1992, pp. 102-103; Hirschel, Hutchison, & Dean, 1992, p. 20; Hirschel, Hutchison, Dean, Kelley, & Pesackis, 1991, p.103). Thus, in comparing rates of failure as measured by incidence, arrest is apparently more effective than the citation treatment but apparently less effective than the advise/separate treatment. However, arrest is not significantly more or less effective than these other two treatments at statistically acceptable levels.

To examine more comprehensively the effect of the advise/separate treatment and to control to some extent for misdeliveries of treatment (38.1% of the misdeliveries were citations delivered as arrests), analysis was undertaken of the informal (advise/separate) versus the formal (citation and arrest) treatment responses. Analysis of pairwise Scheffé comparisons indicated that the informal response was indeed more successful at deterring subsequent abuse. It also showed that the contrast between arrest and nonarrest (advise/separate and citation combined) was not statistically significant at the .05 level. Similar results were obtained through analysis of all cases except those that entered the experiment in the final 6 months ($N = 513$). Analysis of repeat cases treated as new cases ($N = 686$) and delivered-as-assigned cases ($N = 545$) produced results that were insignificant at the .05 level. Although the prevalence analysis of the delivered-as-assigned cases had shown the arrest treatment to have the highest recidivism rate (though with a p value of .44), the incidence analysis showed the citation treatment to have the highest recidivism rate (.211, as compared with .191 for the arrest and .130 for the advise/separate treatment: F ratio = 1.44, $p = .24$). Analysis using treatment as delivered as the independent variable produced results that were insignificant at the .05 level (F ratio = 1.56, $p = .21$). Finally, analyses of incidence controlling for relevant offender, victim, and incident variables yielded no significant interactions with treatment effects.

Incidence of Failure as Reported by Victims

The overall 6-month incidence rate of repeated abuse, based on victim reported data, was 2.16 incidents per victim; more specifically, the rate was 2.15 for arrest cases, 2.23 for citation cases, and 2.08 for advise/separate cases, statistically a chance rank ordering ($p = .88$; see Table 5.2).

Time to Failure

Prevalence and incidence measures are not sensitive to significant fluctuations in the relative effectiveness of the three treatments that may occur during the 6-month period. To identify such time fluctuations in deterrence, survival analysis was conducted on the data. This approach indicates what proportion of a group "survives" a given time period without being abused again.

Arrest and Time to Failure

The survival analysis indicated that at no time was the arrest treatment more effective in deterring subsequent abuse than the other two treatments. Initially, for the first 3 weeks, the arrest treatment was slightly more effective than the combined advise/ separate and citation treatments. However, the differences were small, were not sustained, and were not statistically significant. When the formal (citation and arrest) treatments were combined and compared with the advise/separate treatment, a statistically significant difference did emerge, particularly toward the end of the 6-month measurement period (for more details, see Hirschel, Hutchison, Dean, Kelley, & Pesackis, 1991, pp. 108-113).

Time to Failure Based on Victim Reports

The survival rates for most of the follow-up period were close, with the arrest cases producing a survival rate of 40.8, the advise/ separate cases a rate of 40.1, and the citation cases a rate of 39.1 after 180 days. None of the analyses produced statistically significant differences (for more details, see Hirschel, Hutchison, Dean, Kelley, & Pesackis, 1991, pp. 129-136). These analyses underscore the fact that the victim interview data are unambiguous in indicating a lack of treatment effect in deterring or escalating subsequent abuse.

Summary of Prevalence, Incidence, and Time to Failure Results

The preceding data analyses demonstrated little treatment effect. The best generalization based on these data is that arrest is not an effective deterrent to subsequent abuse. This generalization is supported by extensive analysis of prevalence data, by incidence data, and by time to failure data. The generalization is supported by both official police records and victim interview data. The generalization is supported by looking at different kinds of arrests and taking into account specific demographic characteristics (e.g., race, marital status, employment status). There are some exceptions to the overall pattern, but very few. If enough comparisons are made, researchers are bound to find some differences somewhere.

Does Arrest Escalate Abuse Rates?

These data appear to produce an overall pattern (indicate a *direction*) of the advise/separate treatment exerting the greatest deterrent effect and the citation the least, with the arrest response generally nestled in the middle. Most of the analyses, however, do not produce results that are significant at the .05 level. Although we have concluded in previous reports that "the results of the Charlotte experiment are decisive and unambiguous, and indicate that arrest of misdemeanor spouse abusers is neither substantively nor statistically a more effective deterrent to repeat abuse than either of the other two police responses" (Hirschel, Hutchison, Dean, Kelley, & Pesackis, 1991, p. 154), Sherman (1992a, 1992b) has declared that the Charlotte experiment showed arrest to have a clear escalation effect. We believe that such a conclusion is based on three errors: first, discounting the victim data; second, substituting direction for scientific convention of statistical significance; and third, ignoring the contaminating effect of the citation option.

We recognized earlier in this chapter that our victim interview response rate was not as high as we would have liked and acknowledged that the statistical power of the tests employed to determine treatment effects in the victim interview data was not as great as desired. We hope we have demonstrated, however, that it is reasonable to generalize from the sample of interviewed cases to the larger pool of experimental cases; that there are inherent weaknesses in official data; and that it is wrong to dismiss the victim data as being less complete or less reliable than the official data. The victim interviews show the citation response to have the highest recidivism rates (65.3 for prevalence, 2.226 for incidence), whereas the arrest and advise/separate treatments are too close to call: arrest with a prevalence rate of 58.9 and an incidence rate of 2.152, compared with rates of 59.8 and 2.078 for advise/separate.

It is correct that our data show the advise/separate treatment generally produces a lower rate of recidivism than arrest or citation or the two of these combined. We agree that the *direction* of the data often indicates a greater deterrent effect of the advise/separate treatment than of the other two treatments. The vast majority of the numerous statistical analyses, however, indicate *no statistically significant treatment effect*, either deterrent or escalation. In addition, different analytical approaches produce different results. Defining *incidence* as the ratio of number of offenses divided by the number of active (as opposed to total) cases, Garner et al. (in press) report that the direction of our incidence results for the arrest versus the combined citation and advise/separate treatments is reversed: Their analyses show the official data producing a deterrent and the victim data an escalation effect of arrest, although none of these results is statistically significant. To report that the Charlotte study found an escalation effect of arrest is to ignore accepted scientific convention of statistical significance.

Another possible reason for the error or confusion in reporting the true results of the Charlotte study lies in the contaminating effect of the citation option, and in particular the results obtained when the arrest and citation (formal) treatments are combined and compared with the advise/separate (informal) treatment. No analytical comparisons of arrest with advise/separate produced statistically significant differences (either deterrence or escalation). Occasionally, when citation was combined with arrest and then compared with the advise/separate treatment, statistically significant differences did emerge in some of the data (e.g., incidence and time to failure as measured by official police arrest records). We think the combination—with the addition of citation—"tipped the balance" onto the arrest side and made it appear as if arrest was doing something significant when, in fact, it was not. This contamination of citation with arrest is used most visibly by Sherman to advance his argument that the Charlotte experiment produced an escalation effect (1992b, p. 133).

The NIJ mandate was to determine whether arrest, not arrest in combination with some other treatment, was a relatively more effective deterrent to subsequent spousal abuse. Our data are very clear that arrest does not produce the hypothesized deterrent effect. Moreover, even when arrest is combined with citation, there is still scant statistical evidence that this combination produces—despite Sherman's claims—an escalation effect. Finally, even if there were statistically convincing evidence of an escalation effect when arrest and citation are combined, this alleged effect would still be *relative only to the other treatment(s)*. In the sometimes contradictory and often confusing claims made about the results of these experiments, it is easy to lose sight of the fact that all treatment effects are relative to the other treatments. It would be easy, but totally erroneous, to conclude that one treatment produces an escalation effect relative

to no police response at all. None of the projects are in a position
to demonstrate this because all used misdemeanor calls for service
as the entry into the experiment. Other research (e.g., Langan &
Innes, 1986, p. 1) has shown that women who do not call the police
are more likely than those who do call to be abused again. We reject
the claim that the Charlotte data demonstrate an escalation effect
for arrest, but we do acknowledge that the citation option does
contribute some confusion.

Why should citation have such an impact? The answer is not
clear because citation as a treatment has never before been investigated. We speculate that the citation treatment often produced the
highest raw rate of recidivism (but rarely at statistically significant
levels) because it was new, untried, unfamiliar, and somewhat
ambiguous.

CONCLUSION

Although there may be some conflict about whether the arrest
treatment shows an escalation effect, there is no dispute about the
lack of a deterrent effect. Thus, we are left to face the policy
implications of an experiment that clearly does not support the
findings of the Minneapolis study.

As we mentioned at the beginning of this chapter, the focus of
all the NIJ-funded spousal abuse experiments has been on the
rather narrow research issue of whether arrest is more effective than
other police responses at deterring subsequent abuse. This is the
primary issue we have examined in this chapter and in our previous
writing on the Charlotte experiment. This narrow focus on specific
deterrence explains why so little attention has been paid to the
victims, an omission decried by a number of critics (e.g., see
Lerman, 1992; McCord, 1992). It should perhaps be noted for the
record that, in our extensive victim interviews, we have gathered
data that examine numerous victim perspectives, such as their
assessment of the police response and the nature and effect of prior
help-seeking behavior. However, we have as yet published few of
these findings.

Although we are not comfortable with the potential policy implications of the narrowly focused NIJ experimental studies, Sherman
(1992b) categorically asserts that "the primary goal of police inter-

vention is to *reduce the risk of repeat violence by the suspect against the same victim in the future"* (p. 10). We could not more fundamentally disagree. A detailed discussion of the purposes of law and law enforcement is clearly outside the ambit of this chapter. Suffice it to say that we recognize that specific deterrence is an important consideration, although we would define it more broadly to include other victims. However, we have been at pains in all of our previous writings on the Charlotte experiment to follow up our discussion of the research findings with an epilogue in which we stress the significance of the rationales of just deserts and general deterrence and the symbolic importance of arresting offenders (e.g., see Hirschel & Hutchison, 1992, pp. 118-119; Hirschel, Hutchison, & Dean, 1991, p. 15; Hirschel, Hutchison, Dean, Kelley, & Pesackis, 1991, pp. 158-160). As we concluded in our final report to NIJ:

> Even though arrest has not been shown to have a particular deterrent value, and even if arrest may not have much of a punitive value, it may still constitute a more conscionable choice than non-arrest. Not to arrest may communicate to men that abuse is not serious and to women the message that they are on their own. It may communicate to children, who very often witness abuse of their mothers, that the abuse of women is tolerated, if not legitimated. It may communicate to the public at large that a level of violence which is unacceptable when inflicted by a stranger is acceptable when inflicted by an intimate. (Hirschel, Hutchison, Dean, Kelley, & Pesackis, 1991, pp. 159-160)

NOTES

1. A total of 573 (83.5%) of the 686 eligible cases were delivered as assigned; 113 of the cases (16.5%) were misdelivered (not delivered as assigned). These misdeliveries were delivered by 84 officers, exactly one third of those who had contributed any eligible cases (252). As would be expected, misdeliveries were not equally distributed across the three treatments. The misdelivery rate for the arrest treatment was 9.1%; for the advise/separate treatment, 12.8%; and for the citation treatment, 26.7%. Clearly, delivery of the citation treatment as assigned was lower than for the other two treatments. Misdeliveries were of four general types: (a) advise/separate delivered as arrests (28 cases), (b) citations delivered as arrests (43 cases), (c) citations delivered as advise/separate (20 cases), and (d) arrest delivered as advise/separate (17 cases). The movement from less severe to more severe treatments is underscored by the fact that the most common reason given for misdelivery was "escalation of imminent danger" (52 cases, or 46% of all misdeliveries).

2. For example, when a citation treatment was delivered as an advise/separate treatment because the offender could not be issued the citation as he had left the scene after the officers had arrived.

3. The other statistically significant difference to emerge was that cases that produced interviews were less likely to have victims who were under the influence of alcohol or drugs at the time of the presenting incident (9.3% vs. 15.2%, χ^2 = 6.24, p = .04).

REFERENCES

Berk, R. A., Campbell, A., Klap, R., & Western, B. (1992). A Bayesian analysis of the Colorado Springs Spouse Abuse Experiment. *Journal of Criminal Law and Criminology, 83*(1), 170-200.

Berk, R. A., & Newton, P. (1985). Does arrest really deter wife battery? An effort to replicate the findings of the Minneapolis Spouse Abuse Experiment. *American Sociological Review, 50*, 253-262.

Binder, A., & Meeker, J. W. (1988). Experiments as reforms. *Journal of Criminal Justice, 16*, 347-358.

Bowman, C. G. (1992). The arrest experiments: A feminist critique. *Journal of Criminal Law and Criminology, 83*(1), 201-208.

Dunford, F. W. (1990). System-initiated warrants for suspects of misdemeanor domestic assault: A pilot study. *Justice Quarterly, 7*, 631-653.

Dunford, F. W., Huizinga, D., & Elliot, D. S. (1989). *The Omaha Domestic Violence Police Experiment: Final report*. Washington, DC: National Institute of Justice.

Dunford, F. W., Huizinga, D., & Elliot, D. S. (1990). The role of arrest in domestic assault: The Omaha Police Experiment. *Criminology, 28*(2), 183-206.

Dutton, D. G. (1987). The criminal justice response to wife assault. *Law and Human Behavior, 2*(3), 189-206.

Elliot, D. S. (1989). Criminal justice procedures in family violence crimes. In L. Ohlin & M. Tonry (Eds.), *Family violence* (pp. 427-480). Chicago: University of Chicago Press.

Garner, J., Fagan, J., & Maxwell, C. (in press). Published findings from the spouse assault replication program: A critical review. *Journal of Quantitative Criminology*.

Hirschel, J. D., & Hutchison, I. W. (1992). Female spouse abuse and the police response: The Charlotte, North Carolina, experiment. *Journal of Criminal Law and Criminology, 83*(1), 73-119.

Hirschel, J. D., Hutchison, I. W., & Dean, C. W. (1991). The Charlotte Spouse Abuse Study. *Popular Government, 57*, 11-16.

Hirschel, J. D., Hutchison, I. W., & Dean, C. W. (1992). The failure of arrest to deter spouse abuse. *Journal of Research in Crime and Delinquency, 29*(1), 7-33.

Hirschel, J. D., Hutchison, I. W., Dean, C. W., Kelley, J. J., & Pesackis, C. E. (1991). *Charlotte Spouse Assault Replication Project; Final report*. Washington, DC: National Institute of Justice.

Hirschel, J. D., Hutchison, I. W., Dean, C. W., & Mills, A. M. (1992). Review essay on the law enforcement response to spouse abuse: Past, present, and future. *Justice Quarterly, 9*(2), 247-283.

Langan, P., & Innes, C. (1986). *Preventing domestic violence against women*. Washington, DC: U.S. Department of Justice.

Lempert, R. (1989). Humility is a virtue: On the publicization of policy relevant research. *Law and Society Review, 23*, 145-161.

Lerman, L. G. (1992). The decontextualization of domestic violence. *Journal of Criminal Law and Criminology, 83*(1), 217-240.

McCord, J. (1992). Deterrence of domestic violence: A critical view of research. *Journal of Research in Crime and Delinquency, 29*(2), 229-239.

Pate, A. M., & Hamilton, E. E. (1992). Formal and informal deterrents to domestic violence: The Dade County Spouse Assault Experiment. *American Sociological Review, 57,* 691-697.

Pate, A. M., Hamilton, E. E., & Annan, S. (1992). *Metro-Dade Spouse Abuse Replication Project technical report.* Washington, DC: Police Foundation.

Sherman, L. W. (1992a). The influence of criminology on criminal law: Evaluating arrests for misdemeanor domestic violence. *Journal of Criminal Law and Criminology, 83*(1), 1-45.

Sherman, L. W. (1992b). *Policing domestic violence: Experiments and dilemmas.* New York: Free Press.

Sherman, L. W., & Berk, R. A. (1984a). *The Minneapolis Domestic Violence Experiment.* Washington, DC: Police Foundation.

Sherman, L. W., & Berk, R. A. (1984b). The specific deterrent effects of arrest for domestic assault. *American Sociological Review, 49,* 261-272.

Sherman, L. W., Schmidt, J. D., Rogan, D. P., Gartin, P. R., Cohn, E. G., Collins, D., & Bacich, R. (1991). From initial deterrence to long-term escalation: Short-custody arrest for poverty ghetto domestic violence. *Criminology, 29*(4), 821-850.

Sherman, L. W., Schmidt, J. D., Rogan, D. P., Smith, D. A., Gartin, P. R., Cohn, E. G., Collins, D., & Bacich, R. (1992). The variable effects of arrest on criminal careers: The Milwaukee Domestic Violence Experiment. *Journal of Criminal Law and Criminology, 83*(1), 137-169.

U.S. Bureau of the Census. (1988). *County and city data book.* Washington, DC: Government Printing Office.

Zorza, J. (1992). The criminal law of misdemeanor domestic violence, 1970-1990. *Journal of Criminal Law and Criminology, 83*(1), 46-72.

6

The Preventive Conceit
The Black Box in Market Context

PETER K. MANNING

Despite the rather ineffectual character of law enforcement approaches to deterrence via arrests in the control of drunk driving (Ross, 1992), illegal drug use (Manning, 1992), juvenile crime (Nagin & Paternoster, 1991), domestic assault (Dunford, Huizinga, & Elliott, 1990), and crime as indicated by rising per capita incarceration rate (Bureau of Justice Statistics, 1992), the preventive conceit retains its grip on criminal justice practitioners and researchers. The shared presumption or conceit is that the law should and does deter and that official data on arrest are an adequate surrogate measure of deterrence. The process by which such deterrence works (e.g., self-control, recognition of future consequences of actions) is assumed, rather than studied. A useful case in point in the research literature on domestic violence argues the merits of the "arrest treatment" in atheoretical "black box" terms (Sherman & Cohn, 1989, p. 133).

A belief in the deterrent effects of arrest is a "conceit" because it is mental activity organized by a misguiding metaphor that animates policy and research. Arrest in domestic conflict echoes the "crime attack" notion (Sherman, 1992) that validates police belief in pragmatic "crime control," rather than the theoretically shaped pursuit of knowledge. As such, advocating an arrest policy in domestic disputes begs the question of the context of the arrest, the limits of formal social control, and the preferred role of policing in a democratic society.

In this chapter, I argue that the presumption of the effectiveness of the legal sanction of arrest is based on a flawed deterrence doctrine and a confused understanding of the diverse meanings of *arrest*. Furthermore, criminalizing domestic conflict and the corollary belief in arrest as a solution to social conflict is, at least in part, a product of the reduced legitimacy of the police and their increasing vulnerability to "market pressures," "management dicta," and vaguely understood community demands. I first review the recent advocacy of arrest sanctioning and philosophical and logical objections to these claims and then review the varied meanings of arrest. I conclude by considering the current vulnerability of the police to market pressures.

THE POLICE AND ARREST

The vast relevant literature on the impact of arrest on crime(s) resists brief summary (Blumstein, Cohen, & Nagin, 1978). It is useful, however, to consider that (a) specifying the deterrent effects of arrest (or indeed of any formal sanction) is difficult and entails fundamental philosophical problems (Gibbs, 1975); (b) arrest is unconnected to any known systematic theory of criminal behavior in a positive, direct fashion; (c) the claimed deterrent effects of arrest on re-arrest are the product of a series of rather dubious methodological and operational definitions and arbitrary measurement decisions; and (d) the isolation of arrest from the consequences and sequelae created by arrest underestimates the costs to the police, the participants, and society of an arrest-focused policy.

Deterrence

General deterrence was articulated by theorist Jeremy Bentham as a means to reduce the use of vengeful and ex post facto punishment and to increase more humane forms of legal control. It is one of the stated aims of modern law. The most systematic reviews of the concept of deterrence (Gibbs, 1975, 1989; Nagin, 1978) conclude that the general deterrent effects of the law are difficult to establish. Both measurement and conceptual problems remain resistant to solution. In part, this is because the conceptual link between the law (or a set of legal norms), potential sanctioning, actual sanctioning, and behavior change is predicated on unknown cognitive and epistemological assumptions about citizens' knowledge of and response to legal norms: confusion between legal norms (authoritative standards supported by the state on violence) and sanctioning norms (standards for determining response to a violation) and confusion between individual beliefs (whether individuals believe they are deterred) and beliefs in general deterrence (whether others are deterred). Because of the unknown number of unsanctioned violators and because of the problems of determining what acts are deterred (two kinds of unknown effects), the arrest rate is a small sample of violations.

From a policy point of view, it is not clear whether the aim of deterrence is to deter individual criminal acts or to reduce the crime rate (Pepinsky, 1980). The aim of deterring individuals may conflict with reducing the crime rate, and these two aims may be mutually exclusive or interact complexly. In other words, punishing individuals may increase the rate by escalating a criminal career, whereas focusing on matters that reduce a rate, such as environmental changes, modifications in law, or other means of reducing opportunities for crime, may decrease the rate of punishment or arrest. There is no evidence that arrests reduce crime or even reduce the likelihood of re-arrest.

Establishing specific deterrence effects has also been problematic. Arguments continue about whether severity, certainty, or alacrity of the sanction is the most effective (Nagin & Paternoster, 1991). Specific deterrence has been studied with respect to the impact (typically) of arrests on subsequent arrest rates or recidivism. The results are unsupportive of legal deterrent doctrine: homicide (Klein, Forst, & Filatov, 1978; Sellin, 1980), drunk driving (Ross, 1992), burglary (Wilson & Boland, 1978), traffic offenses (Chambliss, 1966), drug offenses (Schur, 1969), corporate crime (Braithwaite, 1989), and recently, domestic assault (Dunford et al., 1990; Sherman & Berk, 1984; Sherman et al., 1991). Quasi-experiments weakly support the claim that arrest or direct police intervention reduces or modifies, for brief time periods, the targeted rate (see Sherman, 1990, 1992).

The logical and empirical links between knowledge of the law and sanctions, arrest, consequences of an arrest, and alteration in future behavior have never been adequately presented. They remain inside a black box labeled *crime control* or pragmatic policy interventions.

Criminological Theories

The arrest approach to crime control is systematically disconnected from any known theoretical perspective. In a rhetorical flourish, Sherman et al. (1991) asserted that the impact of time in custody (one aspect of "arrest") on future criminality is a central question in criminological theory: "Does length of time in custody affect the odds of future criminality? This question is central to public policy and criminological theory, yet it remains virtually unanswered" (p. 822). They cited the prevalence of arrest, noting that police in 1989 made some 14 million nontraffic arrests and equating it metaphorically at one point with a dosage of medicine and at another with "aspirin" (p. 822). They might have noted that arrests clear somewhere around 50% of all reported crimes. This percentage is offense specific. The prevalence of arrest as a variable in research studies surely does not establish arrest time as a central focus of criminological theory. (No supporting evidence is cited for this claim.) No systematic criminological theory claims that time in custody or even arrest has an unmediated specific impact on criminal behavior.

Considerable evidence suggests that, consistent with the labeling hypothesis, arrest and other forms of sanctioning have a negative and criminogenic impact on individuals, although variation in rates may not be possible to establish clearly (Pepinsky, 1980). As Black (1980, 1990) and colleagues (Baumgartner, 1988) have repeatedly shown, governmental social control, indicated by arrest, is a dependent variable, a reflection of other social variables. Clearly, the context of the arrest decision and the relational status of those arrested pattern the probability of arrest. The impact of the arrest cannot be understood outside a longitudinal analysis of the consequences of the arrest policy to those arrested, to the families, and to the criminal justice system (Buzawa & Buzawa, in press).

Methodological Objections

A number of important critiques of the work on arrest in domestic conflict have been published (see Buzawa & Buzawa, 1991, in press). My focus here is the assumptions lying behind the research and the analysis. Sherman and Berk (1984) and Sherman (1990, 1992; Sherman et al., 1991) did not base their research on a clearly stated theoretical rationale derived from philosophical analysis or criminological theory that links arrests to prevention or deterrence. Sherman and Berk (1984) claimed that a version of labeling theory (one unpublished study by Lincoln is cited) that posits incremental deviance based on applications of sanctions was "falsified" by their research. In none of the published Sherman research is the precise linkage between arrest sanctioning and repeated arrests spelled out. It remains unspecified or defined on pragmatic grounds.

The article by Sherman et al. (1991), which was based on Milwaukee data on the effects of arrest, was sprinkled with ad hoc interpretations about why and how length of time in custody might affect future law-breaking behavior, and called on "frustration" and "anger" as commonsense variables. Operational definitions of length of time in custody were called "short" or "long" in terms of hours (2 vs. 8 or more) in custody. Furthermore, meanings of the arrest to the police, to the offender(s), to those in the domestic relationship, or to the risk of future arrest in any relevant sense were not discussed. The authors stated that the Milwaukee data do not support the specific deterrence of arrest premise (p. 845).

The analysis assumed that arrests play an important role in social control: to deter or reduce criminal behavior, violence, and re-arrest. Findings were related to posited policy implications of arrest or nonarrest or other forms of legal intervention. An operational definition of deterrence based on arrest—re-arrest correlations is a specific, rather narrow, and operational approach to the problems of deterrence and social control. Thus, the link between arrest and re-arrest is created by measurement by fiat (Cicourel, 1966). In conclusion, Sherman et al. (1991) suggested that other

variables, such as unemployment or impact on the domestic relationship, might modify the pattern discovered, but they did not
elaborate on this possibility.

DIVERSE AND HISTORIC
FUNCTIONS OF ARREST

A number of ethnographic and sociolegal studies have suggested
that the term *arrest* is a slippery one (e.g., Lafave, 1965). Historically, the citizen's authority to arrest and hold for adjudication any
known offender was originally and is still possessed by citizens in
common law. The purpose was to ensure the citizen's appearance
for judicial proceedings (e.g., hearing, trial). Lafave (1965), in a
functional sociolegal catalogue, listed some functions of or reasons
for arrest. In an important two-part article, Sherman (1980) analyzed the diversity of arrest's meaning in law (varying across states
and other jurisdictions) and concluded that the concept of arrest in
law is difficult to pin down precisely.

The evolution of the idea of arrest has drawn it closer and closer
to ideas of moral punishment and revenge by using legal means
rather than self-help (Black, 1980). Police view arrest as a mode of
control, of shaming, of asserting authority, covering themselves
from criticism, ensuring compliance with their commands, and the
like. Prevention, deterrence, and the like are distant objectives of
little relevance to police decisions. Retention for questioning produces "transaction costs" to offenders regardless of their guilt or
innocence. These costs radically increase if their cases go to court.
Moral shaming and constraint are an intimate part of the process.
Feeley (1979) argued cogently, on the basis of a study of New Haven
courts, that the process of arrest and being brought to trial is the
punishment. This conclusion is consistent with ethnographic studies suggesting that not only the propensity to arrest (Bayley &
Garofalo, 1989) but also the context of arrest are variables, not
constants (Bayley & Bittner, 1985; Ericson, 1981, 1982; Muir, 1977;
Skolnick, 1977). This is marked in domestic disputes (Davis, 1983;
Parnas, 1966). Scant attention is given in the arrest-focused research to the interactional context in which the arrest results
(Buzawa & Buzawa, in press; Lempert, 1989; Stark, 1991). Buzawa

and Buzawa (1991) argued that an entire series of decisions—from the decision to call the police to the report of the incident to the final outcome—is context dependent. Furthermore, because the vast majority of domestic assaults are not reported to the police, to define control of "domestic assault" by differential rates of re-arrest under several treatment conditions does not speak to the incidence or prevalence of domestic assault, but only of re-arrest on that charge.

The deterrent effects of arrest in "domestic assaults" derived from a single controlled experimental study are a narrow basis for extrapolating deterrent effects. Even differences in custody effects on subsequent re-arrest cannot be understood solely by such a carefully restricted case study in a single city (Lempert, 1989).

Perhaps the issues central to criminology are not the philosophical or operational problems of studying the deterrent effects of arrest in domestic assaults, as further research will establish the limits of the treatment. One might better ask why such research and policy recommendations should have had such an impact (Binder & Meeker, 1988; Buzawa & Buzawa, 1991, chap. 6; Sherman & Cohn, 1989). What do these changes in public policy communicate about the police mandate? They are one aspect of a changing picture of policing.

CHANGES IN POLICING IN THE PAST 20 YEARS

Many changes have occurred in the internal and external environment of U.S. urban policing in the past 20 years (see Manning, 1992). External changes make the police more vulnerable to political pressures and trends. The infrastructure of cities has deteriorated even as city budgets have grown massively, and the costs of governance exceed the capacity of taxpayers to meet them. As a result, the police continue to face serious budget cuts, layoffs, and hiring freezes in many large cities. These affect morale and loyalty, as well as increasing personnel turnover. The degree of support for policing, especially in urban areas, has declined; concurrently, the public's fears of violent crime and drugs have increased. Despite police efforts, unanticipated and negative consequences have resulted from law enforcement efforts. The media play an increasing role in policing and social control. The media focus on policing and police figures (see Ericson, 1989, 1991) and consider the quality of police leadership and police leaders as meaningful national issues. Television "cop" shows created from "bits of life" stories, reconstructions and re-creations, fabrications and docudramatizations, and even cinema verité shows like *Cops* are found in abundance on every network. Police have developed sophisticated media skills and create "media reality" through manipulating the conventions of the media, such as providing predigested sound bites, granting "indepth" interviews (3 or more minutes in length) and on-the-scene statements for minicameras, and providing formatted press releases (Altheide & Snow, 1991; Ericson, 1989). The police have orchestrated and amplified the media-driven "moral panics" associated with drugs and violent crime and are directly linked to the production of crime news (Surette, 1992). The police have strong political allies and are an active part of police reform movements. Organizations like the Police Executive Research Forum (PERF), the Police Foundation, National Institute of Justice (NIJ), (the International Association of Chiefs of Police (IACP), and the National Council of Mayors influence policing, shape police leadership, and provide rhetoric. Reform movements, such as "community policing" (see chapters by Manning, Mastrofski, and Bayley in Greene & Mastrofski, 1988; see also Trojanowicz & Bucqueroux, 1990) and problem-oriented policing (Goldstein, 1990), have had a wide, if not deep, impact on the rhetoric of policing in the United States. The degree to which police practice has changed remains to be established (Ferraro, 1989), and the percentage arrested in domestic incidents varies widely (Buzawa & Buzawa, in press). In total, these external changes increased public awareness of the limits and constraints on policing while sensitizing police to the need for reform (see Cordner, 1990).

Important changes are taking place within policing. These include changes in the level of education of officers (Mastrofski, 1990), in the conception of police, in the role of the law in policing, and in the social roots of the police mandate.

Police, like many other public service occupations and bureaus (Wilson, 1989), are now viewed by many observers as businesses. One indication of this perception is the use of the mannered euphemisms of business management to describe policing. Police chiefs are seen as analogous to CEOs: managing businesses and taking risks to increase their market share. Law enforcement institutes and universities are offering seminars on such topics as advanced management for law enforcement executives and law enforcement management. Policing is termed a "service," analyzed by using the concepts of market strategies and tactics, viewed as competing for a precarious market niche, and called "corporate" in character (Moore & Trojanowicz, 1988). No longer a secure monopoly, police compete with private security firms, community action groups, and the media for the right to provide legitimate application of social control (Shearing & Ericson, 1991). Researchers raise questions of efficiency and effectiveness in policing (Clarke & Hough, 1980), and innovations are advocated on the grounds that they will increase efficiency or reduce policing costs (Hough, 1980a, 1980b; Tien & Colton, 1979).

Both criminal and civil law have grown as determinants of police practice. Procedural aspects of criminal law continue to shape policing practice. The role of civil law has also expanded. Where once they were protected from civil suits, police are now liable, and out-of-court settlements and court-mandated payments are major expenditures in large cities (Mastrofski, 1990).

Policing increasingly acknowledges its highly discretionary modality, its emphasis on ordering and compliance and restitutive modes of dispute resolution. Modern police claim something like the coproduction of order, rather than order resulting from law enforcement. Despite the controversy about domestic violence, police aim for skillful avoidance of violence and arrest (Bittner, 1991) and dispute resolution.

As a result of these changes, the traditional or "sacred" (Manning, 1977) bases of the police mandate are changing. Commitment to maintaining the collective good, serving with honor and loyalty, and observing tradition are in conflict with pragmatic obligations, concern for avoiding legal liabilities and civil suits, and budgetary constraints. The mandate fits uneasily with a concern for order management, compromise, and negotiated order, and is it less loosely linked to criminal law (Weick, 1979) and tied more to considerations of practical management and administration.

CURRENT VULNERABILITY
OF POLICE TO MARKET FORCES
AND LAW ENFORCEMENT CLAIMS

The massive response of the media, political action groups, and law enforcement to the 1984 Sherman and Berk study suggests a number of inferences. Their work did not urge arrest in domestic disputes as a police policy, but instead urged a presumptive preference for arrest. The response to this work had a number of important consequences.

It tapped a new concern with the rights of members of domestic units and a decline in legal protection of private relations from intrusion of the law. Concern for protection of females was dramatically associated in the media with the ideological and moral outrage of political interests, some called "feminist," seeking to control abuse mainly by men through expanding the application of the criminal law. Belief in law as a democratic mechanism for producing justice was consistent with the experience of the civil rights groups who are the model for civil protest in the last part of the 20th century. As a symbolic tool, the law stands as a representation of the good, the right, and the proper in the United States (Edelman, 1966). The application of law in private relations has a less consensual position. Because arrests in domestic disputes are disproportionately of lower class, minority residents of large cities (Buzawa & Buzawa, 1990), the policy extracts yet an additional cost, or "crime tariff" (Packer, 1965), from them. Not all families are being policed for "violence."

The position of leaders in U.S. law enforcement since the 1930s has been that law enforcement was an objective, nondiscretionary matter unaffected by either high or low politics. The success in altering public police policy (see Ferraro, 1989) suggests that publicity, political forces, and movements increasingly shape policing. This has been true historically, but police were loath to admit it in an era of reformist and scientific policing.

The changes in policy and practice show dramatically the increasingly elevated position of law as a form of social control and the weakness of informal controls in this society. Edelman (1991) argued that the use of arrest and criminal law generally converts private relations into public spectacles. Like Prohibition, MADD, and SADD, the pressure to criminalize domestic conflict is a moral reform movement. This shows the explicit political relevance of policing for the political economy of the control of risk generally. Political pressures on the police to enforce drunk driving laws, drug laws, and domestic assault laws suggest the changing nature of the mandate from an insular activity restricted in range to service functions with modest legal and criminal law obligations shaped by national political activity. Growth in the demand for "law enforcement," and the transition of policing to a demand-focused "service" industry rationing its "services," is revealed in the police response to the movement to criminalize domestic conflict. Police are under pressure, some of it self-created, to make explicit their market strategy, how they differentially serve target groups and "submarkets," and manage demand. The police are moving away from an explicit egalitarian allocational and distributional function and toward a rationing, market-based corporate strategy that assumes a distributional bias. This strategy entails explicit service goals, sets differential levels of response, and seeks to manage demand. This strategy creates tensions and contradictions because the public position of 24-hour available response coupled with secret, private, discretionary rationing decisions is being replaced with reduced service, public statements of priorities, and explicit policies that ration police services. Quantitative measures of efficiency and effectiveness can become reified and be used to rationalize differentially serving needy and demanding groups.

The focus on a narrow intervention claimed to alter behavior is a change in police orientation. Anglo American policing has been incident driven, anti-intellectual, and ahistorical. It has eschewed problem-solving preventive approaches. The controversy about intervention in domestic conflict could be a model for other policy-driven innovations, but it contains the seeds of a powerful "sting" or response. The focus is on the victim and the powerless. The audience is the middle class whose experience with police intervention in family problems is less common. The espousal of the arrest policy is a public adjustment directed to a middle-class audience and lower-class target groups. It opens the police to new charges of unjust treatment should they begin arresting middle-class spouses or if they do not.

CONCLUSION

The purpose of this brief chapter was to review the validity of the deterrence conceit and its atheoretical basis in the case of criminalizing domestic conflict. On the one hand, the deterrence doctrine is well established as a philosophical belief within the criminal justice fraternity. On the other hand, it is empirically problematic. The impact of the idea of arrest on stated policy and the view that it serves as a deterrent in domestic conflict have exceeded that which might be expected from a single case study. This suggests that policing is vulnerable to new pressures, eager to be seen as reforming and sensitive to market trends, and willing and able to change its corporate strategy (Moore, 1992). On balance, the preventive conceit remains unproven, and further evidence—for example, longitudinal panel studies or ethnographic analyses—is needed.

Alternatively, it is possible that policy in policing will continue to be shaped by applied aims and research examining the practical problems of the policing, rather than scientifically derived and theoretically inferred problems. How to attack crime, exert social control expediently, avoid scandal, increase public support for police, and reduce violence are police problems. As valuable as these aims may be, they are not questions derived from criminological theory or deterrence theory. They are issues that lie at the heart of the craft.

REFERENCES

Altheide, D., & Snow, R. (1991). *Media worlds*. Hawthorne, NY: Aldine.

Baumgartner, M. P. (1988). *The moral order of a suburb*. New York: Oxford University Press.

Bayley, D., & Bittner, E. (1985). The tactical choices of police patrol officers. *Journal of Criminal Justice, 14*, 329-348.

Bayley, D., & Garofalo, J. (1989). The management of violence by police patrol officers. *Criminology, 27*, 1-25.

Binder, A., & Meeker, J. (1988). Reforms as experiments. *Journal of Criminal Justice, 16*, 347-358.

Bittner, E. (1991). *Aspects of police work*. Boston: Northeastern University Press.

Black, D. (1980). *Manners and customs of the police*. San Diego: Academic Press.

Black, D. (1990). *Sociological justice*. New York: Oxford University Press.

Blumstein, A., Cohen, J., & Nagin, D. (Eds.). (1978). *Deterrence and incapacitation.* Washington, DC: National Academy of Sciences.

Braithwaite, J. (1989). *Crime, shame, and reintegration.* Cambridge, UK: Cambridge University Press.

Bureau of Justice Statistics. (1992). *Statistical update.* Washington, DC: Government Printing Office.

Buzawa, E., & Buzawa, C. (1990). *Domestic violence.* Newbury Park, CA: Sage.

Buzawa, E., & Buzawa, C. (1991). Changing the police response to domestic violence. In J. Bizzack (Ed.), *Issues in policing.* Westport, CT: Auburn House.

Buzawa, E., & Buzawa, C. (in press). Arrest is no panacea. In M. Gelles (Ed.), *Controversial issues in family violence.*

Chambliss, W. (1966). The deterrent effects of punishment. *Journal of Crime and Delinquency, 12,* 70-75.

Cicourel, A. (1966). *Method and measurement in sociology.* New York: Free Press.

Clarke, R. V. G., & Hough, M. (Eds.). (1980). *Organizational effectiveness.* Aldershot, UK: Gower.

Cordner, G. (Ed.). (1990). On the future of policing [Special issue]. *American Journal of Police, 9*(3).

Davis, S. (1983). Restoring the semblance of order: Police strategies in the domestic dispute. *Symbolic Interaction, 6,* 261-278.

Dunford, F. W., Huizinga, D., & Elliott, D. (1990). The role of arrest in domestic assault: The Omaha Police Experiment. *Criminology, 28*(2), 183-206.

Edelman, M. (1966). *The symbolic uses of politics.* Urbana: University of Illinois Press.

Edelman, M. (1991). *Constructing the political spectacle.* Chicago: University of Chicago Press.

Ericson, R. V. (1981). *Making crime.* Toronto: Butterworths.

Ericson, R. V. (1982). *Reproducing order.* Toronto: University of Toronto Press.

Ericson, R. V. (1989). Patrolling the facts: Secrecy and publicity in policework. *British Journal of Sociology, 40,* 205-226.

Ericson, R. V. (1991). Mass media, crime, law, and justice. *British Journal of Criminology, 31,* 219-249.

Feeley, M. (1979). *The process is the punishment.* New York: Russell Sage.

Ferraro, K. (1989). Policing women battering. *Social Problems, 36,* 61-74.

Gibbs, J. (1975). *Deterrence.* New York: Elsevier.

Gibbs, J. (1989). *Social control.* Urbana: University of Illinois Press.

Goldstein, H. (1990). *Problem-oriented policing.* New York: McGraw-Hill.

Green, J., & Mastrofski, S. (Eds.). (1988). *Community policing.* New York: Praeger.

Hough, J. M. (1980a). Managing with less technology. *British Journal of Criminology, 20,* 344-357.

Hough, J. M. (1980b). *Uniformed police work and management technology* (Research and Planning Unit, Paper No. 1). London: Her Majesty's Stationery Office.

Klein, L., Forst, B., & Filatov, V. (1978). The deterrent effect of capital punishment: An assessment of the estimate. In A. Blumstein & J. Cohen (Eds.), *Deterrence and incapacitation: Estimating the effects of criminal sanctions on crime rates* (pp. 336-360). Washington, DC: National Academy of Sciences.

Lafave, W. (1965). *Arrest.* Boston: Little, Brown.

Lempert, R. (1989). Humility is a virtue. *Law and Society Review, 23*(1), 145-161.

Manning, P. K. (1977). *Police work.* Cambridge: MIT Press.

Manning, P. K. (1992). The police and information technologies. In M. Tonry & N. Morris (Eds.), *Modern policing* (Vol. 15, pp. 349-398). Chicago: University of Chicago Press.

Mastrofski, S. (1990). The prospects of change in police patrol: A decade in review. *American Journal of Police, 9*(3), 1-79.

Moore, M. (1992). Community policing. In M. Tonry & N. Morris (Eds.), *Modern policing* (pp. 99-158). Chicago: University of Chicago Press.

Moore, M., & Trojanowicz, R. (1988). The concept of community. In *Perspectives on policing* (Vol. 10). Washington, DC: U.S. Department of Justice, National Institute of Justice.

Muir, W. (1977). *Police: Street corner politicians.* Chicago: University of Chicago Press.

Nagin, D. (1978). General deterrence. In A. Blumstein, J. Cohen, & D. Nagin (Eds.), *Deterrence and incapacitation* (pp. 95-139). Washington, DC: National Academy of Sciences.

Nagin, D., & Paternoster, R. (1991). The preventive effects of the perceived risk of arrest. *Criminology, 29*(4), 561-585.

Packer, H. (1965). *The limits of the criminal sanction.* Palo Alto, CA: Stanford University Press.

Parnas, V. (1966). The police response to domestic disturbance. *Wisconsin Law Review, 2,* 914-960.

Pepinsky, H. (1980). *Crime control strategies.* New York: Oxford University Press.

Ross, L. (1992). The law and drunk driving [Review essay]. *Law and Society Review, 26*(1), 219-230.

Schur, E. (1969). *Crimes without victims.* Englewood Cliffs, NJ: Prentice Hall.

Sellin, T. (1980). *Murder and the death penalty.* Beverly Hills, CA: Sage.

Shearing, C., & Ericson, R. (1991). Culture as figurative action. *British Journal of Sociology, 42*(4), 481-506.

Sherman, L. (1980). Enforcement workshop: Defining arrests (Parts 1 and 2). *Criminal Law Bulletin, 16,* 376-380, 468-480.

Sherman, L. W. (1990). Police crackdowns: Initial and residual deterrence. In N. Morris & M. Tonry (Eds.), *Crime and justice annual* (Vol. 12, pp. 1-48). Chicago: University of Chicago Press.

Sherman, L. W. (1992). Attacking crime: Police and crime control. In N. Morris & M. Tonry (Eds.), *Crime and justice annual* (Vol. 15, pp. 159-230). Chicago: University of Chicago Press.

Sherman, L. W., & Berk, R. (1984). The specific deterrent effects of arrest for domestic assault. *American Sociological Review, 49,* 261-272.

Sherman, L. W., & Cohn, E. (1989). The impact of research on legal policy. *Law and Society Review, 23*(1), 117-144.

Sherman, L. W., Schmidt, J. D., Rogan, D. P., Gartin, P. R., Cohn, E. G., Collins, D., & Bacich, R. (1991). From initial deterrence to long-term escalation: Short-custody arrest for poverty ghetto domestic violence. *Criminology, 29*(4), 821-850.

Skolnick, J. (1977). *Justice without trial* (2nd ed.). New York: John Wiley.

Stark, E. (1991, November). *In defense of arrest.* Paper presented at the Annual Meeting of the American Society of Criminology, San Francisco.

Surette, R. (1992). *Media, crime, and criminal justice.* Monterey, CA: Brooks/Cole.

Tien, H., & Colton, K. (Eds.). (1979). *What works? LEAA.* Washington, DC: Government Printing Office.

Trojanowicz, R., & Bucqueroux, B. (1990). *Community policing.* Cincinnati, OH: Anderson.

Weick, K. (1979). *The social psychology of organizing* (2nd ed.). Reading, MA: Addison-Wesley.

Wilson, J. Q. (1989). *Bureaucracy.* New York: Basic Books.

Wilson, J. Q., & Boland, B. (1978). The effect of police on crime. *Law and Society Review, 12,* 367-390.

7

Battered Women and the
Criminal Justice System

BARBARA HART

Domestic violence victims are both similar to and strikingly different from other victims of violent crime. Thus, they require all of the information, assistance, and input that facilitates the committed, informed participation of other victims and witnesses, but beyond these, they require enhanced protection and advocacy.

Battered women are often similar to other victims of violent crime in that they want perpetrators to stop their conduct, to pay dues for the crimes committed, and to compensate victims for the losses sustained as a result of their criminal conduct. They are also similar to other crime victims in that they have interests in justice that may differ from the interests of the justice system. They may want privacy or anonymity in the prosecution process, whereas the criminal justice system values public accountability. They may want speedy disposition, whereas the justice system labors at a snail's pace. They may want input in decisions about plea negotiations and sentencing, whereas the justice system concludes that this inclusiveness precludes the expeditious handling of criminal cases, unduly interferes with prosecutorial discretion, or intrudes on the rights of defendants. They may want sentences for perpetrators that are specifically crafted to protect victims, whereas courts may focus on offender rehabilitation and ignore victim safety.

What is also true about battered women, as it is of other victims of violent crime, is that they are not all cut from the same cloth and do not all want the same outcomes. Battered women have varied interests in participation in the prosecution process and in outcomes. No profile of a battered woman witness fits all or most battered women.

BARRIERS TO VICTIM PARTICIPATION
IN THE CRIMINAL JUSTICE SYSTEM

Although each battered woman's experience should be recognized as unique, many commonalities are found among battered women victim-witnesses. Perhaps the most critical commonality is that battered women confront significant barriers to safe and effective participation as victim-witnesses in the criminal justice process.

Recidivism and Retaliation

Like other victims of violent crime, battered women fear retaliation. Fully 50% of all victims of violent crime report being fearful that perpetrators will seek reprisal if victims participate in prosecution. Like other victim-witnesses who are threatened by the perpetrator (or his agent) during the pendency of prosecution, they are twice as likely to resist participation in prosecution as are those not threatened (Davis, Smith, & Henley, 1990).

The National Crime Survey (NCS) from 1978 to 1982 showed that an estimated 32% of battered women were revictimized within 6 months after the assault that gave rise to criminal justice intervention. They were victimized an average of three times each. In contrast, the 1982 NCS data on violence committed by strangers showed that only 13% of the victims of stranger-committed crimes were subsequently assaulted during a 6-month period. Unlike domestic violence victims, victims of stranger-committed crime were assaulted only once during that period (Langan & Innes, 1986).

For many reasons, battered women appear to be at elevated risk for retaliatory violence. Most other victims of violent crime are not in a relationship with the defendant and are not living with (or did not formerly reside with) the defendant. Most have not previously suffered attacks or sustained injury at the hands of the defendant. Most have not been held hostage by the defendant or experienced his terroristic threats, targeted graphically at the victim or members of her family. Most other victim-witnesses are not economically dependent on the defendant during the pendency of prosecution and potentially thereafter. Most will not be compelled into continuing contact with the defendant during the criminal process and after disposition because of shared parenthood. Most other victims of crime are not integrally interconnected with the criminal assailant. Most other victims of crime are not at elevated risk of violent assault after intervention by the criminal justice system. Battered women, however, are most often killed when attempting to seek legal redress or when leaving an abusive relationship (Browne, 1987; Sonkin, Martin, & Walker, 1985).

Criminal justice system personnel too often believe that battered women will be safer and less exposed to life-jeopardizing violence once they are separated from the offenders and once prosecution has commenced. Quite to the contrary, evidence of the gravity of violence inflicted after separation of a couple is substantial. A batterer may, in fact, escalate his violence to coerce a battered woman into "reconciliation," to retaliate for the battered woman's participation in the prosecution process, or to coerce her into seeking termination of the prosecution. If the batterer cannot "recapture" the battered woman as his ally, he may seek retribution for her desertion and for her disloyalty in exposing him to criminal consequences. Although not all batterers engage in escalated violence during the pendency of prosecution, as many as half threaten retaliatory violence (Davis et al., 1990), and at least 30% of batterers may inflict further assaults during the predisposition phase of prosecution (Goldsmith, 1991).

A battered woman who has made prior attempts to seek prosecution or civil protection orders, only to have the perpetrator escalate his violence, may be unwilling to face the risk that prosecution will further endanger rather than protect her (Family Violence Prevention Fund, 1991). Men who batter have kidnapped victims or seriously injured and even killed battered women to prevent their participation as witnesses (Gwinn, 1991; Hart, 1984).

Battered women may thus be much more concerned about preventing future violence than about vindicating the state's interest in penalizing the defendant for crimes previously committed. This orientation of the battered woman toward future safety may create a tension with those in the criminal justice system singularly focused on winning criminal convictions.

Victim-Blaming Attitudes

Unlike other victims of violent crime, battered women are often viewed by the police, the prosecutor, judges, jurors, and probation/parole staff as responsible for the crimes committed against them—responsible either because battered women are believed to "provoke" the perpetrator into violence or because they are believed to have the power to avoid the criminal assault through accommodating the perpetrator's demands. Other victims of violent crime are not seen as culpable for the crimes inflicted on them, but battered women frequently report that criminal justice system personnel appear to consider them "unworthy victims" who are clogging up the courts with unimportant family matters. Some, therefore, impose barriers to a battered woman's use of the criminal justice system. Police fail to arrest or to file incident reports. Prosecutors delay charging, require substantial corroboration, or impose fees on the victim (Ford, 1991).

Even though justice system actors may eschew victim-blaming attitudes, the criminal process may be confounded by similar attitudes embraced by either the defendant or the battered woman herself. Uniformly, the perpetrator of domestic violence blames the victim for his conduct, claiming that she provoked him so profoundly that his crimes are excusable, if not justifiable. Batterers often persuade battered women of the correctness of this perspective. Beyond this, the battered woman may also blame herself, believing she should have been smarter and figured out a way to prevent the violence or should have been more courageous and found a way to safely leave the relationship. This self-blame may go as far as believing it is not fair to arrest and prosecute the perpetrator.

Systemic Resistance to
the Prosecution of Batterers

Unlike many victims of assault by strangers, but like other victims known to defendants, victims of domestic violence may be reluctant witnesses or may be assumed to be so (Cannavale & Falcon, 1976). There are many reasons for this. Many battered women who earnestly seek prosecution find substantial resistance to the appropriate charging of defendants. National data reveal that law enforcement routinely classifies domestic assault as a misdemeanor even though the criminal conduct involved actually included bodily injury as serious or more serious than 90% of all rapes, robberies, and aggravated assaults (Langan & Innes, 1986). When serious assaults are trivialized and charged as misdemeanors or cited as summary offenses, victims of domestic violence may conclude that the costs and risks of prosecution outweigh the potential consequences for assailants. Thus, battered women may lose interest in criminal prosecution.

Furthermore, some battered women, initially committed to prosecution, become discouraged with the criminal process because of delays (Ford & Burke, 1987), lack of witness protection (Family Violence Prevention Fund, 1991), or prosecutor indifference or insensitivity (Hart, 1991; McGuire, 1991).

Victim Reluctance

Similar to other victims of crime, when battered women are poor, have few personal or financial resources, or find participation in prosecution costly, they may be reluctant to proceed. Rural battered women may not have transportation and thus may find it impossible to arrange for multiple trips to the courthouse. Women with school-age children may have to find expensive and inconvenient child care for all court appearances outside school hours. Seriously injured battered women may find employers unwilling to accommodate court appearances after they have been considerate about many medical appointments. A battered woman who has resided in a rental unit leased from the defendant's parents may face eviction if she prosecutes.

Although it is commonly believed that battered women withdraw cooperation because of decisions to reconcile with defendants, research reveals that this is not typically the reason for the request to terminate prosecution (Ford & Burke, 1987). Some battered women seek to terminate prosecution because the initiation of charges has effected the changes sought in defendant behavior such that victims no longer conclude that prosecution will be necessary to protect them from future abuse (Ford, 1991).

Other battered women who have found that the best protection against perpetrators' violence has been the protection offered by the community with which the women affiliate, rather than by the criminal justice system, may resist prosecution if they conclude that the community will abandon them or withdraw critical support if they pursue prosecution. Women of religious, ethnic, and racial communities sometimes identify community abandonment as an untenable, adverse consequence of cooperation with prosecution.

Battered women may be reluctant to expose the fathers of their children to public accountability because of their children's attitudes toward the criminal justice system. Others are fearful that prosecution will wreak economic ruin on their families. Even smaller numbers of battered women oppose prosecution for political reasons, believing that the criminal justice system selectively penalizes men of color or other politically unpopular constituencies. Some believe that the exposure of batterers to the criminal justice system and its coercive controls will facilitate, rather than deter, future violence.

An understanding of victim reluctance is critical for informed decision making about the role of the battered victim in prosecution, strategies to enhance victim cooperation, and ultimately, disposition by the prosecutor or the court.

STRATEGIES TO
FACILITATE VICTIM PARTICIPATION

Despite these potential barriers to battered women's committed participation in the criminal process, many battered women and justice system personnel have found that these hurdles can be eliminated with careful attention to the particular requirements of each battered woman. A variety of strategies have been embraced to facilitate the informed, protected, and committed participation of battered women in criminal prosecution.

Victim Rights and Services

One strategy enumerated in the Pennsylvania Crimes Code is the requirement that police responding to domestic violence calls "notify the victim of the availability of a shelter, including its telephone number, or other services in the community." The responding officer must also provide the victim with the following statement, either orally or in writing:

> If you are the victim of domestic violence, you have the right to go to court and file a petition requesting an order for protection from domestic abuse pursuant to the . . . Protection From Abuse Act, which could include the following: (1) An order restraining the abuser from further acts of abuse. (2) An order directing the abuser to leave your household. (3) An order preventing the abuser from entering your residence, school, business or place of employment. (4) An order awarding you or the other parent temporary custody of or temporary visitation with your child or children. (5) An order directing the abuser to pay support to you and the minor children if the abuser has a legal obligation to do so. (18 Pa. Cons. Stat. § 2711(d))

Responding officers are also required to advise victims of the potential availability of crime victims compensation (71 Pa. Cons. Stat. § 180-7.17).

Another strategy adopted to enhance victim participation is the statutory articulation of victim rights. Pennsylvania's Crime Victims Bill of Rights specifies that victims of crime have the following rights:

- To have included in any presentence report information concerning the effect that the crime committed by the defendant has on the victim, including any physical or psychological harm or financial loss suffered by the victim, to the extent that such information is available from the victim or other sources
- To have restitution ordered as a condition of probation whenever feasible
- Upon request of the victim of a feloniously assaultive crime, to be promptly informed by the district attorney whenever the assailant is to be released on parole, furlough, or any other form of supervised or unsupervised release from full incarceration (71 Pa. Cons. Stat. § 180-9.3)

An additional strategy is the statutory mandate for victim-witness service funding. The Pennsylvania Commission on Crime and

Delinquency (PCCD) is required to provide technical assistance and make grants to district attorneys and other criminal justice agencies to provide crime victims with notification and protection services that include the following:

- Information concerning financial assistance and other social services available as a result of being a victim of crime
- Notification that a court proceeding to which they have been subpoenaed will not go on as scheduled in order to save the victim an unnecessary trip to court
- Notification of the final disposition of the case
- Protection from harm and threats of harm arising out of their cooperation with law enforcement and prosecution efforts
- A secure waiting area during court proceedings that does not require them to be in close proximity to defendants and families and friends of defendants
- Procedures for the expedited return by law enforcement officials of any personal property of victims that is held for prosecutorial purposes
- Services related to the rights of victims
- Other services as defined by PCCD (71 Pa. Cons. Stat. § 180-9.4)

These rights and services are helpful but often not sufficient to engage the cooperation of victims of domestic violence. The following sections outline additional strategies.

Outreach and Investigation

Police departments in a few jurisdictions in Pennsylvania have established follow-up systems whereby patrol officers or detectives make telephone or house calls to apparent victims of domestic violence in the days immediately following the request for emergency police assistance. When contacting the battered woman, the outreach officer undertakes further investigation into criminal domestic violence, identifies the risks of batterer retaliation that may suggest particular conditions on bail or release, and offers women clarification about legal options to protect them. In completing the outreach interview, the officer gives the victim specific contact information should she have further questions or information to share. Outreach is effective only when responding officers obtain confidential contact information from battered women at the crime scene; such information should include a telephone number where a message can be left for a victim if she cannot be reached in her own home.

Some domestic violence programs have adopted outreach efforts whereby they attempt to contact battered women by telephone the day following police response to an emergency domestic violence call. Communication by the domestic violence program after the immediate crisis of the criminal incident enables battered women to learn about legal options and community services in a context that is supportive, fosters an exchange of information, and engages a battered woman in critical thinking about safety strategies. Outreach thus often facilitates victim participation in and commitment to the criminal justice process.

District attorneys prioritizing the prosecution of domestic violence cases have undertaken outreach to domestic violence victims immediately after preliminary arraignment in order to provide victims with notice about charges filed; information about bail and any special conditions thereon, as well as any victim intimidation order under 18 Pa. Cons. Stat. § 4954; and notice of the defendant's release from custody. Outreach initiates a dialogue and relationship early in the prosecution process. It enables the victim to consider civil legal remedies and human services options for protecting herself and her children during the pendency of prosecution. Outreach often gives prosecutors substantial supplementary information about the crime committed.

Some prosecutors have instituted victim-witness clinics wherein victims learn about the criminal justice system, their role in it, and the likely dispositions upon conviction or a guilty plea. They learn how to craft victim impact statements and how to articulate the specific dangers they believe are posed by their assailants. They learn how to become more effective witnesses. Most significantly, they begin to network and bond with other victims and thereby gain support and eliminate the isolation that domestic violence perpetrators use to dissuade battered women from prosecuting. Clinic workers often provide child care and are available at times convenient to victim-witnesses.

Victim Protection

Because battered women are at elevated risk of violence during the pendency of prosecution, police, prosecutors, and courts should attend specifically to the safety requirements of victims. Systems should be developed to assess the potential lethality of defendants. The police should advocate for cash bail and specific protective conditions on release at the preliminary arraignment. District justices should carefully evaluate the continuing threat the defendant poses to the victim and set bail and conditions thereon that will best safeguard the victim and her family during the pendency of the criminal process. The prosecutor might undertake a periodic review of victim safety with the battered woman and seek additional protections should they be required. When a victim seeks to maintain the confidentiality of an undisclosed address, the police and the prosecutor should very carefully safeguard any contact information and delete any reference to an address on materials disclosed to the public and defense counsel. Beyond this, all criminal justice system personnel should refer battered women to domestic violence programs so that they can carefully construct safety plans to minimize exposure to perpetrators and to engage the community in vigilance for the safety of battered women.

Victim Advocacy

Victim advocacy is a key component in the prosecution of domestic violence. Battered women who find themselves abruptly thrust into the legal system because of the violence of their partners are swamped with new information, sometimes are dislocated, and invariably are confronted with increased demands for family management in this acute crisis situation. It is critical that victims have an identified contact person within the district attorney's office who can provide information about the criminal process and offer referral to supportive services. For other critical assistance, such as emergency shelter, counseling, safety planning, crisis management, and civil legal advocacy, battered victims should be referred to local domestic violence programs.

When battered women engage in legal proceedings, it is critical that they have support from family, friends, and employers so that their participation can be diligent and unclouded by anxieties that significant others do not approve of the prosecution. Therefore, domestic violence programs may seek to educate and engage those people most important to the victim so that her investment in the process of prosecution is not confounded by their concerns and so that they can help her form strategies for safe participation in the criminal justice system.

Specialized Prosecution

Specialization has improved the success of prosecution in domestic violence cases (Fagan, 1988). District attorneys have established domestic violence units in large offices or created specialists in smaller offices to enhance the relationship of the prosecutor with the victim, to better investigate and prepare a case against the perpetrator, and to specifically tailor safeguards to protect the victim from further abuse. Specialized prosecution enhances the expertise of those handling domestic violence cases and facilitates outcomes satisfactory to both the prosecution and the victim-witnesses.

In many jurisdictions in Pennsylvania, the victim of domestic violence must undertake prosecution at the preliminary hearing if the case is to proceed. Crime victims are uninformed prosecutors; they are often incapable of presenting the evidence of the criminal conduct of the suspect and are invariably intimidated by defense counsel and the perpetrator. Thus, many domestic crimes fall through the cracks and are dismissed. The success of prosecution at the preliminary hearing phase sometimes improves when police officers carry the burden, but issues of victim safety are routinely ignored. If district attorneys are to upgrade efforts to prosecute domestic violence crimes, preliminary hearing prosecution by an assistant district attorney is essential.

Timely Prosecution

Victims of crime are not entitled to timely prosecution under the current statutory scheme; however, research suggests that timeliness is essential to victim cooperation (Ford & Burke, 1987). Prosecutors should investigate domestic violence cases expeditiously and not seek or acquiesce in procedural delay if there is no compelling reason. Domestic violence victims grow weary of prosecution if many lengthy appearances are required; thus, the district attorney should require victims to attend only those proceedings in which their testimony is critical to the case. When feasible, the prosecutor should minimize the time that victim-witnesses expend at any court appearance. In scheduling court proceedings where victim

attendance is required, the prosecutor might inquire about significant demands on the time and resources of victims that would
compete with court attendance; these should be accommodated
whenever possible (American Bar Association, 1986).

Victim Participation and Empowerment

District attorneys seeking to upgrade efforts at domestic violence
prosecution often employ other victim-engaging strategies. Victim
input in plea negotiations and dispositional alternatives is a strategy
believed to enhance victim cooperation (Family Violence Prevention
Fund, 1991; McGuire, 1991). Some prosecutors have developed
court schools in which they enable the victim to learn how to be an
effective witness. Many battered women report that prosecutors fail
to adequately prepare for trial; sometimes, it appears that the
prosecutors are not even conversant with the documents in the
prosecution file as trials are about to begin. Careful and periodic
preparation in which the victim is engaged will facilitate successful
prosecution and victim investment in the process. As victims
understand that they have a vital and respected role in the prosecution, reluctance may subside. Data suggest that the more that
domestic violence victims are invested in the prosecution process,
the more powerful its deterrent effect and the stronger the message
to perpetrators that their violence will not be tolerated and that the
benefits of desisting will far outstrip the cost of continued violence
(Goldsmith, 1991).

Victims should not be penalized for their reluctance to participate
in prosecution. Policies should be developed in each prosecutor's
office and within the court that limit the use of compulsion in
achieving victim participation. Victims of domestic violence should
not be incarcerated for refusal to serve as victim-witnesses. Battered
women should not be prosecuted for filing false police reports
because they seek to terminate prosecution, except in those unusual
circumstances in which there is independent evidence of false
swearing or perjury and the interests of justice will be served
thereby. Although it is appropriate to issue subpoenas to compel
victim appearance at trial, bench warrants should not be issued
routinely when victims fail to appear. Rather, continuances should
be sought and investigation should be undertaken to ascertain the
whereabouts of the battered woman and the reasons for her failure

to appear. If reluctance is based on fear or intimidation, strategies should be employed to protect her from the dangers anticipated. Battered women should not be threatened with refusal to prosecute perpetrators for future violence if they fail or refuse to participate in the current prosecution.

Beyond this, prosecutors and courts should be cognizant of the potential adverse ramifications of coercive process with victims of domestic violence. The repercussions of coercive process may be as far-ranging as the loss of custody, the loss of employment, the loss of reputation, eviction from leaseholds, and abandonment by significant support persons. All efforts should be made to gain the cooperation of domestic violence victims, rather than to compel participation.

The interests of justice must seriously consider the interests of victims. On the one hand, their interests in safety and their reputations as law-abiding citizens should not be compromised in pursuit of prosecution unless there are overriding reasons for subordinating victim interests. On the other hand, it may be helpful for victims that the public posture of a prosecutor's office is that the state controls the prosecution. Many in the criminal justice system believe that at least the appearance of no victim discretion on the question of whether the prosecution will proceed reduces batterer intimidation directed at getting charges dropped. This public posture may even enhance victim safety because the perpetrator understands that further violence will not effect a dismissal of the charges but will result in incarceration during the pendency of the initial prosecution and in an additional prosecution for the retaliatory violence. It is important to recognize that prosecution solely controlled by the district attorney will not universally buttress victim investment or protect victims from retaliatory violence. In those instances where termination of the prosecution is critical to protect victims, the public posture should not preclude such prosecutorial discretion.

Sentencing

After conviction and before sentencing, the county probation and parole office undertakes a presentence investigation, from which it develops recommendations to the court for sentencing. A battered woman is entitled to submit a victim impact statement to advise the investigator and the court of the ramifications of the crime(s) for which the offender was convicted on the battered woman and her family. Although investigators are usually receptive to hearing about the emotional, physical, and financial losses sustained by victims, they are too often resistant to hearing of the dangers the perpetrator continues to pose to the battered women and children and reluctant to suggest that these risks of violent recidivism should be considered aggravating circumstances supporting longer sentences or factors to be addressed in crafting protective conditions on probation. Thus, sentencing recommendations typically do not fully inform the court of information relevant to sentencing deliberations in many jurisdictions.

Furthermore, prosecutors frequently rely on the presentence report and the statement of the victim at sentencing, rather than produce testimony or evidence at a sentencing hearing to buttress arguments in favor of incarceration and victim safeguards. This prosecutorial advocacy may not be necessary in jurisdictions where the presentence investigator attends carefully to the risks of recidivism; however, in jurisdictions where the court is not otherwise given information about recidivism prediction and the dangers posed by many batterers long after divorce or incarceration, prosecutors should undertake to inform the court of these risks.

Unless battered women believe that sentences comport with justice and effect specific victim safeguards, they will be most reluctant to participate cooperatively in the criminal process should their assailants recidivate. When courts craft sentences that clearly call batterers to account and safeguard victims, battered women, the general public, and other components in the justice system become confident that criminal justice efforts are meaningful interventions in domestic violence and warrant serious attention.

Restitution and Victim Compensation

Battered women in Pennsylvania have reported that neither restitution nor victim compensation has been predictably awarded or achieved in a timely fashion despite the substantial losses sustained as a consequence of domestic violence. Courts should institute policies whereby victim restitution precedes the collection of other court costs and fines. Moreover, courts can impose timetables that are tight and that require significant payment at the front end, rather than a balloon payment at the end of the payment schedule.

As to crime victims' compensation awards, battered women have received few, even though they are eligible. The lack of awards appears to be a failure of advocacy. Although many district attorneys' offices afford victims clerical assistance in the preparation of compensation claims, they do not follow up to advocate for the issuance of awards. If advocacy for compensation occurs during the pendency of prosecution, victims may invest more fully in the prosecution.

The Protection From Abuse Act permits the court to order payment for many losses that may not be compensable either through restitution or crime victims' compensation. Therefore, the office of the district attorney may alleviate some of the stress and burden imposed by victim losses if it directs domestic violence victims to the civil courts for economic awards as well as protection. Meanwhile, when all else fails, if losses affect a victim's capacity to work, financial assistance might be forthcoming from the Bureau of Vocational Rehabilitation.

Particular attention to these economic matters renders a great service to victims and simultaneously enhances their investment in prosecution. Both crime victim compensation and protection order economic relief can be initiated, and sometimes awarded, early in the prosecution process and thereby have the potential to cement victim cooperation with the criminal process.

Postdisposition Issues

Victims of crime have articulated concerns that prosecutors will lose interest once a conviction or plea has been achieved and sentencing imposed. The only statutory obligations of district attorneys to victims after disposition are notice of parole hearings and the right to participate therein, notice of furloughs, notice of transfer to community facilities, and notice of discharge from incarceration. Actually, victims are entitled to this information only if they request it from the district attorney and provide that office with current contact information. Crime victims may not appreciate the importance of providing the district attorney with this information, and few prosecutors have developed systems that expedite timely notification. These systems may be particularly crucial in domestic violence cases because perpetrators frequently engage in further assaults after incarceration. It is important that contact information be kept confidential so that newly released perpetrators cannot access it to determine the whereabouts of battered women.

Where probationers or parolees have violated conditions imposed on probation or parole, prosecutors and probation staff should engage in outreach to battered women and implement all the strategies outlined earlier in this chapter to facilitate victim protection and participation. Where domestic violence victims believe their safety is jeopardized by early parole of perpetrators, coordinated efforts by the office of the district attorney and the local domestic violence program can provide the parole board with information essential for its informed decision making, about both whether parole should be granted and conditions that might be imposed on any parole.

THE CHALLENGE TO
THE CRIMINAL JUSTICE SYSTEM

Domestic violence victims are increasingly turning to the criminal justice system for assistance in ending the violence that jeopardizes their lives and well-being. They often are uninformed about the criminal justice process and naive about its power to end the violence in their lives. For battered women to be effective, committed participants in the criminal justice system, care must be taken to minimize the barriers to access and investment that historically have impeded empowered participation by battered women. The adoption of protocols attentive to victim issues by every component of the criminal justice system will greatly enhance justice-seeking efforts in domestic violence cases. The strategies outlined here can be used to engage and protect battered women as victim-witnesses and can also greatly advance the success of prosecution and perpetrator accountability.

REFERENCES

American Bar Association. (1986). *ABA suggested guidelines for reducing adverse effects of case continuances and delays on crime victims and witnesses.* Chicago: Author.

Browne, A. (1987). *When battered women kill.* New York: Free Press.

Cannavale, F. J., Jr., & Falcon, W. D. (1976). *Witness cooperation.* Lexington, MA: Lexington Books.

Davis, R., Smith, B., & Henley, S. (1990). *Victim-witness intimidation in the Bronx courts.* New York: Victims Services Agency.

Fagan, J. (1988). Contributions of family violence research to criminal justice policies on wife assault: Paradigms of science and social control. *Violence and Victims, 3*(3), 159-186.

Family Violence Prevention Fund. (1991). *Domestic violence: The crucial role of the judge in criminal court cases.* San Francisco: Author.

Ford, D. A. (1991). Prosecution as a victim power resource: A note on empowering women in violent conjugal relationships. *Law & Society Review, (25)*2, 313-334.

Ford, D. A., & Burke, M. J. (1987, July). *Victim-initiated criminal complaints for wife battery: An assessment of motives.* Paper presented at the Third National Conference for Family Violence Researchers, University of New Hampshire, Durham.

Goldsmith, S. (1991). Taking spouse abuse beyond a "family affair." *Law Enforcement News, 17*(334), 7.

Gwinn, C. (1991, October). *From investigation to trial: The strategy for successful intervention.* Lecture for the National College of District Attorneys, Las Vegas, NV.

Hart, B. (1984, Winter). Testify or prison? *AEGIS: The Magazine on Ending Violence Against Women.*

Hart, B. (1991). Domestic violence intervention system: A model for response to women abuse. In *Confronting domestic violence: Effective police response.* Harrisburg: Pennsylvania Coalition Against Domestic Violence.

Langan, P. A., & Innes, C. A. (1986). *Preventing domestic violence against women: Discussion paper* (Bureau of Justice Statistics Special Reports Series). Washington, DC: Bureau of Justice Statistics.

McGuire, L. A. (1991). *Prosecution of domestic violence in Iowa.* Des Moines: Iowa Prosecuting Attorneys Training Coordinator Council.

Pennsylvania Protection From Abuse Act, 23 Pa. C. S. § 6101 et seq., amended, 1994.

Sonkin, D., Martin, D., & Walker, L. E. A. (1985). *The male batterer: A treatment approach.* New York: Springer.

8

Mandatory Arrest of Batterers
A Reply to Its Critics

EVAN STARK

THE CONTEXT AND THE PLAYERS

As a long-time activist in the battered women's movement, I welcome the debate about mandatory arrest.

There is a certain irony in defending the police powers of the state against critics who helped lay the basis for the proarrest policy in the first place. Larry Sherman's conversion is the most remarkable. Relying on recent evidence that certain men become more violent after arrest, Sherman has replaced his erstwhile ardor for arrest with an equally passionate belief that mandatory arrest laws should be immediately repealed, especially in cities "with substantial ghetto poverty populations with high unemployment rates." As Richard Gelles points out (Chapter 3, this volume), there are profound methodological flaws in both Sherman and Berk's original Minneapolis Domestic Violence Experiment and the replication studies that are the basis for Sherman's current position. Although I concur with these criticisms, here I want to respond to the negative assessments of mandatory arrest that Gelles, Schmidt, and Sherman share with Straus, Manning, and Buzawa and colleagues (Chapters 2, 6, and 9, this volume).

The participants in the debate represent a range of orientations. Embedded in these different approaches are contrasting assumptions not only about the specific changes we are debating, such as the struggle for women's rights, but also about social change in general—whether it is desirable or likely, for instance—and about whether change comes about primarily as the result of structural factors (e.g., poverty), shifts in cultural attitudes because of interventions by elites (be they professional or political) or because of strategic initiatives "from below." These hidden assumptions—as much as empirical evidence—determine how the issues at hand are assessed.

Manning draws on structuralism, phenomenology, and neo-Marxist theories to sketch an elegant picture in which policing is integrated vertically into the social control mechanisms of the capitalist state (relying on Donald Black's conception of law as all-pervasive) and horizontally into the selective manipulation of social problems (and those who inhabit them) to express symbolic control and to reproduce prevailing patterns of domination. In this volume, he cites the transformation of police into a market-driven service focused on specific problems (e.g., woman battering) that have been identified nationally as targets of "moral reform." In passing, Manning notes the increasing importance of social movements in determining the police agenda. The overall thrust of his argument, however, is that arrest in domestic cases elevates the social control function of law (hence, of the state) in private relations and thus relegates community-based movements to self-help.

In contrast, Sherman's picture is constructed from a bygone devotion to positivist criminology. His is a world defined by the technological optimism of the pre-1960s, yet to be polluted by culture, politics, gender, and history. Crime, causality, and, indeed, social efficacy of any kind are invisible in Manning's world. In Sherman's, causality is singular, universal, and unidirectional, and social science research guides professional/government intervention to right injustice. In the post-Law Enforcement Assistance Administration (LEAA) era, this neo-Keynesian belief in state intervention appears as naive as an early Doris Day film. Still, there is something seductive about a "preventive conceit" (Manning's term) that envisions modifying such complex behaviors as violence with minor adjustments in the criminal justice response (arrest vs. no arrest). Would it were so.

Because the aim of the battered women's movement is to define a broad social interest in preventing violence against women, I try to accommodate these divergent views, rather than confront them head-on. Clearly, however, their basic assumptions shape how the authors read what evidence there is about mandatory arrest. Manning's model of social control suggests that arresting batterers will simply exacerbate prevailing inequalities by targeting minorities and low-income people and by reinforcing the state's authority to shape "private" life. Sherman's faith in the instrumentality of professional intervention—including the instrumentality of his own research—supports his belief that arrest increases violence. Hence, eliminating mandatory arrest will reduce the violent response. Both are almost certainly wrong. The point, however, is that they are wrong because the paradigms from which they arise, each in a different way, discredit the role of social initiative—in this case, the role of the community-based women's movement—in shaping the outcome of policy change.

My more pedestrian approach falls between the extremes represented by Manning and Sherman. I suspect that most people view policing as a body of available resources, like schooling or health care, say—a sort of lottery that circumstances periodically force us to enter.[1] Given the complex political realities that shape crime (as well as, e.g., health, welfare, learning) and mediate how police and the public interact, it is hard to predict whether one's welfare will be helped or hindered in any given encounter or, more globally, what determines how a given set of actors (offenders, patients, students, police) will respond to a specific class of interventions (e.g., mandatory arrest). If people "play" nonetheless (call police, attend school, go to the emergency room), it is not because they believe they *will* win, but because this is one of the few shows in town at which they *can* win and because winning—in this case, having police resources at your disposal—is a highly desirable outcome in the long run.[2]

Individual imagination is usually all one can rely on to make the odds in a lottery more favorable. But political action has and will continue to alter the odds favoring a positive response to male violence.

To someone who rejects neoclassical assumptions (and with them, deterrence theory), nothing in the National Institute of Justice (NIJ) replication experiments reveals why arrest should affect violent behavior one way or another. They are more usefully interpreted, in my opinion, as addressing the classic Malthusian problem of how the state should package its resources (in this case, the package associated with police intervention) to satisfy consumer demand (battered women and their supporters) at the lowest "cost" to providers. Lest this appear to trivialize the dynamic between offenders, victims, and the state, let me quickly add that "demand" in this schema is a political construct that takes shape around particular events or objects (e.g., battering) at many levels simultaneously and is formed through historically specific combinations of what people need, what they believe is possible, what they think they deserve, and what they think they can get.

From this vantage, one can think of the proarrest strategy as a "basket of goods" that may include everything from a mere warning, handcuffing, or an arrest warrant through a weekend in jail, mandated treatment, a stalker's law, the community intervention programs described by Gelles, real prison time, the provision of court-based advocates, and so forth. Hart (Chapter 7, this volume) provides the clearest articulation to date of the package of reforms needed to protect and empower battered women once they enter the criminal justice system. But, of course, arrest is a precondition for most of what she proposes. In essence, Sherman and the other critics are recommending that this keystone to reform be removed from the basket because it fails to fulfill an important policy objective—the reduction of violence. Sherman's implication and the thrust of the arguments by Straus and Gelles (in this volume) are that the criminal justice system should no longer be the focal point of society's response to woman battering.

Even before we can ask whether the replication experiments are sufficiently robust to justify abandoning mandatory arrest, we need to question their fundamental premise: that the wisdom of arrest should be assessed solely in terms of its effects on violent behavior, *whatever they are*. To do this, we need to conceptualize the presumed object of the arrest policy—woman battering—and unpack the "demand" that arrest is designed to satisfy. Buzawa et al. (Chapter 9, this volume) and Straus also examine other aspects of this issue, the former from the perspective of individual consumers ("victim preference") and the latter by distinguishing the needs of a small group who face life-threatening violence from the majority of victim-consumers whose needs could be best served by a more flexible policy of informal supports and treatment. In critiquing the police experiments and contrasting the results with evaluations of alternative interventions, Gelles addresses the issue more globally—namely, how various packages of criminal justice resources affect consumers.

However critical I may be of Sherman, Straus, Gelles, or Buzawa, along with Manning, these scholars deserve praise for venturing into practice and public policy, where the "factors" so neatly manipulated in research designs reappear with all the vanity, unpredictability, and courage of flesh-and-blood people. If the winds have changed direction and we must now be as concerned with the effects of criminalizing abuse as we formerly were with its invisibility, I can think of no group better qualified to make the announcement.

BATTERING:
THE SOCIAL PHENOMENON

Feminists have hardly been unambivalent about the wisdom of a proarrest strategy. Who is more aware that depending on protective intervention by a male institution is a two-edged sword? As the concern with "wife torture" emerged from the movements in the 1970s to protect animals and children, British feminist Frances Power Cobbe addressed the same questions we are debating today, and she did so, incidentally, with the same sort of evidence.

Cobbe (1878) believed that battering was rooted in women's status as men's property and that the only effective response was full economic and political independence. Women's subordinate position in the public sphere and their private vulnerability were inextricable, each a precondition for the other. Cobbe supported the arrest and prosecution of batterers as means to reduce women's political isolation. Like Manning, Cobbe emphasized the class and sex biases inherent in law enforcement. She understood that, if left to their own paternalistic devices, the protective services enforced women's oppression like other state institutions. Noninterference when women were assaulted constituted active support for male dominance. As in the 1860s, so too in the 1960s, leaving the response to woman battering to police discretion was like relying on Sheriff "Bull" Connor in Birmingham to protect Alabama blacks registering to vote.

Despite her support for arrest, Cobbe no more thought that outlawing wife torture would change the political nature of male dominance than her abolitionist sisters in the United States thought they could end racial hatred and violence by outlawing lynching. In fact, after studying arrest and court statistics, she concluded that the courts were focusing only on the most extreme cases of violence. As a result, she believed, criminal justice was effectively establishing a permissible level of harm: By punishing only "severe" injury, the court response actually caused the minimum levels of domestic violence to rise. Nor was she sanguine about the response of individual men. Opening the door to male dominance in the home might easily cause any number of men to try even harder to keep that door closed. Cobbe also understood how publicity about the "kicking districts" in working-class Liverpool was used by middle-class men to reinforce their own "relatively mild" power tantrums. She predicted that Irish workingmen "dislocated by mercantilism" would bear the brunt of punishment, much as minority males do today.

I share Cobbe's fundamental conviction that violence against women is a political fact. This means that everything about it— when, how, why, and where it is used, whom it affects, the nature of intervention, and most important, the consequences of intervention for all involved—reflects the relative power of men over women and the struggles by particular men to assert and women to escape this power. Whether this violence is expressed through child sexual abuse, harassment, rape, or battering, the key is the selection of females as victims on the basis of their gender. Because of its roots in sexual inequality, whatever occasions violence in a given encounter, the ultimate cause of "battering" (as well as its consequence) is the denial of women's *civil rights*. When men, children, or the elderly are victimized, this is not structural inequality. Thus, although a proarrest policy reflects the growing power of women to command greater due process *in and of itself*, there can be no expectation—and in the battered women's movement, there is none—that criminalizing male violence against women, no matter how broadly defined, can have more than an incremental effect on women's vulnerability to male domination.[3]

Understanding violence against women as a civil rights issue goes to the very heart of the abusive experience. What distinguishes violence that exploits the structural inequality between men and women from acts of violence generally is neither the greater physical strength of men nor their greater propensity to aggress, both of which have been exaggerated. Rather, its distinctive character derives from how the convergent supports for male authority "enter" an actual conflict and merge with the batterer's pattern of control during and *after* a conflict arises, regardless of who initiates physical violence, particularly if women try to leave the relationship or seek outside help. As historian Linda Gordon (1988) explained, "One assault does not make a battered woman; she becomes that because of her socially determined inability to resist or escape" (p. 285).

In trying to conceptualize battering, we need to picture ongoing forms of control that are at once both personal and social, including economic exploitation, isolation from family and friends, intimidation, and a host of rules governing everyday activities. Ann Jones and Susan Schecter (1991) use the term *coercive control* to describe the systemic fusion of social and individual dominance that undermines the physical, psychological, or political autonomy of even the strongest, most aggressive and capable women.

Because the control elements in battering are visible only negatively, through women's adaptations, coercive control gives a particular man far more power in the eyes of his mate than an outsider without expert knowledge of the situation can perceive. This is why the risks inherent in abusive situations are consistently underestimated even after helpers have been sensitized to intervene (Kurz & Stark, 1988). Emphasizing the cultural factors that make police resistant to change (Manning, Buzawa) neglects the fact that, prior to mandatory arrest, the police response to battering was no different from the response by doctors, judges, psychiatrists, or social workers.

Coercive control is the proper frame for understanding male violence against women, whether it appears as harassment, child sexual abuse, rape, or battering. By contrast, little of the essential reality is captured by models that rely on "a discourse of injury" in which the location, nature, and severity of physical "damage" provides the basis for assessment, arrest, or disposition and assignment to a specialist. In any case, when we speak about "battering," we refer to both the pattern of violent acts and their political framework, the pattern of social, institutional, and interpersonal controls that usurp a woman's capacity to determine her destiny and make her vulnerable to a range of secondary consequences— attempted suicide, substance abuse, mental illness, and the like. The term *entrapment* describes the cumulative effects of having one's political, social, and psychological identity subordinated to the will of a more powerful other who controls resources that are vital to one's survival.[4]

BATTERING: THE CRIME

How does conceptualizing *battering, the social phenomenon*, in terms of sexual inequality, coercive control, and entrapment help us understand *battering, the crime*? Most notably, it highlights the contrast between criminal acts of domestic violence and the pattern of coercion and control that is not currently proscribed by law. Intuitively, it shifts from the class of crimes associated with assault (in which injury is emphasized) to those associated with a history of restraint, such as kidnapping or hostage taking. In Chapter 2, this volume, Straus reminds us that domestic violence abrogates the basic trust implied by family connections, hence the term *abuse*. His analogy to child abuse and his belief in the sanctity of family connections lead him to question legal sanctions in any but the most extreme instances of spousal violence. But highlighting coercive control and entrapment moves us from an abuse model, in which otherwise legitimate authority is exercised illegitimately, to a model in which violent restraint is placed on a continuum with the normative authority men exercise over women. Whatever informal codes of trust it offends, battering also violates women's affirmative rights to liberty and equality, rights that children do not possess. To reiterate, the civil rights violation is the use of control and violence to exploit sexual inequality and obstruct women's self-determination as legally independent adults.

The emphasis on restraint also underlies the social interest in criminalizing battering. Cobbe assumed that women possess affirmative rights to liberty and equality and that society reaps the benefits of women's contribution only when these rights are protected. Starting here shifts the rationale for antibattering laws from protecting the innocent—an emphasis that relies heavily on paternalistic stereotypes of women—to removing an obstacle to social progress.

We may anticipate what this frame implies for policy. Because sexual inequality is not merely an unpleasant sociological fact, but rather a condition of existential risk, women's safety is always contingent and context specific, their "fear" chronic, and their self-inhibition of desired social activities routine.[5] Thus, although safety and the reduction of fear remain important goals, their realization depends on making women's "empowerment" the ultimate standard against which the efficacy of various interventions is judged.

In summary, *battering, the social phenomenon,* occurs at three levels simultaneously: the political level of female subordination, the level of interpersonal assault, and the level of coercive control at which women's social vulnerability is exploited for personal gain. *Battering, the experience,* arises from the particular ways in which these three levels interrelate in a given relationship over time. The challenge is for criminal justice to recontextualize the sorts of disembodied acts of assault recorded by medicine, such as "punched with fist," or by research instruments, such as the Conflict Tactics Scale, in terms of entrapment and control. Sherman recognizes that this episodic focus also governs police work. The same could be said of the calculus of harms that guides criminal proceedings in the courts. Lacking a conceptual frame to understand the historical nature of battering, police, judges, physicians, and other professionals fall back on kitsch psychology or on cultural stereotypes to explain the patterns they observe among individuals, families, or entire groups who appear "violence prone." Absent a theory of coercive control, the traumatic effects of battering seem to be derived from victim psychology.

The question is how to bring these three levels of causality to bear in a criminal justice policy response to *battering, the crime,* and in making and assessing arrest decisions. A democratic society is unlikely to punish normative behaviors as such, even when these reproduce social inequalities and evoke consistent emotional and social harms. Thus, the law acknowledges only extraordinary harms, no matter how pathological the standard. We may not be ready to imprison the physician who abandons his wife after she puts him through medical school, but we have reached a level of social development consistent with sanctioning those who forcibly exploit the inequalities that result from discrimination—even in their homes—to deny minorities such personal liberties as the right to go and come freely, to exercise sexual self-determination, or to freely access helping services, family and friends, money, food, and other personal resources, services, education, and so forth.

Because the element of control is what links the assaultive dimensions of abuse to the political fact of female inequality, there can be no hope of preventing battering simply by regulating the degree of violence. This is why we call for "zero tolerance" of force in interpersonal relationships and oppose basing police intervention on a calculus of physical harm. At the same time, no level of "treatment" (for women or men) will substantially reduce force until the political dimensions of sexual inequality are addressed. The dilemma was illustrated when a man in one of our batterer programs asked whether the government that wanted him to stop his violence was the same one that had trained him to kill in Vietnam. Thus, male violence and inequality must be addressed simultaneously.

Asking police to help free women from a historical process of entrapment and control by men involves them directly in the politics of gender.[6] Even if this is not made explicit during their training, police are quite aware of the political implications of the laws against battering, just as police in the South were aware of what was involved in protecting voting rights demonstrators 30 years ago.[7] Ethnographic descriptions of the informal codes governing how police function on the street and theoretical pictures of how policing reproduces social inequality may add substantially to other dimensions of criminal justice thinking. But they can also obscure what is, at bottom, a political process of negotiation that involves every aspect of law enforcement, from personal attitudes and departmental priorities through who sits on local police boards. Buzawa and Manning predict that the basic function and behavior of police will not change because we mandate arrest of batterers. What they miss is that implementing the mandate is inextricably linked to a range of challenges to basic police functions. As Hart makes clear, we see laws against battering as part of a broad strategy of justice for women. But before we can debate the wisdom of this strategy or the role of police in its implementation, we must reach a consensus that an affirmative conception of women's rights is the proper basis for reform.

Reframing *battering, the crime*, in terms of inequality, coercive control, and entrapment allows us to think in new ways about mandatory arrest. The critics make three powerful points:

1. *Mandatory arrest does not work.* Although arrest might reduce violence in some instances, it may actually increase it in others. Only in allowing police to exercise informed discretion—what Sherman termed *structured discretion*—can we meet the objectives of deterrence. Manning goes further. By "disqualifying" minorities, using force to intrude in private life, arrest actually exacerbates social inequalities based on class, race, and gender.

2. *Mandatory arrest is inhumane.* Arrest does little for the victim and less for the offender. Worse, it jeopardizes the fundamental integrity of family life. It is far better to limit arrest to the most dangerous cases, use treatment for batterers, and offer a range of compassionate family supports. What police need, simply, is an instrument to identify the most severe cases. The child protection system offers a model for this approach.

3. *The very people we are trying to protect do not want it.* It appears contradictory for us to value a woman's claim to liberty as a fully endowed citizen and then to devalue her assessment of a policy carried out in her name, such as mandatory arrest. Allowing women—and police—the discretion to decide whether arrest should occur satisfies the consumer interest of the former and sustains the morale of the latter.

DOES MANDATORY ARREST WORK?

In one of the more dramatic self-critiques in the history of criminal justice research, Larry Sherman, an architect of the Minneapolis Domestic Violence Experiment, now argues that mandatory arrest does not deter domestic violence, except among very select groups (e.g., married, employed men). If the replication experiments failed to show the deterrent value of arrest, they did show, Sherman claims, that arrest actually *increases* violence in the long run, particularly among unemployed, unmarried, and minority males. Although Sherman bemoans the rush to implement the earlier research findings, on the basis of current findings he argues that as a general practice mandatory arrest should be ended immediately, particularly in cities with large ghetto populations. In place of mandatory arrest, he favors "structured police discretion," presumably so that alternatives can be used in cases in which arrest has been shown to increase risk. Because one logical outcome of this position is clearly absurd—namely, to arrest only white, married, employed batterers—in effect, Sherman's argument would virtually end arrest in domestic violence cases, at least in all major urban centers, except in the most severe cases.

No mea culpas are required from Sherman because the results of his Minneapolis Domestic Violence Experiment were misinterpreted. As Lindblom (1980) repeatedly argued, the primary role of analysis in policy making is to influence partisan negotiations. Research findings that fail to enhance a private interest are simply disregarded. This is no less true in police work, in which consumer satisfaction has always been the driving force. Thus, early criticisms of the Minneapolis Domestic Violence Experiment by Gelles and others were swept aside by mounting political pressure for police action from the women's movement, the courts, and the federal government. To this extent, whatever Berk and Sherman intended, the Minneapolis Domestic Violence Experiment was part of the proarrest policy process, rather than its stimulus.[8] Had that experiment not existed, less elegant analyses would have been brought to bear in negotiations. Conversely, recession-driven cuts in basic services and the resulting move toward community policing provide a climate that discourages the sort of open conflict with local (male) norms evoked by mandatory arrest. Although the replication experiments are hardly sufficient to reverse the administrative commitment to arrest, without constant pressure, arrest practices are likely to slowly atrophy (as they did in the 1870s).

Line officers react quite favorably to the news that arrest works in domestic violence. But the major importance of the Minneapolis Domestic Violence Experiment was to give women's advocates (who already favored arrest) a powerful weapon to use with lawmakers who viewed domestic violence, like child abuse, as a social welfare rather than a criminal justice problem. Gelles similarly fails to recognize the partisan role of research in the policy process and hence also exaggerates the influence of the Minneapolis Domestic Violence Experiment. The major influences on police administration were political pressure and fears of liability. For instance, in

Connecticut, the head of the Police Chiefs' Association was on the telephone 48 hours after the *Thurman* decision, offering to support "any law" that would protect his towns from liability. By contrast, in states where battered women's coalitions had the greatest political power—Oregon, Pennsylvania, Minnesota, New Jersey, and Illinois—public pressure had changed the normative consensus about how police should respond to domestics even before arrest became official procedure. To reiterate, the Minneapolis results were accepted so uncritically because, as a management strategy, police discretion in domestic violence cases had already become *politically* untenable.

But what did the battered women's movement hope to accomplish through arrest? After all, having established an unprecedented woman-run, community-based alternative service movement, why risk losing our identity by placing so much emphasis on a male-run system that, as Buzawa reminds us, we located on the far right of the political spectrum in terms of community participation, access to influence, attitudes toward women, and bureaucratic isolation?

The first reason for mandating arrest was to control police behavior. Gelles presents a dismal picture of police behavior in cases of domestic violence prior to the proarrest mandate. By contrast, Buzawa challenges "feminists" for assessments she regards as undeservedly negative. Both are right. The fact is that, in disregarding battering, minimizing its consequences, and blaming the victims of abuse, police were no different from other professional groups. Contrary to what Manning claims (citing Ferraro), there can be little question that police behavior has changed significantly with mandatory arrest. Whereas street-level resistance by police remains widespread, arrests for assault had risen 70% between 1984 and 1989, largely because of domestic violence laws.

However individual officers responded to calls for help, the absence of a standard for police practice increased women's sense of powerlessness and thus posed a major obstacle to their empowerment. As Manning points out, informal practices emphasize the authority of dominant groups even more than arrests. Buzawa makes the interesting point that police behavior may actually be less consistent under mandatory arrest than before. What is more important than consistency—after all, *noninterference* was consistent—is a standard against which to judge variation.

The interest in controlling the police response had as much to do with accountability to shelters as to women generally. The legal mandate that expands the package of services that shelters can offer, including services to police, increases the safe mobility of shelter residents and advocates, provides a rationale for a regular shelter presence in the courts, and lays an empirical basis that shelters can exploit for custodial orders, orders of protection, and expanded services. These functions, in turn, provide the substantive basis for ongoing negotiations among shelters, the criminal justice system, and family and children's services, negotiations that have been formalized in many cities through coordinating councils, networks, or other forums that assume quasi-official oversight responsibility for the law. Because shelters often secure temporary restraining orders (TROs), their power has been greatly enhanced in places where police liability for failing to arrest has been extended to failure to enforce orders of restraint and protection. Liability is a particularly important source of redress because the Supreme Court's 1989 *DeShaney* decision leaves open the question of whether a procedural due process entitlement might exist in situations in which the state fails to protect people it knows to be at risk.

The second reason for mandatory arrest involved immediate protection from current violence. Arrest provides a meaningful opportunity for battered women to consider their options and gives those women ready to end the relationship time to go elsewhere or to obtain a protective order. The amount of time the batterer is physically out of the picture is crucial. In Milwaukee, for example, a woman was three times as likely to be assaulted if police left without an arrest than if the batterer was arrested and then released (7% vs. 2%). Here, too, a major component is the jurisdictional space that arrest opens for shelters and other providers, not simply for battered women.

Third in importance was the desire to reduce the overall incidence of domestic violence both directly, because arrest might deter recidivism, and by sending a clear message that battering was unacceptable. Whereas the replication studies clearly do not support the Minneapolis findings, other studies do. In Lincoln, Nebraska, for example, implementing a mandatory arrest law reduced recidivism dramatically—from 83% to 53%. Interestingly, in the baseline prior to the law, both arrest and citation were associated with *more* recidivism. In Marion County, Indiana, although recidivism at 6 months was higher for those arrested on the scene than for those arrested on a victim complaint, in only 13 of 386 cases did there appear to be retaliation for arrest (Ford, 1990).

According to deterrence theory, the function of mandatory arrest is to convey the criminal nature of battering. Although arrests have risen for domestic violence, because prosecution and sentencing patterns in domestic assault cases have changed very little since battering was criminalized, it is unclear what the NIJ experiments were actually measuring. The results could just as readily be interpreted to mean that arrest is ineffective in isolation from other sanctions. Indeed, just as violence may increase where orders of protection are unenforced, so too is it likely that arrest without serious follow-up is interpreted by some as a license to abuse. By contrast, where arrest has been combined with treatment and prosecution, as in a Canadian experiment reported by Dutton (1986), batterers were 10 times less likely to be recidivists than when arrest alone was used (40% vs. 4%). The policy of mandatory arrest also has the indirect function of setting a standard of zero tolerance for battering that other institutions can emulate.

Fourth, making battering the only crime in which police discretion is removed acknowledges a special social interest in redressing the legacy of discriminatory treatment of women by law enforcement. It also forces the law to juxtapose the subjective experience of women and its traditional accommodation to the interests of propertied (male) strata. Setting the crime of battering apart in this way also helps distinguish battering from the two sets of crimes with which it is commonly confused: *familial* abuse, in which the victim is a minor or a frail elderly dependent, and assaults or muggings by strangers. Mandating arrest communicates how seriously we take the crime of battering and may have an effect on subsequent violence that is independent of arrest as such. This is underlined by the findings from Lincoln, Nebraska. Mandating equal protection in this way also helps counter the general reluctance of courts to extend to women the civil rights protection granted to racial minorities.

A final reason for supporting mandatory arrest was what might be termed its "redistributive" function: the perception that police service is a resource that had heretofore been hoarded by others and now should be made available to women on a more egalitarian basis. Notice that the concern here is with the sheer quantity of services consumed by various groups and with neither their substance nor their outcomes.

The same historical and political context in which the proarrest strategy originated explains its uneven implementation. Differences in community response to mandated arrest reflect differences in this context. Where the law has been delivered from on high, enforcement has been sporadic and police passive-aggressive. In Connecticut, the Family Violence Prevention and Response Act (1986, §§ 466-58a-f) emerged from administrative negotiation, but police were under relatively little local pressure to arrest. So they continue to make "dual" arrests 20% of the time and have limited liability if they fail to enforce protection orders. By contrast, in Oregon, legal reform was the product of intense communitywide struggle, and the implementation of arrest reflected incremental gains in women's power *in that community.* As a result, Oregon's mandatory arrest laws are widely accepted, few dual arrests are made, and police can be held liable for failing to enforce protection orders. Pennsylvania provides an interesting test case for the political hypothesis: There, despite the absence of a mandatory arrest law and the relative backwardness of the state's judiciary, powerful oversight of police practice by the battered women's coalition has made arrest of batterers routine.

The Minneapolis Domestic Violence Experiment also reflected this; with its twin city of St. Paul hosting the nation's first shelter and a police chief who believed oppression by race, class, and gender to be the roots of most crime, no area more supportive of battered women could have been chosen to prove the efficacy of arrest. But if the context strongly biased the outcome of the experiment, so too did the experiment influence the political context, although not nearly to the extent that Sherman and Gelles imply. Some policymakers undoubtedly misconstrued the Minneapolis Domestic Violence Experiment and so implemented mandatory arrest without adequate evidence. But the fact remains that the researchers, the Police Foundation, the NIJ, and those who supported and attacked the findings from Minneapolis failed to set their evidence in a historical, structural, or political context that could have made the contingent nature of deterrence intelligible to local policymakers. Whatever the replication experiments may or may not say about arrest, they speak eloquently to our failure to learn from our mistakes because they, like the original experiment, do not consider the political chain that might help us understand why arrest works in one setting but not in another. At a time when community support for police efforts is widely recognized as the single most important factor in police effectiveness, it is surprising that the NIJ gave no consideration to the political context that set the tone for enforcement either in selecting the research sites to replicate Minneapolis or in evaluating the findings. Shifting the blame to policymakers for implementing arrest prematurely simply makes it easier to curtail arrest now—a right hard-won by the battered women's movement—amid broad cuts in other services to women.

What are we to make of Sherman's conclusion that arrest works mainly with men who are employed and married and that recidivist violence after arrest in certain cities appears highest among minorities and the unemployed? Obvious structural factors are at work here. The correlation between crimes of violence (including assault) and the business cycle has been well known in criminology for some time (Henry & Short, 1977; Ogburn & Thomas, 1922, Table 1, p. 326). Because the replication experiments were conducted when the economy was entering the worst recession in three decades, with the most dramatic effects on minorities and the working poor, the most appropriate baseline is not prearrest levels of violence, but rather rates of violence in similar cities where no change was made in police policy. Beyond this, Otto Kirscheimer showed that rates of violence and the severity of punishment for such crimes increased together, probably because the economic climate that produced one also produced the other. In any case, an adequate model of deterrence must combine what Gelles calls "respect for the law" and socialization models with shifts in motivational and opportunity structures.

Elementary Emile Durkheim would suggest that the normative message sent by punishment would be received best by those whose access to opportunity structures (e.g., family, housing, job) allowed them to realize their goals in "legitimate" ways, a point Gelles makes well. In other words, deterrence is most successful when other provocative factors have at least been neutralized. The problem with applying this formulation here, however, is that the goals of many of the men involved in battering entail denying women access to basic entitlements. Thus, although the employed, white, middle-class husband may be less violent following arrest, he is also more able than his unemployed, black counterpart to leverage resources other than physical force to continue subjugating his wife. Open warfare may be temporarily over in his household, but the control and coercion go on undisturbed. Has arrest worked in this situation?

This point raises the larger issue of what the replication experiments mean *even if we accept the evidence as Sherman presents it*. Our assumptions about the three levels of battering give us no hint what a change in postarrest violence signifies in terms of coercive control, entrapment, and/or inequality. As Dutton, Hart, Kennedy, and Williams (1992) point out, violence may cease because, following arrest, threats of repeat violence may be sufficient to maintain a power advantage over a spouse, as in the case of the employed middle-class husband described above. Conversely, violence may increase because women are empowered by arrest and/or threaten to leave or to have the man arrested again. On the basis of evidence that abuse escalates when males perceive their control threatened, as during separation and divorce, we would predict that postarrest violence would be greatest—as Sherman's data show it is—among those who are least integrated into the job market or other structures from which men garner their authority—namely, the poor, black, or unemployed. Again, violence may increase in this group because arrest works to empower women and undermine male control, the reverse of Gelles's thesis that arrest works for those who have something to lose.

Evidence suggests that even men who become angry following arrest may be no more violent as a result and that men who are violent after arrest are not necessarily angrier than others about arrest itself (Ford, 1990). Even if we assume that arrest provokes greater violence among a substantial number of men, Sherman's proposal that we respond by eliminating mandatory arrest appears perverse (to say the least). A far more humane and rational response would be to expand protection for the most vulnerable female populations—namely, single, minority, and low-income women—as well as to better integrate batterers into opportunity structures *without diminishing women's access to resources*. The bottom line, however, is that assault is merely one among many means available to men in battering relationships and that its absence, even for some extended period, may signify greater equality or greater dominance.

Let's assume that violence increases following arrest among certain groups and that little can be done to inhibit it. Even this worst case scenario barely affects the most important rationales for mandatory arrest—namely, controlling police behavior, setting a public standard for police response, offering immediate protection, embodying women's civil rights claims, and affording women access to a new "package of resources." Moreover, as Gelles reminds us, the rationale of reducing the overall incidence of violence is only negated if we focus on those who are actually arrested, rather than on the larger class of offenders or potential offenders.

To the contrary, other data sets—some of which Gelles examines—indicate that mandatory arrest may meet a number of our more important objectives. With respect to protection and control, for instance, recent Supreme Court and appellate court decisions suggest that battered women in states with mandatory arrest laws have far stronger claims to police protection than do battered women in states without such statutes. Furthermore, states with broad mandatory arrest laws are far more likely to allow liability of police officers than might states without such laws, such as New York.

Minority women deserve particular attention because they are most likely to use the service system (including police) and to suffer powerlessness as a result of institutional discrimination. As Manning predicts, the replication experiments indicate that minority women bear the major brunt of postarrest violence. As a result, argues Sherman, minority women would be the major beneficiaries if mandatory arrest is eliminated.

That arrest poses a series of unique dilemmas to minority women goes without question. But if police were reluctant to intervene generally in domestic violence cases prior to legal reform, they provided virtually no protection to blacks. As Buzawa reminds us, many police conceive of blacks as what sociologist Darnell Hawkins terms "normal primitives" and only intervene in "domestics" when violence overflows into the public arena. This is one reason why violence—almost always by a spouse or a lover—is the major cause of death among black women under 44 years of age (Stark, 1991). That such attitudes are self-fulfilling is suggested by Sherman's observation that police can "predict" which couples (and which apartment buildings!) are chronically violent. Eliminating mandatory arrest, then, would do little more than reestablish a brutal status quo.

IS ARREST HUMANE?

Straus (Chapter 2, this volume) opposes a proarrest policy in domestic violence cases because of its insensitivity to the moral and practical realities of family life. The unique nature of the family, he insists, distinguishes domestic violence from other forms of assault.[9] Having documented the extent of physical force used in families, he quickly reminds us that the vast majority of instances involve infrequent and/or minor episodes for which arrest is inappropriate. He contrasts our moral repugnance with force and the state's obligation to protect family members with society's affirmative interest in maintaining the integrity of families. Families are complicated systems. No single criminal justice response (e.g., mandatory arrest) can be equally sensitive to the best interests of the victim, the offender, and the family as a whole. Because women use force as frequently as do men, a consistent standard would result in women and men being arrested equally, a practice that Straus presumably finds unacceptable.

As a practical solution to these problems, Straus wants to grade sanctions according to the relative physical risk posed to the victim by the offender's profile and behavior. Sanctions would range from the pretrial option of a batterer's program for cases in which injury is minor to postprosecution diversion to treatment for those whose background and behavior place their victims in life-threatening danger.

To implement this policy, Straus offers police a screen for "life-threatening violence" (LTR), which ranks the severity of injury and chronicity of injury with behaviors thought to be associated with homicide, including threats, use of weapons, child abuse, attacks on property, assault on nonfamily members, injury to pets, history of psychological problems, substance use, forced sex, jealousy, extreme male dominance, abuse as a child, and severe violence between the offender's parents. Even for cases in which violence is determined to be life-threatening, Straus only recommends steps that will safeguard victims and offenders' postprosecution diversion to treatment.

With respect to the major premise, suffice it to reiterate that feminists do not regard battering as a family crime primarily, but rather as an assault directed at women because of their gender— hence, more closely linked with rape, harassment, and dating violence than with familial abuse against children or the elderly. Despite the ideological bias that has excluded unmarried women from population surveys of domestic violence, the vast majority of battered women (75% or more) are single, separated, or divorced, with separated and divorced women facing the greatest risk of severe ongoing violence, including homicide (Stark & Flitcraft, 1991). It would be hard to argue that the state's interest in maintaining these relationships overrides its obligation to protect women.

Admittedly, special problems are present in cases in which victims are married or living with their assailants. The term *abuse* evokes a powerful adult on whom the victim is dependent, as in elder or child abuse. With respect to battering, the relative inequality in power originates in social roles and differential access to resources that may or may not be reflected in individual differences in the use of force.

Straus's focus on wife abuse constrains claims for redress to the dependent status implied by the role. As a normative set of expectations, the wife's role is presumed to be functional for family life. However undesirable, violence is seen as requiring outside management only when the *level* of harm or risk (as determined by the severity and chronicity of assault) makes the maintenance of the unit morally indefensible. For Straus and his collaborators, the key difference between spousal violence initiated by men or by women lies in the greater risk of injury that results from men's innate physical superiority.

Feminists identify the functional dependence of women in families as an expression of their *political* vulnerability, much like the vulnerability of blacks reflected in their having to assume a range of dependent occupational roles. Women's attempts to meet their needs within the constraints of sex roles lead to conflicts over the most basic aspects of interpersonal life, including sex, access to money, friends and family, opportunities to work, and so on. The *coercive* control at the heart of battering exploits women's dependent status to gain consistent advantage in these conflicts. Thus, the right of a married woman to be free from coercion is backed up by the same civil rights claim that affects *all* women and is independent of their relationship to their assailants, who initiates violence in a particular case, or the severity of any given injury. The social interest in arrest is even greater when the double vulnerability implied by marriage is violated. Because we invest the parent with

responsibilities for caretaking, which no other institution can similarly discharge, it may be reasonable to set aside sanctions in cases
of child abuse if we believe the victim is no longer at risk. Responsibility for caretaking has no place in cases of battering.

ASSESSING RISK

These opposing conceptions of justice lead to different interpretations of relative risk, as well as of the importance of future risk in
evoking present sanctions. One of the earliest domestic violence
assessments for homicide was developed by Jacqueline Cambell
(1984). Ever since, advocates have employed a variety of instruments to determine the emergent nature of abuse and to assist
battered women in identifying the relative dangers of returning
home. Straus would take us a step further and assess the need for
police protection by screening the severity of injury and the extent
of offender pathology.

Assessment criteria obviously must suit the particular service
encounter. In the medical complex, where the major concerns are
the woman's capacity for self-protection and whether she can return
home safely, assessment is based on factors associated with the
overall level of entrapment, her level of fear and isolation, for
instance, as well as her "trauma history." Because severe injury
could result from a relatively minor assault (e.g., a push might lead
to a severe head wound), severity might not be prognostic. Conversely, minor episodes of injury (even old wounds aching) may
signify more serious injury to follow or that the woman has been
prevented from presenting more serious problems in the past. The
low spontaneous remission rate seen among battered women in the
hospital strongly suggests, contrary to Straus's recommendations,
that early and decisive intervention that separates the couple is the
key to prevention.

Straus acknowledges that his screening instrument lacks empirical foundation. Addiction, mental illness, exposure to parental
violence as a child, and conviction for an unrelated crime may be
disproportionately associated with abuse. But each affects only a
small proportion of batterers—fewer than 10% in some cases—and
none has been tested prospectively for its effects on battering.
Angela Browne's (1987) study of women charged with homicide is

the only evidence that the *combination* of these factors is any more likely to predict subsequent violence for *individuals* than might any of the factors taken alone. Notice, however, that Browne draws her sample from women who have killed their batterers, hardly a basis for assessing "successful" batterers. Indeed, such traits as alcohol abuse and mental illness, which Straus draws from Browne to predict risk for women, may signify the reverse—that is, risk of homicide to offenders. As yet, no research has been done on batterers who have killed their wives.

The large number of false positives produced by a broadly based screening instrument poses few problems so long as the primary goal in assessment is client education or determining the range of needs. In the hospital, we can eliminate many false negatives with a few simple questions about the client's level of fear and entrapment. But in police work, an instrument so lacking in sensitivity and specificity as Straus proposes would produce a completely unacceptable number of false positives and false negatives.

The Straus profiles might be useful in forensic work with women who have used force against their batterers. The number of prior assaults in cases of spousal homicide, the reduction in such fatalities in cities with gun control, and complementary evidence that homicide by friends and acquaintances begins in "fights" suggest that most homicides by batterers are assaults that have gotten out of hand; this point is argued persuasively by Lachman (1978). Therefore, it appears logical—though by no means proved—that, in addition to previous violence, coercive control, and the level of fear, the probability that violence will be fatal is increased by factors that would usually signify loss of control, such as substance use, mental illness, presence of weapons, rape, violence against children or property or pets, threats to kill, and serious injury in the past. Again, however, these same factors would make offenders vulnerable to murder by their victims. Unfortunately, because of the large number of false negatives they yield, instruments based on profiles such as these could also be used to dismiss a woman's claims if the batterer exhibits few high-risk traits. I am repeatedly confronted in my forensic work by long-term batterers who test normal on a range of psychological and behavioral assessments.

Apart from the issue of validity, of what relevance is this sort of profile in police work, where the consequences of being classified include sanctions for offenders and services for victims? A prior question involves the aims of police intervention. As Sherman recognizes, if the aim is prevention, historical patterns are more important than the current episode. Here, the relationships that would benefit most from arrest and treatment are those that Straus would screen out, where coercion and violence are infrequent and less severe and the fewest comorbidity factors are present. By contrast, even if the aim is short-term violence reduction, those whom Straus would mandate into treatment—men whose violence threatens the lives of their victims—have the worst prognosis.

Or should the risk of severe injury be the main criterion? In this case, as in the child abuse field, the poor quality of prognostic research would quickly lead to stigmatizing a subgroup of "deviants," primarily minority males. Straus is on particularly thin ice here. Having taught us that domestic violence is normative behavior, he now suggests we target a group of severely violent males who fall outside the range covered by the Conflict Tactics Scales. But his composite portrait is drawn from anecdotal, second-person reports (e.g., shelter interviews), rather than from control comparisons of actual offenders. To reiterate, the insensitivity of such a screen to the large number of "normal" and very dangerous batterers is a fatal flaw.

The major determinant of a woman's future risk is *her* present capacity for autonomy, *not* the personal characteristics or history of the batterer, and this status is a function of the *degree of coercive control* in the relationship, a factor that may or may not be related to frequency or severity of injury or to the presence of such comorbid factors as addiction or mental illness. Straus recognizes chronicity but fails to understand that its importance is primarily as an indicator of *control*.

Or, as with assaults by strangers, should police intervention be gauged to the severity of harm already inflicted? Apart from the implicit message this sends to the victim, that "if you *really* want protection, you must be *really* hurt," there is the larger issue raised by Cobbe: that nonintervention in so-called minor episodes effectively defines a moderate level of violence as "acceptable." How long would it take in any given community for the level of violence that resulted in no police action to once again become normative? Then, too, the severity of injury that police witness may be inversely related to the degree of coercive control in the relationship because calling the police is an act of *opportunity* and often not associated with the most severe episodes.

By dividing the sanctions for abuse along a continuum of severity, chronicity, and related behavioral problems, the law would be reverting to its pre-1960s status, essentially adapting a modern rule of thumb similar to the "10-stitch" rule, shifting from the assertion that woman battering is a crime to the rearguard position that family violence is a pathology—like child molestation, say, or alcoholism—that should be prosecuted only when it poses a clear and present danger to life and limb.

Straus finesses the issue of women's justice claims by urging victim preference in certain cases. Suffice it to say here that none of the above criteria—prevention of future abuse, reduced risk of severe injury, or severity of the precipitating assault—adequately supports women's right to redress for a crime that involves the use of violence and coercive control to deprive them of basic civil rights. Except in cases of life-threatening injury, for which Straus urges "protection" for victims, he sees law functioning to support the family and to help offenders get into treatment.

TREATMENT:
A HUMANITARIAN ALTERNATIVE?

Straus stratifies sanctions into pretrial and postprosecution diversion to "treatment." Apart from the civil liberties issues this raises for men arrested on the basis of a dubious psychosocial profile that includes witnessing abuse as a child, addiction, and mental illness, it is interesting to ask what exactly he thinks is being treated and whether there is any basis to suppose that "treatment" is suitable for the groups that Straus identifies.

Unlike behavioral problems that have been identified with distinctive psychiatric and/or physiological syndromes, such as addictions or sex crimes, battering has not been identified as a "disease" or even with a set of precipitating etiological factors that might form a coherent object of treatment. Certainly, a large number of batterers present with profiles classifiable for insurance purposes under *DSM-IV* as psychiatric conditions. For most offenders, however, coercive control is a rational strategy completely consistent with a range of positive messages from peers as well as from the surrounding culture, what I call a "normal pathology," a point that Straus has made repeatedly.

The epidemic proportions of battering and the reluctance to imprison offenders have produced a growing consensus that diversion into some sort of treatment or reeducation process is the most humanitarian alternative. Although most states now have batterers' programs, these vary enormously in quality and, in many cases, are capable of handling only a tiny proportion of the batterers arrested each year. Model programs in Boston, Duluth, Rhode Island, Denver, Pittsburgh, and Seattle are clear about victim safety and supplement cognitive-behavioral techniques with political education about coercive control as well as violence. But in the vast majority of jurisdictions, if services are available at all, they are likely to emphasize traditional mental health approaches, including couples therapy, that are insensitive to issues of sexual inequality and victim safety. Thus, treatment is being used as a residual in many jurisdictions despite the dearth and general irrelevance of available mental health services for batterers. What is the evidence that such programs work?

Adele Harrell (1991), at the Urban Institute, has conducted the most comprehensive evaluation to date of court-ordered treatment. She compared offenders ordered to treatment (both pre- and post-prosecution) in three different 8- to 12-week programs to those not ordered to treatment.[10] Data gathering ranged from interviews 6 months after treatment through a review of court records across a period of 15 to 29 months following case disposition.

The results are sobering. Treated offenders found treatment helpful in understanding themselves and in taking responsibility for violence. There was little corresponding improvement, however, in getting along with their partners. Although offenders in treatment were as likely as offenders *not* ordered to treatment to abstain from *severe* violence, a significantly smaller proportion of offenders in treatment abstained from physical aggression (88% vs. 57%), including pushing, kicking, shoving, and hitting. Between 80% and 85% of all offenders abstained from severe violence during the treatment period, whereas just under half (47%) abstained from threats. But longer term cessation of violence measured by domestic violence calls to the police was significantly *lower* among treated offenders (50%) than among offenders not ordered into treatment (70%). Also, treated offenders were almost three times as likely to face new domestic violence charges (19%, compared with 7%). Slightly more of the wives of treated offenders sought medical treatment for domestic violence injuries during the study period, but these groups differed little in their overall assessment of safety. Whereas treated offenders were more likely to understand the legal ramifications of domestic violence, both groups rated the *likelihood* of experiencing such sanctions as low. Also suggesting the poor deterrent effect of such programs is the fact that normative beliefs about the use of violence against wives remained unchanged after treatment. Interestingly, given the selection criteria proposed by Straus, tests for significant interactions between treatment impact and such offender characteristics as offenders' history of violence, criminal history, substance abuse, employment and marital status, or case-handling characteristics identified no consistent patterns.

Although the treatment groups studied were limited in their duration, approach, sanctions for noncompliance, and protection offered to victims, these limits characterize the vast majority of programs currently offered as diversionary. Harrell (personal communication, November 1993) suspects that batterers used the treatment process to forge supportive relations with other offenders. Alternatively, increased violence by treated offenders as well as calls to police might reflect victim "empowerment" (and the felt loss of offender control) as a result of arrest and treatment. In any case, the findings are consistent with the belief that battering is a calculated act of coercive control that can be carried out with full knowledge of its causes and consequences. Not only the long-term effects of treatment on violence but also the use of severe violence (20%) and threats (53%) *during* treatment suggest that diversion to treatment is a poor alternative to punitive sanctions that hold offenders accountable for their crimes. Even studies that reach more optimistic conclusions about the effects of treatment report consistently higher levels of recidivist violence than do studies of arrest.[11] To this extent, the proper test of an arrest policy would compare its consequences to the outcomes of alternative interventions.

DOES MANDATORY ARREST
DISEMPOWER WOMEN?

Buzawa raises the most fundamental challenge to feminist support for mandatory arrest: that in setting a uniform standard for how police *must* respond, the policy not only removes police discretion but also deprives women of control over their destiny and thus presumably reinforces the sense of powerlessness already inflicted by the batterer. Interestingly, Buzawa rests her argument on pragmatic rather than moral or political grounds, highlighting the greater consumer "satisfaction" likely to result from respecting victim preference and the apparent willingness of officers to respect preference, even if this means setting aside long-standing biases based on victim, offender, or situational characteristics. She would hold police administratively accountable to victim preference, an admittedly weaker mandate than one based on liability but significantly more constraining than the "structured discretion" proposed by Sherman.

Buzawa acknowledges that whatever police intervention there was in the past relied heavily on ascriptive characteristics. Even today, severe injury is less likely to prompt arrest than is drunkenness or verbal abuse of police. Conversely, police failed to arrest if victims were black, married, or aggressive in their presence or if a couple's violence was seen as "normal." In sum, arrest in domestic violence cases had little to do with the seriousness of a crime or even with evidence that a crime had occurred.

Buzawa reports the findings from a Detroit study of police encounters with 90 randomly selected victims of domestic violence. Interestingly, arrest decisions generally conformed to the criteria that Straus proposes, specifically whether the victim lives with the offender, severity of injury, victim preference, presence of children (or other "witnesses"), and use of guns and knives. Arrest was also directly related to age, a probable indicator of chronicity.

One way to evaluate the relative advantages of Buzawa's approach is to ask how outcomes might have differed were Detroit police under a mandate to arrest. Opponents of mandatory arrest argue that battered women who use police for informal control will stop calling if they know an arrest will occur and thus incur greater danger as a result. In Buzawa's sample, however, the women who were dissatisfied with the response of Detroit police all favored *more* aggressive behavior by police, not less. At the same time, police respected the wishes of a subgroup who requested no arrest. They did arrest almost a third of the offenders who caused no injury, however, again in response to victim preference; this suggests a sensitivity to the historical and/or coercive factors that goes beyond the criteria suggested by Straus.

Considered a model department with respect to domestic violence, the Detroit police arrest approximately three times as many offenders as were arrested by other departments in the past. And female victims are universally satisfied. In Detroit, the Malthusian problem of finding the minimum level of resources that satisfies consumer demand has seemingly been solved.

Relying on victim preference remains problematic for three subgroups, however: (a) women whose physical or psychological entrapment prevents their expressing a preference for arrest, (b) minorities who may view expressing a preference for arrest as a betrayal of cultural norms, and (c) women who may simply not understand the nature of their risk. In addition, as Buzawa acknowledges, victim preference fails to confront redistributive or justice claims represented by mandated protection.

On the one hand, in itself, the severity of injury when police are called may be inversely related to the level of entrapment. On the other hand, severe injury is a routine basis for arrest in stranger-inflicted assault and so provides a good basis for the claims to equity by battered women. Injury also indicates the vulnerability of victims to coercion—hence, their dilemma if forced to express a preference for arrest, particularly if the assailant is present. In this light, what are we to make of the fact that well over half of those offenders who cause visible injuries and even 43% who cause "serious" injury were not arrested in the Detroit study?

I have argued that the entrapment associated with battering justifies a proactive response from the state in anticipation of future assault and coercive control—hence, a proarrest policy. The same process of entrapment may reduce a woman's capacity *as an individual* to make certain decisions about her situation *so long as she remains under the influence of* coercive control. One basis for this is the psychological syndrome described by Lenore Walker as *learned helplessness*, a response to trauma that inhibits women's capacity to share their situation with service providers. Although this reaction is not typical, it does characterize a minority, particularly white, middle-class victims.

An even more common source of inhibition is the sharply restricted access that many victims are afforded by their batterers to such essential resources as money, other family members, and transportation. The isolation, retaliation, and dependence on the batterer associated with entrapment have material as well as psychological dimensions and illustrate the need for outside intervention to help redress the imbalance in power and clear a space for supportive intervention. Although the influence of larger social inequities is difficult to gauge, an additional population may hesitate to react protectively because they lack job skills or education or simply have "no place to go."

In Detroit, remarkably, the race of the couples made no difference in arrest, undoubtedly because 70% of the police officers are black. Other research uniformly indicates that police discretion is directly related to racial bias in arrest decisions. Whereas racial bias generally leads to *greater* arrests of blacks than whites for equivalent crimes, particularly for black youths, the effects in domestic violence cases are more complicated, perhaps because service to black women as well as punishment of black men is involved. The Duluth, Minnesota, Domestic Abuse Intervention Project compared the effect on blacks of total officer discretion, encouragement to arrest, and mandatory arrest. Whereas the number of overall arrests increased dramatically under encouragement to arrest and even further under mandatory arrest, the percentage of black men who were arrested fell and even reached a level close to the population in Duluth under mandatory arrest (Pence, 1985). The implication is that mandatory arrest reduces the expression of police bias in decision making and results in greater equity, the opposite of what Manning predicts.

Arrest may pose special problems to minority or immigrant groups whose citizenship status is ambiguous or whose cultural mores favor obedience to men, or when language and other cultural barriers increase isolation from mainstream services and distrust of "outsiders," including police. Minority women historically have used police to restore order during domestic disturbances and may feel particularly betrayed where arrest is mandated. Beyond this, as Schecter pointed out, poor and minority women often view battering against the torrent of abuses they experience in virtually every social setting. Kenyari Bellefield, of the Harriet Tubman Women's Shelter in Minneapolis, put it well:

> The effect of racism and sexism seems too great to tackle in the face of being victimized by a loved one. The woman often feels powerless to change her situation, tending to feel she is being forced to tolerate the situation longer because the very system which has historically

served to subjugate and oppress her is the only system which can save her from the immediate abusive system. (cited in Forell, 1990-1991, p. 223n)

Finally, a subgroup of women may hesitate to support arrest because they misunderstand the chronic nature of battering and/or its links to other illegitimate controlling behaviors.

The conflicting realities of coercive control and empowerment through victim preference raise what is undoubtedly the most difficult dilemma about mandatory arrest. Too often in women's lives, the question of who speaks in their name has been dealt with fatuously. For battered women, in particular, there is no more important issue in recovery than the restoration of "voice"; the essence of empowerment, we like to say, is allowing women to make the *wrong* decision. At the same time, and although all choices are constrained by an implicit calculus of costs and benefits to a certain extent, for women who are seriously injured or for those whose decisions reflect ignorance of their danger or psychological, material, economic, or racial deprivation, it is hard to see how the benefits of individual choice outweigh the social interest in stopping the use of illegitimate power. Only in situations where there are no injuries and where there is an expressed desire *not* to arrest despite probable cause to believe an assault has taken place is it likely that the arrest decision will be experienced as demeaning. Because this profile may describe the *most* as well as the least dangerous situations, I would prefer to mandate arrest than leave assessment to police.[12]

CRIMINALIZATION
AS SOCIAL CONTROL

Gelles raises a final argument against mandatory arrest: that it reflects a trend to criminalize behaviors and, as such, is a conservative effort to extend "social control." Manning and other radical criminologists offer a variation on the same theme, though on broader theoretical ground, focusing on the use of police violence to reproduce existing structures of dominance and control. Echoes of the social control argument can also be found in Sherman's and Straus's warnings against interference in "family privacy."

An obvious fact bears repeating: Whether criminal justice intervention will be defined as control or as liberation depends on the reference group. From the standpoint of women whose personal lives are governed by norms of male dominance supported by structural inequities, *noninterference* functions to exacerbate control. Conversely, outside intervention that challenges existing power relations is a fundamental precondition for autonomy among the oppressed. That such intervention may *also* become a vehicle for imposing other systemic biases (e.g., race or class prejudice) highlights the problems with enforcement but is not an inevitable consequence of society's legitimate interest in limiting unacceptable behavior. Nor is the control function of the law a reason to abandon women's larger justice claims for the equitable distribution of criminal sanctions.

Like legal control, criminalization may or may not advance personal liberty and social justice. Critics justly fault the designation as crimes of such behaviors as homosexuality, addiction, or abortion simply because they threaten dominant morality. Often missed, however, is a corresponding trend to decriminalize behaviors that support normative patterns of dominance. So, pressure to criminalize pregnancy among women who are addicted to drugs has been complemented by the effective decriminalization of drug addiction among men. Conversely, in decriminalizing child abuse, the focus of state intervention has shifted from men—the main culprits of physical abuse—to mothers. If control is the common theme here, it is evoked as much by decriminalization as by criminalization.

With respect to both control and criminalization, therefore, there is simply no way to avoid the difficult process of making political decisions about where scarce resources will be distributed and on whose behalf. If we think of justice as a good in itself, not merely as a means to an end, we can ask whether the mandatory arrest of batterers represents a more or less equitable distribution of this good.

There is little question in my view that the mandatory arrest of batterers represents a progressive redistribution of justice on behalf of women. One measure of this is a growing suspicion among social scientists and policymakers that, in intervening to counteract the illegitimate coercive power of particular men, the law is being used "politically" to further the larger goals of sexual equality. Would it were so.

NOTES

1. Whereas I would not deny Manning's argument that the criminal justice system uses its resources to deplete the "cultural capital" of subordinate groups and classes, I do think he minimizes the extent to which the presence of police intervention makes a tangible difference in people's ability to earn a living and raise a family, what I would call "the materiality of policing." The economic assumptions implied here do not encompass the alignment of criminal justice with the interests of propertied classes. With respect to police and particularly at the local level, however, I view such an alignment as strategic rather than structural, and hence ultimately accomplished through accommodation rather than brute force.

2. What "winning" entails for ordinary people is far less clear in policing than it is with the lottery. Health care provides a good analogy. The number of prenatal visits is related to positive birth outcomes, but what actually happens during these visits appears to have little relevance. In essence, as the positive public response to the sheer presence of police appears to indicate, simply gaining access to scarce resources enhances one's efficacy in the world. Does this mean that any policing of domestic violence is better than none? At the risk of grossly simplifying the matter, my answer is yes.

3. A parallel here is the relative effectiveness of medicine against infectious disease. Research shows conclusively that the decline in death from infectious and communicable disease predated by many decades the development of effective medical or public health treatments. Another way of understanding this process is to recognize that individual methods of treatment could only "work" after the social conditions that affected infectious disease on an epidemic scale had been controlled (Stark, 1982). From this vantage, the decline in disease—resulting from improved living and working conditions—was a precondition for the success of medicine, not the reverse. In a similar way, police control of individual violence can be expected to succeed only *after* violence has already been *managed* by advances in social equality.

4. In legal terms, entrapment implies choice in response to an enticement. Here, I want to retain both its original meaning—being trapped—as well as the connotation of coerced choice because the battered woman has entered the abusive relationship voluntarily and may have "chosen" to accommodate her assailant because he possesses/controls resources vital to her physical health and/or well-being.

5. Thus, in response to interviews in three cities by Gordon and Riger (1991), women were more than three times more likely than men to avoid doing things they had to do because of fear of being harmed (68% vs. 22%).

6. On a macrolevel, as Manning senses, this reflects a shift in our expectations of government. Pre-Depression Americans saw government creating a favorable climate for business and ensuring that minimum conditions of social life were sustained, particularly for those whom misfortune made unable to compete in the market. Today, both business and the public expect every level of government to problem-solve on a much broader terrain. But it is unclear whether this represents an extension of "control" (Manning's contention) or a recognition that reallocation issues cannot be dealt with piecemeal where there is widespread oppression and structural inequality.

7. Police who embrace domestic violence laws are no less stigmatized by their colleagues than those who stood for the protection of civil rights in the 1960s. One difference, of course, is that police are likely to "marry one" or to have one as a mother, daughter, or colleague.

8. We have had a parallel experience of "distortion." Although the original research I did with Flitcraft, documenting the extent of battering as a source of women's injury, was conducted in the emergency department, the same study also showed that because the vast majority of health visits by battered women were to nonemergency, nontrauma sites, emergency rooms were the *worst* place to begin a process of training in identification and referral. Given the convergence of medical interests in the traumatic dimensions of violence and the investment of battered women's advocates in defining abuse as an "emergency," there could be little question which part of our work would be "heard" and which would be passed on to a footnote in an academic journal.

9. Straus is confusing on this point. After outlining the various reasons why domestic violence is not like other forms of assault, Straus advises that intervention in cases of spousal assault be governed by the same principles applied to intervention in assaults between strangers or acquaintances.

10. Although the assignment of offenders to treatment was not random, it came as close to fulfilling the conditions of random assignment as could be expected in a natural experiment. In this case, two judges handled dispositions: One believed in treatment; the other did not. No prescreening mechanism determined which of the two received which case.

11. This is not to suggest that batterer education programs be eliminated. The availability of batterer reeducation, like arrest, may serve as a resource for women regardless of its effects on violent behavior. This is true particularly where the most likely alternative after arrest is dismissal of the case or a small fine or where there is little mental health care available. Again, the argument for maintaining batterers' programs is their redistributive effects, not whether they work.

12. Interestingly, mandatory arrest would also benefit male victims. Although the 15% of male victims were more likely to be seriously injured (38% vs. 14%) in the Detroit sample, female and male offenders were equally likely to be arrested, a finding that suggests a bias in arrest against male victims. By contrast with the women, *none* of the male victims were satisfied; this finding suggests that police behavior toward male victims may be independent of arrest decisions.

REFERENCES

Browne, A. (1987). *Women who kill.* New York: Free Press.

Cambell, J. (1984). Nursing care of families using violence. In J. Cambell & J. Humphreys (Eds.), *Nursing care of victims of family violence* (pp. 216-246). Englewood Cliffs, NJ: Prentice Hall.

Cobbe, F. P. (1878). Wife torture in England. *Contemporary Review, 32,* 55-87.

DeShaney v. Winnebago County Department of Social Services, 489 U.S. 189 (1989).

Dutton, D. G. (1986). The outcome of court-mandated treatment for wife assault: A quasi-experimental evaluation. *Violence and Victims, 1*(3), 163-175.

Dutton, D. G., Hart, S. D., Kennedy, L. W., & Williams, K. R. (1992). Arrest and the reduction of repeated wife assault. In E. Buzawa (Ed.), *Domestic violence: The changing criminal justice response* (pp. 111-128). Westport, CT: Auburn House.

Family Violence Prevention and Response Act (1986, §§ 466-38a-f).

Ford, D. (1990). Preventing and provoking wife battery through criminal sanctioning: A look at the risks. In D. Knudson & G. Miller (Eds.), *Abused and battered: Social and legal responses to family violence* (pp. 191-210). Hawthorne, NY: Aldine.

Forell, C. (1990-1991). Stopping the violence: Mandatory arrest and police tort liability for failing to assist battered women. *Berkeley Women's Law Journal,* 6(Pt. 2), 215-263.

Gordon, L. (1988). *Heroes of their own lives: The politics and history of family violence, Boston 1880-1960.* New York: Viking.

Gordon, M. T., & Riger, S. (1991). *The female fear: The social costs of rape.* Chicago: University of Illinois Press.

Harrell, A. (1991). *Evaluation of court-ordered treatment for domestic violence offenders* (Final report). Washington, DC: Urban Institute.

Henry, A. F., & Short, J. F., Jr. (1977). *Suicide and homicide.* New York: Free Press.

Jones, A., & Schecter, S. (1991). *When love goes wrong.* New York: HarperCollins.

Kurz, D., & Stark, E. (1988). Not so benign neglect: The medical response to battering. In K. Yllö & M. Bograd (Eds.), *Feminist perspectives on wife abuse* (pp. 249-266). Newbury Park, CA: Sage.

Lachman, J. A. (1978). *A theory of interpersonal conflict with application to industrial disputes* (Discussion paper). Ann Arbor, MI: Institution of Public Policy Studies.

Lindblom, C. E. (1980). *The policy making process.* Englewood Cliffs, NJ: Prentice Hall.

Ogburn, W. F., & Thomas, D. S. (1922). The influence of the business cycle of certain social conditions. *Journal of the American Statistical Association, 18*(139).

Pence, E. (1985). *The justice system's response to domestic assault cases* (Unpublished report available from Domestic Abuse Intervention Project, Duluth, MN).

Stark, E. (1982). Doctors in spite of themselves: The limits of radical health criticism. *International Journal of Health Services, 12*(3), 419-457.

Stark, E. (1991). Preventing primary homicide. In D. Leviton (Ed.), *Horrendous death, health, and well-being* (pp. 109-134). New York: Hemisphere.

Stark, E., & Flitcraft, A. (1991). Spouse abuse. In M. L. Rosenberg & M. A. Fenley (Eds.), *Violence in America: A public health approach* (pp. 123-158). New York: Oxford University Press.

Thurman v. City of Torrington, 595 F. Supp. 1521 (1985).

9

The Role of Arrest in Domestic Versus Stranger Assault
Is There a Difference?

EVE S. BUZAWA

THOMAS L. AUSTIN

CARL G. BUZAWA

One of the greatest concerns of feminists and advocates for victims of domestic violence has been how police prevent violence against women. Literature consistently has documented that relatively few domestic violence incidents result in arrest. Researchers also have observed, however, that police make relatively few arrests in *any* cases of nonaggravated assault. Therefore, a critical question that remains is whether the police have been less likely to use arrest in domestic assault cases, more than 90% of which are reported by women.

In this chapter, we test the proposition that measurable differences may be found in how some police departments treat domestic violence cases, compared with similar offenses. Specifically, although overall police arrest rates for minor assaults may be quite low, we test in one department whether domestic violence cases result in lower rates of arrest compared with similar crimes even when controlling for several key variables. We also study the department's policies, procedures, and incident reports to determine whether they also indicate differential responses to domestic violence incidents.[1]

REVIEW OF LITERATURE

Role and Use of Arrest in Domestic Violence Cases

Virtually all proposals to reform societal responses to domestic violence center heavily on police actions. This emphasis is not misplaced. Although the police function within an overall criminal justice system, their output is perhaps the most visible and important, serving not only as an around-the-clock service provider with the authority to end disputes but also as a gatekeeper to the criminal justice system.

In this regard, police have primary responsibility to arrest offenders. Arrest power is significant in domestic violence cases for several reasons. Many offenders deny criminality or even wrongdoing after beating family members. They believe that as the family patriarch, they have the right to control others—by using physical force if necessary (Pleck, 1989). For such offenders, it is essential to show that this will not be condoned and that violent acts will not be sanctioned.

Not surprisingly, critics of police behavior have long argued that leniency in the criminal justice system legitimates domestic violence in the minds of many potential aggressors (Dobash & Dobash, 1979, 1992; Ferraro, 1989). For others, being arrested may be the first step toward treatment for substance abuse or violent behavior problems. In a related context, considerable attention (whether appropriate or not) has been placed on the deterrent value of arrest.[2] Arrest also serves the criminal justice system by identifying offenders and tracking cases of continued abuse. Similarly, successful interventions by the criminal justice system, via arrests if necessary, may be the vehicle by which victims become empowered to prevent future abuse.

Despite the acknowledged importance of arrests in domestic violence cases and the proarrest policies recently mandated by state statutes and by administrative rules in most major police departments, research has shown that police make relatively few domestic violence arrests, with estimates varying from 3% to 14% (Bayley, 1986; Holmes & Bibel, 1988; Langley & Levy, 1977; Lawrenz, Lembo, & Schade, 1988; Roy, 1977). Viewed in isolation and without knowledge of police practices, this point might be surprising. After all, in domestic cases there is a known victim, often with apparent injury, and a known offender, often at the scene.

Officers may be reluctant to arrest for a variety of reasons. First, departments' priorities may effectively discourage arrests, which from their perspectives may be unjustified for a low-status misdemeanor with relatively poor chances of conviction (Buzawa & Buzawa, 1990). In this context, officers often believe that victims of domestic assault are inherently unreliable and unpredictable (Sanders, 1988). Whereas Stanko (1985) believed this to be simply a pervasive myth, Sanders (1988) argued that such claims, in fact, do have legitimacy. Regardless, studies of police practice have demonstrated that police do not differentiate domestic violence victims from equally problematic complainants for other types of crime (Sanders, 1988; Sheptycki, 1993).

Second, physical risks to the officer also are perceived as dramatically increasing when they abandon official neutrality and attempt an arrest.

Third, some argue that failure to make domestic arrests simply validates the observation that the police culture does not care about victim rights, especially when the victim complains of domestic abuse (Ferraro, 1989; Stanko, 1985).[3] In contrast, many officers we have interviewed over the years appear to believe sincerely that they will be placing the victim in increased danger by making an arrest, rather than disposing of the call informally.

SITUATIONAL NATURE OF ARRESTS

Police do not make arrests in all assault cases, and arrests in general are not commonly made unless necessary (Bittner, 1974; Black, 1976; Elliott, 1989; Parnas, 1967; Skolnick, 1975; Wilson,

1968). For these reasons, Sanders (1988) and Elliott (1989) argued that the police treat all cases that share the same characteristics in a similar manner (they act situationally). Elliott (1989) reported that arrest practices for nonfamily assaults were not significantly different from those for domestic assaults. Similarly, Faragher (1985) reported that nondomestic public violence was treated as lightly as domestic violence, and Sanders (1988) argued that the relevant factor is not whether the assault is nondomestic or domestic, but rather the circumstances under which the assault occurs. Hence, the focus should be on the situational characteristics of incidents, with the assumption that these adequately explain arrest decisions. If followed to its "logical" conclusion, then, failure to arrest in domestic violence cases does not reflect bias, but is merely a logical result of routinized police behavior (Sherman, 1992b).

Certainly, the concept that police base arrest decisions on the situational characteristics of an interaction is neither new nor the topic of much dispute. It is well known that police often base arrest decisions in both domestic and other forms of violence on factors unrelated to the crime itself. What are the situational characteristics of the police-citizen encounter that are most likely to lead to arrest? How do the use of these "nondiscriminatory" factors affect police performance in domestic violence cases? Initially, we noted that most police officers appear to share a common preference regarding when to make an arrest. For example, in one 1980 study of officers from 17 departments, more than 90% identified the following factors in their decisions to arrest: commission of a felony, serious victim injury, use of a weapon, violence against the police, and likelihood of future violence. Prior calls from a household and victim preference were not nearly as important (Loving, 1980).

How might these and other policy preferences affect the decision to arrest batterers and other assailants? First, in terms of their professionally defined roles and missions, most police officers believe that arrest priority should be placed on cases in which public order and authority have been challenged, with only secondary importance attached to individual victims' considerations (Sanders, 1988). Because most domestic violence cases are not "public" in nature, they would be relegated to positions of less importance (Sanders, 1988; Sherman, 1992a).

Second, organizational imperatives at the individual officer and departmental levels drive police officers to spend time on cases that are likely to lead to convictions. The effectiveness of police officers—a key aspect of promotability—is determined, in part, by how many of their major felony arrests lead to convictions. Officers' time spent processing (largely misdemeanor) "domestics" may therefore "waste" time. Similarly, police departments seek to prove their efficacy by emphasizing the number of felony arrests and the percentage of convictions. Because most domestic violence cases are organizationally termed "misdemeanors," having officers spend time on such cases may not be warranted. Many police departments effectively create this disparity when their officers unofficially "downgrade" domestics to misdemeanor assaults even though they would otherwise fit the textbook definition of a felonious assault (Buzawa & Buzawa, 1990; Kemp, Norris, & Fielding, 1992).

Third, the willingness of victims to assist officers and prosecutors in following the case through to conviction is an important determinant of arrest (Sheptycki, 1993). Domestic violence victims are notorious for dropping complaints, ostensibly because they have reconciled with their abusers. This conclusion is often erroneous. Victims drop cases for a variety of reasons. They do so because arrests have accomplished their goals of deterring future abuse, of allowing an easy separation, or of simply ratifying their status as victims (Buzawa & Austin, 1993). In many instances, unique procedural hurdles and a largely impersonal bureaucracy of the police and prosecutor impel victims to drop cases.

Fourth, characteristics of police-offender interactions dramatically affect the chances of arrest, especially what offenders do *after* the officers arrive; for example, if offenders are disrespectful, arrest is justified (Manning, 1978). Dobash and Dobash (1979) found that arrest was far more likely in domestic cases when assailants were hostile to the police. Violence in the officer's presence implies that the officer's ability to control the situation is being threatened (Dolon, Hendricks, & Meagher, 1986; Ferraro, 1989) or that the suspect is personally hostile to the police (Bayley, 1986). Loss of situational control is highly predictive of the threat of officer injury (Manning, 1978). Thus viewed, arrest is a mechanism of asserting authority, rather than of protecting the victim.

HAVE STUDIES
SHOWN DISCRIMINATION?

Police practices toward domestic and stranger assaults have been inconsistent. Several studies lend tentative support to the thesis that police differentially respond to family assaults. In his classic 1980 study, Black reported that rates of arrest for felonies involving strangers were higher than those among family members (88% to 45%), with somewhat smaller differences for misdemeanor assaults (57% to 47%). Black therefore postulated a continuum of responses to assault cases, with sanctions becoming more formal (arrest) as the social distance between victim and assailant increased. However, because of the relatively small sample size for both felony and misdemeanor family assaults, the failure to differentiate violence among intimates from other familial disputes, and the lack of control over level of injury, Black's findings do not generalize to current police practices.

Similarly, using a 1971 sample, researchers at the Vera Institute of Justice (1977) observed that arrests were more likely in stranger assault than in those involving victims with a prior relationship to one another. In contrast, several slightly more recent studies have not reported differences in arrests between "family" and "non-family" assaults. In one study based on the 1977 Police Services Study, Oppenlander (1982) reported that the rate of arrests for assaults within a family was 22%, compared with only 13% for assaults outside the family. This disparity disappeared, however, when injury was controlled as an intervening variable. Oppenlander also reported that, in family cases, the arrest was often for drunk and disorderly conduct, rather than for the assault itself. This claim appeared to be based on the author's impressions, however, rather than on quantifiable data (Elliott, 1989).

Smith (1987) used the same database as Oppenlander (1982) and reported virtually no difference in arrest rates between family and nonfamily assaults (28% vs. 30%). Smith found that when assaults involved only males (typical of assaults among strangers), arrest was substantially higher than when male-female assaults occurred. This finding may explain the disparity in domestic assault cases, which are composed of more than 94% of male assaults on females (Bureau of Justice Statistics, 1994). This was not addressed in Smith's study, however, and led Elliott (1989) to conclude that no research directly compared arrests involving male and female victims.

The Oppenlander and Smith studies are somewhat relevant to this study. They dealt with family versus nonfamily assaults, rather than domestics (husband-wife, girlfriend-boyfriend) versus stranger assaults. In addition, they failed to separate misdemeanors and felonies; that may be crucial because officers may exercise more discretion with felony assaults than with misdemeanors. Further, more nonfamily assaults frequently involve friends, relatives, or acquaintances, and may invoke a response different from those including domestic or stranger cases. To show the importance of this type of analytical detail, Sheptycki (1993) reported that whereas family versus nonfamily calls differed only slightly in arrest practices, when husband-wife assaults were separated out, arrests were *far* less likely.

The failure of researchers to control for various factors that are known to increase or decrease arrest rates led Elliott (1989) to conclude there is no basis for maintaining that the police use differential arrest criteria in family versus stranger assault cases. In fact, Elliott posed the rival hypothesis that factors associated with the decision to arrest are simply more likely in stranger assault cases.

Nonarrest data suggest intriguing but difficult-to-quantify differences in policing between domestic and stranger assaults. For example, according to the Bureau of Justice Statistics (1994) in a report on violence between intimates, a small but consistent trend was found toward more aggressive policing in stranger assault cases when compared with intimate assault cases. According to the National Criminal Victimization Survey (NCVS) (Bureau of Justice Statistics, 1994), police respond within 5 minutes in 36% of cases in which the offender is a stranger and in only 24% of cases in which the offender is an intimate. Similarly, police are more likely to take a formal report if the victim is a stranger (77%), rather than an intimate (69%). Although such data suggest only minor differences between such assaults, the structure of the NCVS is likely to understate disparities in police actions. Specifically, this study used an older methodology, which has been subsequently changed but not included in these figures, that counts only individuals who recognize their victimization as a crime. Many domestic violence victims, even those severely abused, have never regarded this abuse as criminal conduct. Therefore, it would not be surprising that those identifying themselves as victims were more likely the more seriously injured, which in turn would have resulted in a more rapid police response.

Is the Cause for
Differential Responses Important?

Perhaps the causes of differential responses to domestic cases are less important than their effects. Most victims of domestic assault are women, and most victims of public disorder crimes are men. Hence, the system in many locations may effectively offer greater protection to men. Perhaps the criminal justice system considers domestic assault cases more trivial because they are less likely to result in conviction or because the system is inherently sexist (Dobash & Dobash, 1979; Matoesian, 1993; Smart, 1986). Regardless of the reason, if situational factors disparately affect enforcement of laws when a largely identifiable class of victims is involved, then further public attention is merited. Such reluctance may be reinforced by class-based attitudes. Many police officers may simply view violence in families, especially among poor and minority group members, to be "normal" (Black, 1980). Because the police have enormous discretion in what they do on the street, this determination of "normalcy" makes it far less likely that they will exercise their arrest powers.

Therefore, a lack of aggressive law enforcement may typify cases in which the police respond to assaults against members of minority groups and the poor (Black, 1980; Chevigny, 1969; Elias, 1993; Parker, 1985). In short, victims who are powerless, whether they are victims of domestic violence or otherwise, may not receive the same degree of police action as other victims (Dobash & Dobash, 1992; Edwards, 1989; Hanmer, Radford, & Stanko, 1989; Skolnick, 1977).

Variables such as the setting of a dispute (public vs. private) and the presence or absence of witnesses should not affect arrest decisions. Legally, such decisions should be based on officers' determinations of probable cause or their assessment of prospective violence. Although a legal analysis can help in explaining why police do not make many domestic violence arrests, it is important to realize that the situational factors cited earlier are not relevant to determining probable cause. Therefore, it is facile to dismiss differential impact as being merely "situational." Furthermore, although it may be conceivable that arrest rates would also decline in situations in which "strangers" are cohabiting, most of these cases brought to the attention of police are domestic violence incidents, and the vast majority (estimates ranging as high as 95%) involve males assaulting their female partners or former partners.

The situational view of comparative arrest practices, which is apparently favored by Elliott (1989), Sanders (1988), and Sherman (1992b), largely ignores the fact that every state within the last 15 years has passed reform legislation expressly stating the policy of state (and formal) governments to respond aggressively to domestic violence cases, including arrest. No such policy has ever been adopted or even articulated for handling cases of stranger assaults. In short, making the case that similar situational factors are used in arrests in domestic and stranger assaults implicitly concedes that many police officers simply ignore the statutory policy favoring domestic assault arrests, which is a discriminatory action in itself.

RESEARCH DESIGN

Testing for Discrimination

We believe that the foregoing situational explanations of low arrest rates should be tested to see whether they provide an adequate explanation of police behavior in domestic violence incidents. We chose to study whether a department discriminates against domestic violence calls by examining whether police differentially respond to key factors in the decision to arrest. For example, complainant preferences for arrest in both domestic and stranger assaults should be studied because complainant preference for police action has been found in a variety of settings to be a consistent predictor of police behavior (Black, 1976; Smith & Klein, 1984; Worden & Pollitz, 1984) and an essential element in making domestic arrests (Bell, 1984; Berk & Loseke, 1981; Worden & Pollitz, 1984). Similarly, we studied whether the extent and degree of injury affects chances of arrest in cases of domestic and stranger assaults.

For several reasons, we chose arrest as the criterion to gauge disparate treatment between stranger and domestic assaults. As we described earlier, making an arrest is intrinsically important. Arrest decisions are also typically accompanied by factual justifications and thus allow a more detailed analysis of when officers arrest. The choice of official data may be significant. In a practical sense, it was the only data available, given our desire to reconstruct police behavior at the scene of an incident. This measure also had the advantage of being in an officially mandated format that individual police officers followed, pursuant to department instructions. It also maximized officer cooperation, at least to the extent that they filled out forms and participated in the study—an important consideration in police research projects.

In using arrests, we recognize that the data might actually understate differential relationships because police may simply downgrade or not even file reports for offenses in which they do not wish to take official action. Such downgrading might occur when the police report only a simple misdemeanor assault in cases in which severe injury was present or in which they fail to classify an offense as a felony when the aggressor used a weapon or apparently intended to inflict serious bodily harm on the victim, a practice found by Burris and Jaffe (1983), Stanko (1989), and Langan and Innes (1986). Alternatively, officers might delay responding to calls, hoping the situation will "go away" and will be resolved on arrival (Sheptycki, 1993).

If there is a bias against responding aggressively to domestic violence cases, official reports might be effectively prescreened. Screened calls for assistance may result in no response or a response that is assigned a far lower priority. Obviously, if a police unit never responds or if the response is delayed past the period when an offender is on site, then an arrest will not occur. Past research has amply demonstrated that this type of differential response has occurred in many, if not most, departments (Ferraro, 1989; Manning, 1993; Sheptycki, 1993).

Another limitation of using official police reports as a primary data source is that they typically were not designed for research purposes. The form contains categories that are overly specific and do not report important information. In either case, some data transformation is required; this presents the obvious risks of possible event miscategorization.

Despite these shortcomings, we consider official measures the most reliable method of measuring police behavior. When attempting to measure past behavior, it was also the most feasible strategy because perceptions of proper police conduct vary. We believe this method is preferable to having an independent observer measure police behavior.[4] Nonetheless, in recognizing the limitations of official data, we included supplementary analysis of other measures for profiling and characterizing police behavior—that is, official police policies and content analysis of police reports. These measures were used to either confirm the analysis of official arrest data or cast doubt on relationships found therein. This helped us in answering whether observed practices were likely because of individual officer preferences or the result of official or unofficial policy preferences.[5]

Departmental policies illustrate the relative attention accorded to an offense and reflect administrative perspectives. It is likely that such priorities are internalized by officers (e.g., they might be aware that the department is not overly concerned with "domestics" but are extremely concerned with proper processing of traffic violations). A study of one department's policies cannot determine the general impact of policies on police practices, but it can assist researchers in determining whether observed discrimination, if any, is reinforced by organizational structures or, alternatively, whether it appears despite official policy. Similarly, content analysis of officer reports performed in both stranger and domestic assaults, even if somewhat impressionistic, may serve to better explain the actions of police officers.

Sample Selection

This research project was the outgrowth of a study conducted by one of the researchers on behalf of the plaintiffs in a lawsuit against the police department of a midsize, midwestern city. Although the study was commissioned by the plaintiffs' counsel, every effort was made to obtain unbiased data that would fairly test the premise that the department might have disparately treated victims of domestic violence.

The data set consisted of 376 assault cases from the official records of the police department. It covered all cases designated by the department as an "assault" for a period of 10 months during 1986 to 1987, after a domestic violence reform statute was passed that asked police departments to aggressively intervene in domestic assault cases. This time period was chosen because it was relevant to the facts of the case, although there was no reason to believe it was unrepresentative of other periods.

Simple Effect of Type of Assault on Arrest

Table 9.1 contains all variables used in the analyses. Of initial interest is the frequency or univariate distribution of each of the six independent or situational variables. Assaults characterized as Acquaintance ($N = 194$) were more than twice as likely to occur as either Domestic ($N = 89$) or Stranger ($N = 93$) assaults. Most victims experienced no injury or only minor injury, and in more than three quarters of the cases, the type of force/weapon used was the assailant's hands, arms, or feet. Witnesses were present in more than two thirds of the incidents. Similarly, in more than two thirds of the incidents, the offender was not present at the scene when the police arrived, and in about half of the cases, the victim's preference was arrest. With respect to arrest, the dependent variable, it occurs in more than one quarter of the cases.

Two findings from Table 9.1 are most relevant to the current investigation. First, as the level of intimacy characterizing the relationship between the parties changes from more to less intimate, arrest becomes more likely. The relationship is statistically significant, and the gamma coefficient of .23 indicates an association of marginal strength. Although the modal response is to not arrest, when it does occur, incidents involving strangers result in an arrest 33% of the time, compared with 28% for acquaintances and 18% for domestic.

The second notable finding involves the relationship between the remaining five situational variables and arrest. In all cases in which they are either evident or more certain, an arrest is more likely to occur. All five relationships are statistically significant, and the strength of the associations ranges from marginal (gamma of .21 in the case of injury to the victim) to strong (gamma of .73 where the offender is present at the scene of the incident).

These bivariate findings lead to two tentative conclusions. First, although arrest is an unlikely event, it characterizes stranger assaults more than domestic. Second, when an arrest does occur, it is more likely when the situational elements are present or more evident.

TABLE 9.1 Type of Assault and Situational Variables by If Arrest Made[a]*

Variable	Values	No %	Arrest N	Yes %	Arrest N	Row %	Total N
Offender's relationship to victim	Domestic	82	(73)	18	(16)	100	(89)
	Acquaintance	72	(139)	28	(55)	100	(194)
	Stranger	67	(62)	33	(31)	100	(93)
	Chi-square = 5	Probability = .05				Gamma = .23	
Nature of injury to victim	Minor/none	77	(138)	23	(41)	100	(179)
	Minor/apparent	73	(103)	27	(39)	100	(142)
	Major/serious	60	(33)	40	(22)	100	(55)
	Chi-square = 6.23	Probability = .04				Gamma = .21	
Type force/weapon used by offender	Hands/arms/feet	77	(220)	23	(65)	100	(285)
	Object/knife/gun	59	(54)	41	(37)	100	(91)
	Chi-square = 11.12	Probability = .00				Gamma = .40	
Were other witnesses present	No	85	(101)	15	(18)	100	(119)
	Yes	67	(173)	33	(84)	100	(257)
	Chi-square = 12.68	Probability = .00				Gamma = .46	
Offender present at scene of call	Not present	85	(219)	15	(39)	100	(258)
	Yes, present	47	(55)	53	(63)	100	(118)
	Chi-square = 59.99	Probability = .00				Gamma = .73	
Was victim's preference arrest	No	83	(168)	17	(34)	100	(202)
	Yes	61	(106)	39	(68)	100	(174)
	Chi-square = 23	Probability = .00				Gamma = .52	

NOTE: *Base percentage is across rows; thus, comparisons are based on columns.
a. N = 376.

Additive Effects of Type of Assault on Arrest

What remains to be seen is whether the reason for fewer arrests in domestic cases is attributable to the absence of these situational factors in stranger assaults. To assess this possibility, the variables were examined by using logistic regression. The association between type of assault and arrest was examined to determine whether the situational variables alter the bivariate association. All variables were entered into the analysis simultaneously because there was no a priori basis for determining their ordering. Two variables—Type of Assault and Nature of Injury to Victim—were treated as "dummy variables." The category Stranger Assault was recoded to the following values: 0, indicating no or that the assault was by someone other than a stranger; and 1, indicating that a stranger committed the assault. Similarly, an assault by an acquaintance is coded 0 for no and 1 for yes if committed by an acquaintance. Domestic Assault serves as the reference category, and thus the no category for both stranger and acquaintance is referring to domestic assaults. Injury to Victim is similarly coded. The remaining variables are dichotomous, and their coding reflects their ordering in Table 9.1. All variables and their codes are presented in Table 9.2.

Results from this analysis are presented in Table 9.3 and, with minor exceptions, mirror findings in Table 9.1. The exceptions include a small but significant decrease in the effect of assaults involving acquaintances on arrest and the statistically insignificant effect of minor injury to the victim and the presence of witnesses on arrest.

Otherwise, an arrest is about 2.5 times more likely when a weapon is involved, approximately 8 times more likely when the offender is present at the scene, 2 times more likely when the victim's injury is serious, and about 3.5 times more likely when the victim's preference is arrest. Regardless of the situational variables, arrest is still more likely when the incident is characterized as a stranger assault. Compared with domestic assaults, such incidents are more than twice as likely to result in an arrest. Thus, as the level of intimacy between the parties increases, the probability of an arrest for assault decreases.

TABLE 9.2 Variables, Categories, and Their Coded Values

Variable	Code and Categories		
Was offender arrested	0 = No	1 = Yes	
Type of assault			
Stranger	0 = No	1 = Yes	
Acquaintance	0 = No	1 = Yes	
Domestic	Reference category		
Injury to victim			
Major/serious	0 = No	1 = Yes	
Minor/apparent	0 = No	1 = Yes	
Minor/none	Reference category		
Type force/weapon	0 = Hands/arms/feet	1 = Object/knife/gun	
Other witnesses present	0 = No	1 = Yes	
Offender present	0 = No	1 = Yes	
Victim preference arrest	0 = No	1 = Yes	

TABLE 9.3 Regression of Arrest on Type of Assault and Situational Variables[a]

	MLE	SE	MLE/SE	EXP (MLE)
Type of assault				
Stranger	.82	.35	2.34*	2.28
Acquaintance	.59	.31	1.90	1.80
Nature of injury to victim				
Major/serious injury	.79	.40	1.98*	2.18
Minor/apparent injury	.15	.31	0.48	1.15
Type of weapon/force used	.88	.31	2.84**	2.41
Offender present at scene	2.06	.30	6.87***	7.86
Other witness(es) present	.60	.33	1.82	1.81
Victim preference arrest	1.22	.28	4.35***	3.38

NOTE: MLE = Maximum Likelihood Estimate/Coefficient, SE = Standard Error of MLE, MLE/SE = statistical significance of MLE based on t distribution, EXP (MLE) = odds of an arrest of variable category coded 1.
a. $N = 376$.
* < .05; ** <.01; *** < .001; −2 log likelihood = 338.38; χ^2 = 101.17; sig = .00.

Interactive Effects of Type of Assault on Arrest

We examined the additive effects of type of assault on arrest and found, regardless of situational considerations, that assaults committed against strangers are more likely to result in arrests. Inter-

estingly, we also found that four of the situational variables continued to have an effect on the decision to arrest. Because the situational variables did not alter the association between type of
assault and arrest but did affect the decision to arrest, we explored
whether a "washing-out" effect was occurring; that is, one or more
of the situational variables might have an effect on one type of
assault, whereas the remaining variables are affecting the other
categories of assault. If so, this could be characteristic as specification, which in the current context connotes the type of assault under
which the situational variables affect arrest. To test this possibility,
we performed analyses within each of the three types of assault
categories. Doing so would allow us to test the relative importance
of the situational variables and help in determining whether an
interaction was occurring. Results from the analyses are presented
in Table 9.4 and support an interaction effect.

Regardless of the type of assault, the offender's presence at the
scene increases the probability of arrest, whereas the extent of injury
to the victim has no effect on arrest in any of the three types of
assaults. Both type of force/weapon used and presence of witnesses,
however, affect the decision to arrest in domestic, but not in
acquaintance or stranger, incidents. In domestic cases, when witnesses are present or the weapon used is more deadly, an arrest is
more likely. Tentatively, this finding suggests that a higher standard
or level of probable cause is needed for an arrest in domestic
incidents. This tentative conclusion is reinforced by the finding that
victim preference does not affect the decision to arrest in domestic
assaults, but does in cases involving acquaintances and strangers.
More weight seems to be given to the victim's request in the
decision to arrest when the parties are less intimately acquainted.
The latter two findings support the idea of specification and suggest
why arrest in less intimate incidents is more likely. Assaults involving strangers may be viewed by the police as more genuine and thus
do not require corroboration by outside sources. Conversely, the
police may view domestic incidents as family matters and thus, by
their very nature, require independent verification.

Content Analysis of Reports

We conducted a content analysis of 1,000 consecutively num-
bered incidents to obtain a general understanding of how reports for

TABLE 9.4 Regression of Arrest on Situational Variables Within Categories of Type of Assault

	MLE	SE	MLE/SE	EXP (MLE)
DOMESTIC[a]				
Nature of injury to victim				
Major/serious injury	.06	1.21	0.05	1.06
Minor/apparent injury	−.12	.80	0.15	0.88
Type of weapon/force used	2.23	.97	2.30*	9.29
Offender present at scene	2.28	.83	2.75**	9.83
Other witness(es) present	2.16	.88	2.44*	8.61
Victim preference arrest	1.41	.80	1.76	4.07
ACQUAINTANCE[b]				
Nature of injury to victim				
Major/serious injury	.83	.52	1.60	2.30
Minor/apparent injury	.36	.41	0.87	1.43
Type of weapon/force used	.49	.42	1.16	1.63
Offender present at scene	2.07	.39	5.31***	7.89
Other witness(es) present	−.03	.42	0.07	0.96
Victim preference arrest	.83	.37	2.24*	2.29
STRANGER[c]				
Nature of injury to victim				
Major/serious injury	.58	.82	0.70	1.79
Minor/apparent injury	−.48	.66	0.72	.61
Type of weapon/force used	1.07	.69	1.55	2.91
Offender present at scene	2.47	.66	3.74***	11.81
Other witness(es) present	.36	.81	0.45	1.43
Victim preference arrest	2.12	.62	3.41***	8.34

NOTE: MLE = Maximum Likelihood Estimate/Coefficient, SE = Standard Error of MLE, MLE/SE = statistical significance of MLE based on t distribution, EXP (MLE) = odds of an arrest of variable category coded 1.
a. $N = 89$.
b. $N = 194$.
c. $N = 93$.
* < .05; ** < .01; *** < .001; −2 log likelihood = 77.40; χ^2 = 40.99; sig = .00.

domestic assault were written, compared with those for other calls. Initially, it seemed reasonable to assume that officer time in report preparation and detail given to describe the event reflected the perceived relative importance of such incidents. Several observations were made. Of the 1,000 incidents, only 564 actual reports were written. Although we had no way of ascertaining with certainty whether domestic cases were more likely to be screened out, a reading of the reports is certainly suggestive of this possibility.

Traffic offenses were typically a minimum of two to three typed pages, with careful attention to detail. It appears that officers thought convictions likely or were concerned about the possibility of affecting civil liability of participants. As a result, their narrative was fully documented. Conversely, domestic assaults were far more abbreviated and thus subsequent successful prosecution was less likely.

Because it was rare that arrests were actually made on the spot, it appeared that when officers thought an arrest was necessary, they would simply note that they had "advised" the victim to see the prosecutor. This notation was seldom placed in stranger assault reports. In addition, the domestic assault victims were frequently described as "hysterical" and were told to see the prosecutor when they "calmed down." The victim's story was described in terms of "alleged," rather than "fact"; this did not typify police reporting of stranger assaults. Again, this designation and admonition was absent in cases of stranger assaults. Thus, even when an arrest was subsequently made, the process of requiring greater victim initiative and of describing the victim's story in terms of "alleged" rather than fact did not typify reporting of stranger assaults. Although such reported results are impressionistic, it seems reasonable to assume that officer time in report preparation and detail given to describe the event reflects the perceived relative importance of such incidents.

Sheptycki (1993) also made similar observations in London, where he observed that such phrases as "victim claims," "it seems that," and "victim alleges" were used in domestic assaults three times as frequently as in nondomestic assaults. Police are more likely to discourage such victims from pressing charges (Faragher, 1985; Sheptycki, 1993). Victims frequently interpret such police attitudes as a lack of interest, and this interpretation often affects their willingness to pursue criminal charges (Radford, 1987; Sheptycki, 1993).

Policy Review Analysis

A review of this department's policy manual indicated a low level of interest in domestic violence. Initially, we noted this was a department that believed it necessary to have exhaustive written policies, even for many minor items. As a result, the department policy book was several hundred pages in length. Presumably, the police department administrators believed that without such policies, officers would not act appropriately, and the administrators used such policies as a vehicle for developing consistent police practices and as a training guide for officers. In this context, several observations were striking. Despite statutory guidance, there was no policy on handling or complying with the new domestic violence proarrest statute. Furthermore, there was no policy addressing how to respond to protective orders, an important vehicle for protecting victims. There was merely a one-line reference to "ex parte" orders, far too vague to provide officer guidance.

Within the policy for assaults was a call for exceptionally passive police responses. Officers were instructed to "stand by" a short distance away until arrival of the second officer, rather than to respond immediately to the scene unless the officer determines that an emergency exists. The obvious question is how officers can ascertain that such an emergency exists when waiting in patrol cars. This dilemma was verified in reports. For example, in one situation an officer waited for his backup to arrive, noting that all was quiet inside. As soon as his partner arrived and they entered the premises, however, five people were found to be seriously injured and requiring emergency medical treatment.

Domestic assault cases were the only cases singled out for such a cautious response. Such a policy appears to conform with feminist observations that officers in some departments delay their arrival, hoping the call will "go away" (Sheptycki, 1993). In contrast, in cases of shoplifting and "minors attempting to purchase intoxicants" calls, officers were instructed to respond immediately because the suspect may resist or attempt to flee from a merchant before the officers arrive. Although this may be true, the priority of these calls cannot possibly be compared with calls from battered women whose lives (or the lives of minors) may be endangered by a policy to wait deliberately until backup units arrive. Although the ideal organizational goal may be to protect victims and arrest batterers where appropriate (though in this case the goal is not stated), the policy's primary focus is on officers' personal safety, rather than on victims' safety.

The emphasis in the policy manual was on the response to "disturbances," which need to be "quelled," not investigated to determine whether a crime had occurred or an offender should be arrested.

As Wilson (1989) noted, officers are taught to define their job in terms of "handling the situation," rather than enforcing the law.

This policy statement demonstrates that tasks such as handling domestic violence calls were not really valued by the department. In a 14-page, exhaustively detailed description of the knowledge that an officer needs for career development and reimbursement was only a one-line reference to knowledge relating to domestic violence. On page 11 of 14, in a checkoff of approximately 120 items, merely a single check mark was placed on knowledge of "family crisis intervention." By the number of references, this might be considered the same as officers' knowledge of "calculators," "cameras," or "public speaking."

Finally, whereas the department has a very progressive 6-page "posttrauma procedure" on how to ascertain that all of its members are aware of posttraumatic stress disorder and how to cope with stress, this is not in reference to the disorder in victims. Rather, officers are instructed to present a good attitude and to show personal concern for other officers who are involved in a fatal shooting or other trauma. Similar sensitivity toward victims is absent. This once again signifies a police department that appears to be far more sensitive to the feelings of its members than to those of the general public.

In summary, the department studied seems to be striving for professionalism, with its policies on diverse topics relevant to its mission. Other policies were aimed at controlling officers' conduct even to the extent of personal grooming (e.g., female officers are expected to keep their hair in "a condition befitting their sex"). In this context, the lack of a specific and detailed policy on the proper handling of domestic assault cases was incongruous; it suggested that such cases were not very important to the department's mission.

CONCLUSIONS

Perhaps of greatest significance, this project found differential treatment of domestic violence and stranger assault incidents as measured by the likelihood of arrest. Despite the relatively low percentage of arrests made (26%), it became clear that officers made fewer arrests for domestic assault cases than for stranger assault cases. This distinction became magnified when several relevant factors—offender presence at the scene and victim preference—were controlled. Of equal importance, victims' preferences for arrest were ignored in 75% of domestic assault cases, compared with more than 40% of stranger assault cases. Although this finding provides some confirmation for the observation that police disparately treat the problems of the largely female victims of domestic violence, we are unwilling to state that this is symptomatic of overall police behavior.

Future Research

We previously noted that many police departments have changed their behavior regarding domestic violence incidents in response to legislation, training, and research demonstrating the importance of this problem. Throughout the country, many departments have promulgated policies far more conducive to an activist response to domestic cases, and to a lesser extent, they have adopted changes in practice (Buzawa & Buzawa, 1990). As a result, any research should consciously limit its conclusions to the department being studied, other studies providing primarily a road map for future research instruments and designs. The reasons for disparities between domestic violence and stranger assaults are less clear and still must be examined on a department-by-department basis. On the one hand, some may actively discriminate against domestic complaints as a matter of policy. On the other hand, police may simply be acting situationally in a manner that favors aggressive responses to public disorder and that downplays aggressive responses to interpersonal crimes. Although perhaps not overtly discriminatory, this still may be unacceptable. It is now commonly accepted that women are more likely than men to be victimized in private settings. Specifically, female victims of homicides, assaults, and rapes are more likely to be victimized "behind closed doors." As a consequence, the concept of police limiting active intervention to public order violence must be increasingly challenged.

The tendency is to use all such research models to prove a point (e.g., the police discriminate, the police respond to organizational constraints). Although global constructs of police behavior often may provide a powerful tool in analyzing behavior, in this case it may be premature and perhaps too simplistic to adopt rigid theoretical models in which overall police conduct is measured. We need to avoid situations where researchers with preconceived ideas of police organizational behavior or feminist analysis look at the same event and reach diametrically different conclusions.

Ambiguous data often can lead to this result. For example, Hoyle (personal communication, August 1993), in describing her field observations with the London Metropolitan Police, recounted that an officer conducted an exemplary intervention in a domestic assault. However, his final parting comment was, "If I return here again tonight, there will be an arrest." The officer then asked Hoyle how he had done. When she asked why he made his final remark, he appeared surprised and replied that he was only trying to ensure the woman's safety and deter the assailant from a subsequent assault. Because the officer knew he was being observed and because his concern for Hoyle's subsequent opinion was evident, his statement appears genuine. His statement taken in isolation, however, could be used to argue that the organizational priority is to limit repeat calls or to have officers take charge when the parties do not comply (e.g., see Kemp et al., 1992). Instead, it could be used to provide more evidence of an unsympathetic police subculture that still is trying to avoid domestic calls by threatening arrests when victims do not desire such actions (Edwards, 1989). Hence, it would appear that, in some contexts, either perspective may be more accurate. For this reason, contextually based field observations offer considerable insight in explaining seemingly inconsistent empirical findings.

Proof of differences also may be difficult to obtain. Differential arrest rates might provide the most dramatic evidence that certain police departments treat domestic violence cases differently from other cases, but alternative measures should be developed to confirm or reject this observation. As noted in this study, content analysis of official policies and incident reports may serve as a tool to understanding behavior on the street.

Arrest data may be contrasted with other methods of determining whether police departments may be treating domestic violence complaints differently from other similar cases. A study of call screening through an examination of 911 tapes (if preserved) and the actual dispatch of officers or their filing official reports could provide a significant clue whether domestics are being prescreened out of the system prior to any official action. Similarly, as the 1994 Bureau of Justice Statistics data suggested, comparing the time an incident is reported to the police and the time a response occurs would be helpful to determine whether the department has tacitly (or even through informal policies) developed a pattern of delay in responding to domestics (thereby allowing the incident to "cool down," at least by official measures, and giving offenders time to leave the scene) that would dramatically reduce the potential for the police to use their arrest powers. Determining the amount of time spent at the scene (time cleared) also would indicate whether domestics were treated more cursorily or disposed of more routinely than stranger assaults.

Still other projects might determine whether a police department treats calls from some victims less seriously than others. For example, it is possible that such calls are responded to more slowly or with a differential response when the victims call, rather than when neighbors report a public breach of the peace.

Situational characteristics of the incident and of the officers themselves also might be profitably studied. Data concerning the incident would be valuable but might require the presence of an objective, trained observer, with its attendant risk of an experimental effect. Despite this possibility, it may be useful to determine whether arrests in one or both categories were restricted primarily to instances in which arrested persons are disrespectful to the police—as opposed to the merits of the case itself.

Finally, officer-specific data, though difficult to obtain, might prove instructive in measuring whether certain officers' characteristics (e.g., personal beliefs, past experiences, training, gender, race, age, years on the force) make them more or less likely to treat a domestic incident cavalierly. In any event, until many such research projects are conducted in a variety of departments, we believe that results should be reported on a department-specific basis, with broad generalities resisted.

NOTES

1. We note that the same analysis might be used to determine whether the police differentially respond to crimes committed predominantly against other disfavored groups. Put another way, are some complainants disadvantaged prior to victimization, whether through police organizational constraints and/or bias against certain types of complainants?

2. Discussion of the deterrent impact is beyond the scope of this chapter. For analysis of the initial experimental data of the Minneapolis Domestic Violence

Experiment (MDVE), see Sherman and Berk (1984) and Sherman and Cohn (1989). Limitations of this experiment are discussed by Binder and Meeker (1988); Elliott (1989); Hirschel, Hutchison, Dean, Kelley, and Pesackis (1991); Sherman (1992b); and Sherman et al. (1992). These reports were critically analyzed by Zorza (1994). See also independent studies of deterrence by police action reports (e.g., Williams & Hawkins, 1989).

3. Supporting this thesis is past research showing that when police officers are required by departmental policy to adopt a presumptive current arrest policy, mechanisms develop to circumvent such a policy even to the extent of implicitly defying orders of the police chief (Ferraro, 1989).

4. It is well known that many police officers are suspicious of and uncooperative with social policy research. Hence, in using an observer, there is a substantial risk of an experimental effect that contaminates the internal validity. Because of inherent discretion in the police occupation, they might change behavior for the duration of a research project, only to resume when the project and/or official command attention has been refocused.

5. There is no consensus regarding the role of department policy in determining "street practices" of patrol officers, especially in responding to domestic assault. Whereas Ferraro (1989) noted how officers subvert a proarrest policy in Phoenix, others believe that officers by and large reflect the preferences of their departments (Stanko, 1985).

REFERENCES

Bayley, D. (1986). The tactical choices of police patrol officers. *Journal of Criminal Justice, 14*, 329-348.

Bell, D. (1984). The police response to domestic violence: A replication study. *Police Studies, 7,* 136-143.

Berk, S., & Loseke, D. R. (1981). "Handling" family violence: Situational determinants of police arrests in domestic disturbances. *Law and Society Review, 15,* 317-346.

Binder, A., & Meeker, J. (1988). Experiments as reforms. *Journal of Criminal Justice, 16,* 347-358.

Bittner, E. (1974). Florence Nightingale in pursuit of Willie Sutton: A theory of the police. In H. Jacob (Ed.), *The potential for reform of criminal justice* (pp. 17-44). Beverly Hills, CA: Sage.

Black, D. (1976). *The behavior of law.* San Diego: Academic Press.

Black, D. (1980). *The manners and customs of the police.* San Diego: Academic Press.

Bureau of Justice Statistics. (1994). *Violence against women: A national crime victimization survey.* Washington, DC: Author.

Burris, C. A., & Jaffe, P. (1983). Wife abuse as a crime: The impact of police laying charges. *Canadian Journal of Criminology, 25,* 309-318.

Buzawa, E, & Austin, T. (1993). Determining police response to domestic violence victims: The role of victim preference. *American Behavioral Scientist, 36,* 610-623.

Buzawa, E, & Buzawa, C. (1990). *Domestic violence: The criminal justice response.* Newbury Park, CA: Sage.

Chevigny, P. (1969). *Police power: Police abuses in New York City.* New York: Pantheon.

Dobash, R. E., & Dobash, R. (1979). *Violence against wives: A case against the patriarchy.* New York: Free Press.

Dobash, R. E., & Dobash, R. (1992). *Women, violence, and social change.* London: Routledge.

Dolon, R., Hendricks, J., & Meagher, M. S. (1986). Police practices and attitudes toward domestic violence. *Journal of Police Science and Administration, 14,* 187-192.

Edwards, S. (1989). *Policing domestic violence: Women, law, and the state.* Newbury Park, CA: Sage.

Elias, R. (1993). *Victims still: The political manipulation of crime victims.* Newbury Park, CA: Sage.

Elliott, D. S. (1989). Criminal justice procedures in family violence crimes. In L. Ohlin & M. Tonry (Eds.), *Crime and justice: A review of research* (pp. 427-480). Chicago: University of Chicago Press.

Faragher, T. (1985). The police response to violence against women in the home. In J. Pahl (Ed.), *Private violence and public policy* (pp. 123-148). London: Routledge & Kegan Paul.

Ferraro, K. (1989). Policing woman battering. *Social Problems, 36,* 61-74.

Hanmer, J., Radford, J., & Stanko, E. (1989). Improving policing for women: The way forward. In J. Hanmer, J. Radford, & E. Stanko (Eds.), *Women, policing, and male violence: International perspectives* (pp. 185-201). London: Routledge & Kegan Paul.

Hirschel, J. D., Hutchison, I., Dean, D., Kelley, J., & Pesackis, C. (1991). *Charlotte Spouse Assault Replication Project: Final report.* Washington, DC: National Institute of Justice.

Holmes, W., & Bibel, D. (1988). *Police response to domestic violence: Final report.* Washington, DC: U.S. Bureau of Justice Statistics.

Kemp, C., Norris, C., & Fielding, N. (1992). *Negotiating nothing: Police decision making in disputes.* Aldershot, Hants, England: Avebury.

Langan. P., & Innes, C. (1986). *Preventing domestic violence against women.* Washington, DC: U.S. Department of Justice, Bureau of Justice Statistics.

Langley, R., & Levy, R. (1977). *Wife beating: The silent crisis.* New York: Dutton.

Lawrenz, F., Lembo, R., & Schade, S. (1988). Time series analysis of the effect of a domestic violence detective on the number of arrests per day. *Journal of Criminal Justice, 16,* 493-449.

Loving, N. (1980). *Responding to spouse abuse and wife beating: A guide for police.* Washington, DC: Police Executive Research Forum.

Manning, P. (1978). The police: Mandate, strategies, and appearances. In P. Manning & J. Van Maanen (Eds.), *Policing: A view from the street* (pp. 78-94). Santa Monica, CA: Goodyear.

Manning, P. (1993). The preventive conceit: The black box in market context. *American Behavioral Scientist, 36,* 639-650.

Matoesian, G. M. (1993). *Reproducing rape: Domination through talk in the courtroom.* Cambridge, MA: Blackwell.

Oppenlander, N. (1982). Coping or copping out: Police service delivery in domestic disputes. *Criminology, 20,* 449-465.

Parker, S. (1985). The legal background. In *Private violence and public policy.* London: Routledge & Kegan Paul.

Parnas, R. (1967). The police response to the domestic disturbance. *Wisconsin Law Review, 4,* 14-60.

Pleck, E. (1989). Criminal approaches to family violence 1640-1980. In L. Ohlin & M. Tonry (Eds.), *Crime and justice: A review of research* (Vol. 2, pp. 19-58). Chicago: University of Chicago Press.

Radford, L. (1987). Legalizing women abuse. In J. Hanmer & M. Maynard (Eds.), *Women, violence, and social control* (pp. 135-151). New York: Macmillan.

Roy, M. (1977). *Battered women: A psychosociological study of domestic violence.* New York: Van Nostrand Reinhold.

Sanders, A. (1988). Personal violence and public order: The prosecution of "domestic" violence in England and Wales. *International Journal of the Sociology of Law, 16,* 359-382.

Sheptycki, J. W. E. (1993). *Innovations in policing domestic violence.* Brookfield, VT: Ashgate.

Sherman, L. (1992a). The influence of criminology on criminal law: Evaluating arrests for misdemeanor domestic violence. *Journal of Criminal Law and Criminology, 83,* 1-45.

Sherman, L. (1992b). *Policing domestic violence: Experiments and dilemmas.* New York: Free Press.

Sherman, L. W., & Berk, R. A. (1984). The specific deterrent effects of arrest for domestic assault. *American Sociological Review, 49,* 261-272.

Sherman, L. W., & Cohn, E. G. (1989). The impact of research on legal policy: The Minneapolis Domestic Violence Experiment. *Law and Society Review, 23,* 117-144.

Sherman, L. W., Schmidt, J., Rogen, D., Gartin, P., Cohn, E., Collins, D., & Bacich, A. (1992). The variable effects of arrest on criminal careers: The Milwaukee Domestic Violence Experiment. *Journal of Criminal Law and Criminology, 83,* 401-432.

Skolnick, J. (1975). *Justice without trial.* New York: John Wiley.

Smart, C. (1986). Feminism and law: Some problems of analysis and strategy. *International Journal of the Sociology of Law, 4,* 109-123.

Smith, D. A. (1987). Police response to interpersonal violence: Defining the parameters of legal control. *Social Forces, 65,* 767-782.

Smith, D. A., & Klein, J. (1984). Police control of interpersonal disputes. *Social Forces, 31,* 468-481.

Stanko, E. (1985). *Intimate intrusions: Women's experience of male violence.* London: Routledge & Kegan Paul.

Stanko, E. (1989). Missing the mark? Policing battering. In J. Hanmer, J. Radford, & E. A. Stanko (Eds.), *Women, policing, and male violence.* London: Routledge & Kegan Paul.

Vera Institute of Justice. (1977). *Felony arrests: Their prosecution and disposition in New York City's courts.* New York: Author.

Williams, K., & Hawkins, R. (1989). The meaning of arrest for wife assault. *Criminology, 27,* 163-181.

Wilson, J. Q. (1968). *Varieties of police behavior.* Cambridge, MA.: Harvard University Press.

Wilson, J. Q. (1989). *Bureaucracy: What government agencies do and why they do it.* New York: Basic Books.

Worden, R. E., & Pollitz, A. A. (1984). Police arrests in domestic disturbances: A further look. *Law and Society Review, 18,* 105-119.

Zorza, J. (1994). Must we stop arresting batterers? Analysis and policy implications of new police domestic violence studies. *New England Law Review, 28,* 929-990.

10

Prosecution Response to Domestic Violence
Results of a Survey of Large Jurisdictions

DONALD J. REBOVICH

Until recently, local prosecutors' offices had been characterized as major impediments to an activist approach in handling domestic violence offenses (Field & Field, 1973; Greenwood, Wildhorn, Poggio, Strumwasser, & DeLeon, 1973; Lerman, 1981). Prosecutors were said to be at best, apathetic toward, and at worst, disdainful of prosecuting domestic violence cases because of their purported perceptions that domestic violence cases were trivial or difficult to prosecute successfully, especially if victims were reluctant to serve as witnesses. As a result of this pessimism, the past had been

AUTHOR'S NOTE: This chapter was supported by a grant under award 93-IJ-CX-0039 from the National Institute of Justice, Office of Justice Programs, U.S. Department of Justice. Points of view in this chapter are those of the author and do not necessarily represent the official position of the U.S. Department of Justice.

witness to the use of prosecutorial discretion to discourage the filing of domestic violence complaints. In the 1970s, cases of domestic violence were significantly more likely to be screened out or later dismissed, in large part because of prosecutors' expectations that victims would be uncooperative and because of a general misunderstanding of legal options available for prosecution (Williams, 1976).

Recently, however, scholars such as Naomi Cahn (1992) and Louis McHardy (1992) have explained that public interest pressure for domestic violence control, along with the introduction of "proarrest" policies for domestic violence incidents, has led to a dramatic increase in the number of domestic violence cases being brought to court in many jurisdictions. Predictably, these cases have presented the local prosecutor with provocative new challenges to his or her ability to effectively manage and prosecute these cases. Nationally, the National Council of Juvenile and Family Court Judges (McHardy, 1992) has formulated the following recommendations for local prosecutors:

- Prosecutors should initiate, manage, and pursue prosecution in all family violence cases in which a criminal case can be proved, including proceeding without the active involvement of the victim if necessary.
- Prosecutors should have specialized family violence personnel and written procedures for prompt screening and charging in family violence cases.

Fortifying the public pressure for increased prosecution is recent empirical evidence that the withholding of domestic violence prosecution can result in further harm not only to adult victims but to children as well. Waits (1985) and Cahn and Lerman (1991) concluded through their studies that unless abusers are adequately prosecuted, their violence usually continues to cause further physical and emotional damage to victims and their children.

As Cahn (1992) noted, modern-day prosecutors have reached a crossroads and must choose to move in one of two directions: toward ever earlier dismissals or toward the exploration and adoption of innovative methods that effectively address occurrences of domestic violence. For many, this choice will entail self-assessments that pose what may be difficult questions to answer, for example, How are these cases most effectively and judiciously screened? How are "no-drop" policies crafted and executed? What are the variations of no-drop policies, and which are most productive? How should conditional pretrial release policies be handled? What are the most productive means to encourage victim cooperation in the prosecution? What prosecution methods are open to the prosecutor if the victim refuses to cooperate? Which are most effective? What are the most reliable trial techniques to preserve evidence, use experts, and develop effective ranges of sentencing options? What are the most critical factors in predicting the success or failure of prosecuted domestic violence cases?

A number of local prosecutors throughout the United States have already made the decision to forge ahead and mobilize "cutting-edge" programs for the prosecution of domestic violence cases. Some of these programs are established; others are in their infancy. Although some noteworthy exploratory studies have been done on how some of the established programs are structured (Cahn, 1992; McHardy, 1992), scant research has been conducted in the areas of how these programs were organized (planning processes, common pitfalls, methods used to overcome these problems) and how they effectively address the processing of these cases while simultaneously addressing the needs of the victims.

The primary objective of the study this chapter is based on was to conduct a national mail survey of local prosecutors' offices to assess the present level of domestic violence prosecution throughout the United States and to increase this level by promoting effective prosecution practices. The project solicited information on a wide scale on how local prosecutors typically handle these cases now and what their most pressing needs are. In addition, the project has conducted appraisals of the *development* of several existing strategies for coordinated, prosecutor-led domestic violence programs that spotlight the most effective parts of these programs as perceived by program administrators.

BACKGROUND

During the past 10 years, criminal justice research has focused much attention on the enforcement of domestic violence offenses. On May 27, 1984, the National Institute of Justice (NIJ) announced the results of a randomized clinical trial of the use of arrest for misdemeanor domestic violence (Sherman & Cohn, 1989). This pioneering study of 314 domestic violence cases in Minneapolis was followed by research replications in Atlanta, Charlotte, Colorado Springs, Metro-Dade (Miami), Omaha, and Milwaukee. Results from these studies were groundbreaking. Arrest for misdemeanor domestic assault was found to have different effects in different cities (some demonstrating deterrent effects, others showing increased violence) and different effects on different types of offenders (deterrent effects on employed offenders, and increased violence for unemployed offenders; Hirschel, Hutchison, Dean, Kelley, & Pesackis, 1990; Pate, Hamilton, & Annan, 1991; Sherman, 1992; Sherman et al., 1991).

Despite the major gains in criminological knowledge derived from these studies, a number of important questions revolving around the issue of domestic violence remain unanswered. Bowman (1992), Zorza (1992), and Frisch (1992) point out that the Minneapolis study and its replications suffer from some limitations in that no serious monitoring of the domestic violence prosecution processes and their outcomes was conducted and that this lack placed the arrest phase in an unrealistic system vacuum. Isolating one factor in the domestic violence context (arrest) and slicing it into reality at one point in time distorted this reality. In addition, Frisch notes that few of the replication studies paid serious attention to studying the *qualitative* nature of domestic violence and its treatment by the criminal justice system and, instead, concentrated on an exclusively quantitative analysis of this phenomenon. In "The Arrest Experiments: A Feminist Critique," Bowman asserts that the experiments failed to present a comprehensive qualitative/ quantitative picture not only of how the system treats domestic violence but also of how this system treatment is viewed by the victims. Finally, the experiments are somewhat limited in that they provide information on only those cases involving *misdemeanor* domestic violence offenses. It is certainly understandable why the use of an experimental design to study domestic violence felonies is prohibitive (ethical prohibitions associated with the random assignment of cases). Nonetheless, the topic area of how the system defines and treats more serious domestic violence occurrences is still virtually untouched.

The current study fills these informational gaps with regard to the local prosecutor's role in the prosecution of domestic violence misdemeanors and felonies and the perspective of domestic violence victims of the local prosecutor's handling of these cases. Because few empirical studies have been done on the local prosecutor and domestic violence (Ford & Regoli, 1992; Schmidt & Steury, 1989), the current study should be viewed as more of a descriptive analysis than as an explanatory one. The thrust of the approach is (a) to assess the state of domestic violence programs within local prosecutors offices, both formal and informal, throughout the United States; (b) to identify needs of local prosecutors; (c) to explain common obstacles to successful prosecution of these offenses; and (d) to provide recommendations for the improvement of domestic violence prosecution effectiveness.

EXECUTION OF THE
NATIONAL MAIL SURVEY

The American Prosecutors Research Institute (APRI) devised the national mail survey instrument with the help of information gleaned from focus group and advisory committee meetings and personnel from APRI's National Center for the Prosecution of Child Abuse. The survey collected baseline information on the local prosecution of domestic violence and included open-ended question formats to provide a wide range of responses conducive to exploratory studies, as well as closed-ended, Likert-constructed queries. The survey permits a better understanding of the quality and quantity of resources and approaches to the prosecution of domestic violence in the United States.

Intense contact was directed to all offices in jurisdictions with populations between 250,000 and 500,000 (strata 5) and over 500,000 (strata 6), under the assumption that their problems will be more acute and that their program efforts will be more routinized. Of 200 offices surveyed, encompassing the total population of strata 5 and strata 6 offices, 142 responded; this return represented a response rate of 68%. Half of the offices responding reported separate units or sections devoted to the prosecution of domestic violence. Only 22% reported separate units for felonies and for misdemeanors.

The main body of the survey solicited information on how prosecutors typically handle domestic violence cases and the most urgent needs in this area. Specifically, the survey attempted to identify how local prosecutors perceive and address domestic violence cases in the context of all other crime-specific cases. Completed questionnaires supplied valuable information on the extent to which domestic violence cases are prioritized, the decision-making processes used to determine level of seriousness prosecutors afford these cases, and the role of resources in effective domestic violence prosecution. The questionnaire was partitioned into seven substantive sections: (a) case management, (b) case screening/ charging, (c) pretrial release policies, (d) postcharge diversion, (e) trials, (f) sentencing options, and (g) victim support programs. Each section was designed to gather comprehensive information on each of the respective topic areas. The following discussion provides summary information on the results of each of these sections of the survey.

Case Management

The first section of the questionnaire queried prosecutors on how they are organized to manage domestic violence cases (e.g., vertical prosecution, separate unit). Prosecutors were also questioned on how the organization of the office may influence the effectiveness of case prosecutions and assistance provided to victims. This section posed several questions on how these cases are managed in each office and the role that resource availability plays in management organization style. As previously stated, local prosecutors were basically split on whether their offices devoted separate units or sections to handling domestic violence cases. The vast majority of respondents (86% [121]) indicated that their offices handled domestic violence misdemeanors as well as felonies. Only 16% (21) admitted their offices' management style was not effective for domestic violence cases. According to respondents, the availability of resources has a definite impact on how domestic violence cases are handled: 82% (113) replied that the level of resources has a "medium to high degree" of impact on the manner in which domestic violence cases are handled by their offices.

Case Screening/Charging

The second part of the questionnaire was devoted to determining how domestic violence case screening and charging decision making compares with such decision making for other offenses. Of special interest for the survey was the development of guidelines for filing charges, their implementation, and any variation of "no-drop" policies for charge filing. Prosecutors were asked whether they applied special criteria in case screening/charging decision making for domestic violence cases that are fundamentally different from such decision making for other types of cases: 55% (76) replied they did use such unique criteria in case screening/charging decision making for domestic violence cases, and 54% (72) reported their internal policies for domestic violence cases affect case screening/charging decision making. Prosecutors were asked how they proceed with cases when the victim is deemed uncooperative at the case screening/charging stage. Of the 85 who responded to this question, 80% (68) stated that, in such situations, they proceed with the prosecution of the case; only 20% (17) declared that the case is dropped; and 85% (108) stated that they experience screening /charging decision-making problems unique to domestic violence cases. Although a majority of prosecutors were found to have formal office protocols for processing domestic violence cases (65% [90]), only 30% (32) revealed they have separate protocols for misdemeanors and felonies. The majority who responded to the question about the degree to which protocols were followed reported that such protocols were followed to a high degree (60% [55]). Local prosecutors believed these protocols to be effective regardless of whether they pertained to misdemeanor or felony cases. Of 86 responding to the question on effectiveness regarding misdemeanor cases, 90% (77) believed them to be effective. For felony protocol, of the 89 responding, 94% (84) believed them to be effective.

Formal policies adopted for control of domestic violence offenses at the arrest and prosecution stages were found to have a noticeable impact on local prosecutors' offices. The vast majority (92% [125]) of respondents were from prosecutors' offices in jurisdictions where proarrest policies have been adopted by local police departments; and 87% (106) thought proarrest policies had affected the volume of domestic violence cases coming to them, but few thought the increase in volume resulting from proarrest policies affected either general prosecutorial decision-making processes or, more specifically, plea negotiation procedures. Only 17% (23) thought they were forced to modify decision making because of proarrest policies, and an even lower 13% (17) thought the volume resulting from proarrest policies had affected plea negotiation processes. With regard to prosecutorial no-drop policies for domestic violence cases, 66% (92)

indicated their offices had adopted no-drop policies, but of the 97 responding to a question on the flexibility of no-drop policies, 90% (87) reported that some flexibility was built into these policies. Almost all (83% [94]) said their no-drop policies were treated consistently regardless whether the complaint was initiated by the victim or by the police. In the majority of jurisdictions (58% [63]), victims are not contacted by the prosecutors' office prior to prefiling.

A series of questions were asked of local prosecutors on how domestic violence cases are initiated with their offices. A high percentage of respondents in local offices (78% [108]) stated that domestic violence cases are typically introduced to their office through the police, rather than through the victims. In only 12% of the cases (14) did prosecutors state that domestic violence incident filing responsibility rested to a high degree with the victims. However, 53% (65) reported that such filing responsibility rests with the prosecutor. An equal percentage reported that filing rests to a high degree with the police.

The final item in this section of the questionnaire dealt with the extent to which victim injury and the willingness of the victim to cooperate can affect the decision to file domestic violence charges. Of interest to the study is that although responses to the question on victim injury were similar, respondents from stratas 5 (jurisdictions between 250,000 and 500,000 population) and 6 (jurisdictions over 500,000 population) varied across strata regarding how decisions to prosecute are affected by victims' willingness to cooperate; 41% (58) of the sample thought the extent of victim injury affected the filing of domestic violence cases to a high degree. The most striking contrast between strata involved the issue of proceeding with prosecutions in cases with uncooperative victims. Of the 67 from strata 6 who responded to the "victim cooperation" question, only 8% (6) thought the willingness of the victim to cooperate affected their decision to prosecute to a high degree, whereas 36% (25) of the 61 from strata 5 thought victim willingness to cooperate affected the decision to prosecute to a significant degree.

Pretrial Release Policies

The third section of the survey centered on the types and strengths of prosecutor office policies to protect the domestic violence victim from retribution by the offender and the protection of children in the household. Regarding pretrial release of a domestic violence offender, 76% (105) of respondents said their offices tend to recommend bail amounts comparable to those for other offenses. In only 16.5% (18) did respondents report their offices typically request denial of bail in domestic violence cases. However, 95% (124) stated their offices typically request that certain conditions be set on an abuser's release.

Some differences were noted across strata on the percentage of offices that notify victims of the defendants' release in domestic violence cases. For strata 5, 68% (64) of respondents reported that victims are notified of the defendants' release, whereas only half of respondents in strata 6 (59) indicated that they also notify victims. Just over half of the offices responding (58% [77]) have established protocol regarding the issuance of no-contact orders. Only 18% (23) expressed a low degree of reliance on protective orders to protect domestic violence victims; 33% (42) rely on these protection orders to a medium degree; and the plurality (48% [62]) rely on protective orders to a high degree. According to responses of local prosecutors in both strata, there was some question as to the effectiveness of protective orders. Only 11% (14) thought these mechanisms are highly effective, 63% (78) thought them to be of average effectiveness, and 23% (28) concluded that protective orders are of low effectiveness. The survey found that in only 9% (12) of the jurisdictions were violations of protective orders treated as felonies.

Some indication was found that the presence of a child in a domestic violence situation can affect how the prosecutor will proceed with a domestic violence case. In only 29% (34) of the cases did respondents say the presence of a child has a low degree of impact on how the prosecutor will proceed with the case; 45% (53) indicated it affects the case to a medium degree; and 25% (30) related a high degree of impact on how the prosecutor proceeds if a child is involved.

Postcharge Diversion

The fourth section of the questionnaire centered on the extent the prosecutor's office chooses postcharge diversion options used to suspend case processing while the abuser undergoes treatment. The section also surveyed respondents on the implications of the use of these options. Offices were virtually split on the issue of whether they were involved in postcharge diversion programs for domestic violence offenses (50% indicating the presence of these programs, 50% indicating the absence of these programs). In jurisdictions where these programs existed, 63% (35) were pretrial programs, and 37% (21) were postplea programs. Slightly more than half of these programs were licensed. Only about 35% of respondents indicated their state codes established eligibility guidelines for admittance into diversion programs. About 59% of the offices that had diversion programs indicated they had developed eligibility guidelines for admittance into these programs.

Respondents were asked about what happens to offenders after they successfully complete the diversion program. Practically all of those responding (93% [50]) indicated that offenders are *not* convicted of the prosecuted offense once they successfully complete the program. Only 7% (4) stated that offenders successfully completing the program are convicted of lesser charges. A high percentage of respondents thought the diversion programs in their jurisdictions were effective (80% [52]).

Trials

The fifth section of the questionnaire posed questions on special features of domestic violence trials that can make these cases distinct from other trials. This section was focused on methods used to overcome problems arising from the lack of victim cooperation. Respondents were asked whether their offices encountered any of four types of uncooperative victims for domestic violence cases: (a) victims who prefer not to be involved or to come to court, (b) victims who will testify truthfully only on subpoena, (c) victims who will not appear in court on subpoena, and (d) victims who actively undermine the prosecution. Respondents were unanimous in stating they all encounter victims who would prefer not to be involved or to come to court. Between 90% and 94% of respondents also encountered all three of the other possibilities (victims testifying only on subpoena, victims not appearing in court on subpoena, and victims who actively undermine the prosecution).

Respondents were asked in what percentage of their domestic violence cases victims were considered to be uncooperative. The plurality (33% [45]) of respondents reported that over 55% of their cases involved uncooperative witnesses, 16% (22) reported that between 41% and 55% of their domestic violence cases had unco-operative witnesses, 26% (37) reported that between 26% and 40% of their cases had uncooperative witnesses, and 26% (37) indicated that up to 25% of their cases had uncooperative witnesses.

Respondents also described the most common methods used by their offices to overcome the problems connected with uncoopera-tive domestic violence victims. Clearly, the most common method used by local prosecutors was the use of subpoena power, with 92% (129) reporting this. Ranked a close second was the use of photo-graphs of injuries to the victim as evidence (82% [115]). A distant third in ranking was the use of evidence of "excited utterances" at the crime scene (64% [91]). About half of respondents (51%) re-ported common methods of using family/neighbor testimonies and the use of 911 audiotapes to overcome the problem of uncooperative victims. Slightly over a quarter of respondents rely on sworn state-ments of the victims at screening and present sense impressions. The least used methods to overcome lack of cooperation by victims were the use of victim advocate testimony (10% [14]) and the use of videotapes of initial victim interviews (6% [8]).

Reliance on the use of expert witness testimony to help overcome evidentiary problems at domestic violence trials was decidedly low, with 76% (93) reporting a low frequency of employing expert witness testimony on these cases. As expected, the issue of resource avail-ability and its potential prohibiting effect on the employment of these expert witnesses was more of a factor for smaller jurisdictions (strata 5) than larger jurisdictions (strata 6), with 42% (59) in strata 5 indicating a high degree of importance attached to the availability of resources and only 32% (21) in strata 6 reporting a similar response.

Sentencing Options

In the sixth section, several questions were asked about positions on sentencing domestic violence offenders and the degree to which sentences reflect the serious nature of the offenses committed. When asked how they view sentencing patterns of domestic vio-lence offenders in their jurisdictions, few respondents thought sentences were severe enough (5% [7]). Most characterized sen-tences as moderate (66% [93]), with a sizeable number charac-terizing them as lenient (29% [41]).

This section of the questionnaire also attempted to determine the extent to which local prosecutors interacted with representatives of agencies *outside* the prosecutor's office in the interest of domestic violence cases. A special area of the survey dealt with the way local prosecutors' offices interact with probation officers to track offender compliance with probation conditions. Such tracking was found to be rare, with only 28% (36) reporting prosecutor monitoring of domestic violence probationer compliance with probation conditions. A more global question was asked of prosecutors concerning their offices' work with other organizations outside the criminal justice system (e.g., victim advocates, social services, battered treatment programs) in handling domestic violence. The vast majority (91% [122]) stated they did participate with other organizations for domestic violence misdemeanors, and slightly more (96% [124]) stated they did so with regard to domestic violence felonies. Fewer than half (47% [61]) revealed their offices had representatives who participate in formal multidisciplinary teams that handle domestic violence cases. Nearly half (48% [65]) were involved in diversion/rehabilitation programs for domestic violence offenders. Just over half (52% [73]) had established formal policies/procedures for cases in which substance abuse is suspected for the offender in a domestic violence case. Few offices (11% [15]) had any formal policies/procedures for cases in which substance abuse is suspected for the victims in domestic violence cases.

Two questions were asked regarding how the presence of recidivism of domestic violence offenders affects charging decisions and sentencing. Overwhelmingly, prosecutors reported that knowledge of recidivism did affect their charging decisions in domestic violence cases (83% [104]). In only 50% (63) of the cases, however, had offices established policies to address recidivism (felony penalties imposed after a certain number of misdemeanors).

Victim Support Programs

The seventh section of the questionnaire covered the extent and types of support that prosecutors' offices provide to satisfy the needs of domestic violence victims. Of special interest were methods employed to foster victim participation in the prosecution process, level of interaction with external victim support programs, and level of development of any internal victim support programs.

A high percentage of offices surveyed employed at least some formal procedures to encourage victim participation in the domestic violence prosecution process (82% [114]). Most respondents (71% [98]) had incorporated domestic violence victim support programs as part of their offices. Nearly all (98% [92]) contended these victim support programs were effective. In most cases (65% [69]), domestic violence advocacy units within prosecutors' offices were combined with victim/witness units in the offices.

Respondents were asked about the types of services their victim support services offered. The most common service offered was the referral to social services agencies (98% [107]) and court accompaniment of the victim (87% [104]). Also, 84% (100) indicated they provided court preparation for domestic violence victims, and 72% (86) supplied education to domestic violence victims on obtaining criminal/civil remedies. More than half (64% [75]) furnished supportive counseling to domestic violence victims. Some variation was found between strata regarding the office employment of domestic violence advocates. Such in-office victim advocates were more common in larger jurisdictions (strata 6, 65% [43]) than in smaller jurisdictions (strata 5, 44% [28]). When asked about the degree to which offices interact with local victim support programs operating outside the offices, more than half of respondents indicated a high degree of interaction (54% [74]).

DISCUSSION

In the recent past, local prosecutors were widely thought to be insensitive to the needs of domestic violence victims and negligent in the consistent prosecution of these cases. Public pressures for the aggressive prosecution of domestic violence offenders and the continuing evolution of the local prosecutor's role have dovetailed to produce a dichotomy of a select group of local prosecutors' offices that have developed innovative programs for effective domestic violence prosecutions and a larger collection of offices that desire to establish such programs. Until the present, scant empirical information has been available on local domestic violence prosecution programs on a national level. Filling this gap, the results of the

APRI's national survey in this area can be characterized as both encouraging and disheartening.

It can be confidently said that the survey results from prosecutors' offices representing medium to large jurisdictions demonstrate a growing commitment by district attorneys to vigorously prosecute domestic violence. Prosecutors seem to be persistently searching for the most effective means of bringing domestic violence offenders to justice. Examples of this aggressive new stance include the prevalence of no-drop policies and, with it, a pronounced willingness to move forward in cases in which victims do not participate as witnesses and to rely on nontraditional methods to ameliorate the litigation dilemmas presented by this absence. Results also demonstrate how prosecutors are willing to invoke the use of protective orders in efforts to ensure victim safety from retaliation when the victim *does* testify as a witness. At the same time, results indicate that many local prosecutors have also become inclined to support domestic violence diversion programs, offender counseling programs, and the extensive use of victim advocate programs. Taken together, these results point to an encouraging new direction for prosecutors in blending a tough control position with a logical expansion of the prosecutor's community leader role to address all dimensions of the domestic violence problem.

The survey results, however, also bring to light several disturbing aspects of the domestic violence prosecution scene that indicate more must be done before one can conclude that the struggle to upgrade the local prosecutor's response to domestic violence has been won. A most dispiriting result of the survey concerns the issue of offender retaliation against victims of domestic violence who testify as witnesses. On the basis of survey responses, it appears that prosecutors continue to rely heavily on the use of protective orders as a remedy even though they concede that the effectiveness of this option is questionable and that violations of such orders often result in minimal punishments.

The results also illustrate how a lack of adequate prosecutorial resources—particularly in the less populous jurisdictions—can be a factor in the priority level afforded domestic violence cases (e.g., the addressing of cases with victims who will not participate as witnesses, victim notification of the offender's release, the employment of victim advocates). Clearly, the results here underscore how the presence of a comprehensive approach to domestic violence can be dependent on jurisdictional size and the ability to designate sufficient resources to the problem in the context of all other crime problems faced by the prosecutor.

All things considered, the finding that deserves the most immediate attention by prosecutors is the high percentage of respondents who report the occurrence of cases in which the victim will not serve as a witness. This finding should signal to prosecutors that it is incumbent on them to devote increased efforts to explore the full range of methods that can be applied to successfully solicit the participation of the domestic violence victim in the criminal justice process. Without the victim's assistance in the prosecution, prosecutors of domestic violence will undoubtedly continue to wrestle with the same problem: that of testing alternative means of compensating for what can prove to be an essential ingredient in determining the success or failure of the domestic violence prosecution. Although it has been shown that such replacement modes have the potential to be effective, it remains to be seen whether they truly convey the same degree of credibility to jurors as does the courtroom testimony of the victim of domestic violence. To date, no empirical research compares the relative strengths of alternatives to victim testimony in domestic violence trials. There still are no clear answers on how effective these alternatives are in convicting the domestic violence offender and what weight the threat of their use carries with the defense attorney during plea negotiations. In the quest to enhance the quality of domestic violence prosecutions, answers to these questions are necessary and require that future, rigorous studies be initiated to address them.

REFERENCES

Bowman, C. (1992). The arrest experiments: A feminist critique. *Journal of Criminal Law and Criminology, 83*(1), 201-208.

Cahn, N. (1992). Prosecuting domestic violence crimes. In E. Buzawa & C. Buzawa (Eds.), *Domestic violence: The changing justice response* (pp. 162-179). Westport, CT: Auburn House.

Cahn, N., & Lerman, L. (1991). Prosecuting woman abuse. In M. Steinman (Ed.), *Woman battering: Policy responses.* Cincinnati: Anderson.

Field, M., & Field, H. (1973). Marital violence and the criminal process. *Social Service Review, 47*(6), 221-240.

Ford, D., & Regoli, M. (1992). The preventive impacts of policies for prosecuting wife batterers. In E. Buzawa & C. Buzawa (Eds.), *Domestic violence: The changing justice response* (pp. 182-207). Westport, CT: Auburn House.

Frisch, L. (1992). Research that succeeds, policies that fail. *Journal of Criminal Law and Criminology, 83*(1), 209-216.

Greenwood, P., Wildhorn, S., Poggio, E., Strumwasser, M., & DeLeon, P. (1973). *Prosecution of adult felony defendants in Los Angeles County: A policy perspective.* Washington, DC: Government Printing Office.

Hirschel, J. D., Hutchison, I. W., III, Dean, C. W., Kelley, J. J., & Pesackis, C. E. (1990). *Charlotte Spouse Assault Replication Project: Final report.* Washington, DC: National Institute of Justice.

Lerman, L. (1981). Criminal prosecution of wife-beaters. *Response to Violence in the Family, 4*(1), 1-19.

McHardy, L. (1992). *Family violence: State-of-the-art court programs.* Charleston, SC: National Council of Juvenile and Family Court Judges.

Pate, A. M., Hamilton, E. E., & Annan, S. (1991). *Metro-Dade Spouse Abuse Replication Project draft final report.* Washington, DC: National Institute of Justice.

Schmidt, J., & Steury, E. (1989). Prosecutorial discretion in filing charges in domestic violence cases. *Criminology, 27*(3), 487-510.

Sherman, L. (1992). The influence of criminology on criminal law: Evaluating arrests for misdemeanor domestic violence. *Journal of Criminal Law and Criminology, 83*(1), 1-45.

Sherman, L., & Cohn, E. (1989). The impact of research on legal policy: The Minneapolis Domestic Violence Experiment. *Law and Society Review, 23*, 117-144.

Sherman, L. W., Schmidt, J. D., Rogan, D. P., Gartin, P. R., Cohn, E. G., Collins, D., & Bacich, R. (1991). From initial deterrence to long-term escalation: Short-custody arrest for poverty ghetto domestic violence. *Criminology, 29*(4), 821-850.

Waits, K. (1985). The criminal justice system's response to battering: Understanding the problem, forging solutions. *Washington Law Review, 60*, 267-329.

Williams, K. (1976). The effects of victim characteristics on violent crimes. In J. R. Chapman & M. Gates (Eds.), *The victimization of women* (pp. 143-174). Beverly Hills, CA: Sage.

Zorza, J. (1992). The criminal law of misdemeanor domestic violence, 1970-1990. *Journal of Criminal Law and Criminology, 83*(1), 46-72.

11

Re-Abuse in a Population of Court-Restrained Male Batterers
Why Restraining Orders Don't Work

ANDREW R. KLEIN

Since first enacted in Pennsylvania in 1976, every state and the District of Columbia now provide for the issuance of restraining or protective orders (ROs) to protect victims of spousal/partner abuse (National Council of Juvenile and Family Court Judges, 1992). The issuance of these civil orders has become the chief means of protecting victims of domestic abuse in many jurisdictions. In Massachusetts, for example, 46,515 ROs were issued against abusers in 1992, whereas the total number of defendants brought to criminal court for any kind of assault, of which only a small fraction were domestic, was 73,609.[1]

Despite their popularity, scant quantitative research has been conducted on whom ROs are being issued against, for what, and what effect, if any, the issuance of such orders has in terms of new abuse. In addition, no effort has been made to predict future risk of abuse based on the characteristics of the abuse, the victim, the defendant, or the criminal justice system's means of inter-

192

vention. The following research was conducted to address these questions.

THE RESEARCH DESIGN

Every RO case successfully brought in the Quincy Court in 1990 in which the defendant was a male and the victim was a female spouse, current or former, or girlfriend, current or former (who either cohabited with the abuser or had a child by him) was examined. The total was 663.[2]

Various victim, incident, abuser, and defendant characteristics were examined and broken down as follows:

Independent Variables to Be Examined

Abuser Characteristics
1. Age
2. Relationship to petitioner/victim: wife, former wife, not wife
3. Living arrangement with victim at time of incident: separated, not separated
4. Presence of children in household: at least one, none
5. Prior criminal record: at least one prior criminal complaint, none
6. Number of prior complaints
7. Prior alcohol/drug prior complaints: at least one, none
8. Number of alcohol/drug prior complaints
9. Prior crimes against person complaints: at least one, none
10. Number of crimes against person complaints
11. Gender of victim of prior crimes against person complaints
12. Prior history of ROs: at least one, none

Victim Characteristics
1. Relationship to abuser (see above)
2. Living arrangement with victim at time of incident (see above)
3. Presence of children in household (see above)
4. Length of RO held by petitioner/victim (in days)
5. Victim response: dropped order before 365 days, kept order for 365 days or more

Incident Characteristics
1. Type of abuse: physical assault, threats/fear, other
2. Alcohol/drug use reported: yes, no

   3. Mental illness reported: yes, no
   4. Town where incident occurred: Quincy, Weymouth, Braintree, Randolph, Holbrook, Milton, Cohasset

Police/Court Characteristics

   1. Simultaneous police arrest with RO: yes, no
   2. Court RO provisions: vacate (yes, no); custody (yes, no)
   3. Length of court RO (see above)

Dependent Variables to Be Examined

   1. Re-abuse: new arrest, new RO for new incident (does not include extension of existing order)
   2. Interval between re-abuse and original 1990 RO: new arrest, new RO

Each defendant was tracked for 2 years to determine further abuse, which was defined by (a) a criminal complaint anywhere in Massachusetts for abuse against the same victim, either an arrest for a criminal violation of the RO or a new assault and/or threats arrest, and/or (b) a new RO based on a new incident of abuse filed in the Quincy court.

Because victims were not interviewed to determine new abuse, findings of re-abuse are admittedly conservative. Prior research has indicated that arrest records represent only a small percentage of actual abuse cases (e.g., see Hirschel, Hutchison, Dean, Kelley, & Pesackis, 1991).[3] Survival analysis was completed to determine which independent variables correlated with re-abuse.

Findings

Abuse Incident

Although the abusers were brought to civil court by their victims, the vast majority physically assaulted their victims (64.4%). Another third threatened to kill or otherwise harm them, their children, or a relative.

Police were involved in over 10% of the cases, also arresting the abuser for the incident that formed the basis of the RO request.

Alcohol or drugs were used by the abuser in at least 39% of the incidents as reported by the victims in their affidavits. Greater use may have occurred but was unnoted by the victim.

Abuser Characteristics

Age. The age of the abusers ranged from 17 to 70, with the average being 33. Two thirds were between the ages of 24 and 40 (see Figure 11.1).

Marital Status. Just over half of the males were either married or divorced from their victims (46.6% currently married, 3.9% formerly married, 49.5% not married).

Prior Criminal History. Almost 80% of the abusers had prior criminal histories within the state of at least one criminal complaint. Prior complaints ranged from underage drinking to murder. Thirty of the abusers had inactive records or records that were more than 15 years old. Not only did most have prior records, but also the average record length was 13 complaints. In 1990, the average arrest resulted in 1.95 complaints; this means the average abuser had probably been in criminal court for six separate incidents. The breakdown of prior criminal history is contained in Figure 11.2.

In analyzing the prior record, 54% had at least one prior record for an alcohol or drug crime, usually drunk driving; 43% had at least one prior complaint for a crime against persons. In checking those with prior crimes against persons lodged in Quincy Court ($N = 155$), victims were males as well as females in two thirds of these cases; in other words, most of the abusers with past histories of crimes against persons appeared to be generally violent, as opposed to being violent exclusively against females or spouses/partners. Only a third restricted their past violence to women.

Victim Characteristics

All the women came to court to obtain the initial temporary order, valid for 5 days. The overwhelming majority (75%) returned for the contested hearing, at which time the abuser may also testify before the court. All the women who requested were given a longer-term order, valid up to 1 year. The vast majority let the orders lapse after that year, with only 27 returning after a year to request an extension.[4]

Notwithstanding the high return rate after the initial 5-day order, almost half of the women returned to court to drop their ROs prior

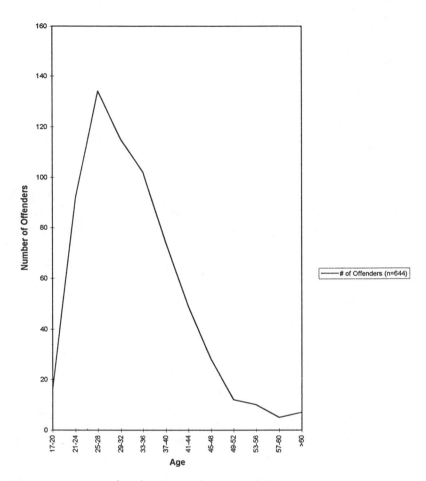

Figure 11.1. Age of Male 209A Subjects as of 1990

to the 1-year termination date (see Figure 11.3). Victims may request orders be dropped because they reconcile with their abusers or because they are effectively coerced into doing so by their abusers.

Interestingly, no statistically significant difference was found between victims who maintained their ROs and those who asked that their ROs be dropped early, except that those who had prior ROs were more likely to maintain the 1990 RO. A third of the victims had prior ROs against the same abuser (see Table 11.1). Other research suggests that victims are more prone to keep orders each time they come to court seeking assistance (Kramer, 1989).

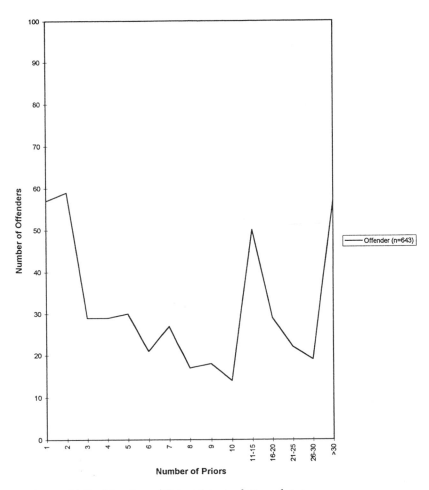

Figure 11.2. Number of Prior Criminal Complaints

Although the RO and record documents that were relied on were not fully revealing, it appears from the affidavits filed by the victims in their requests for the ROs that at least a third of the women had physically separated from their abusers prior to the abuse incident that led to the request for a RO. In addition, 8% of the women who had been married to their abusers had divorced them prior to the incident that precipitated the RO. In other words, a significant number of these women had taken significant steps to protect themselves prior to coming to court to request the RO. This finding

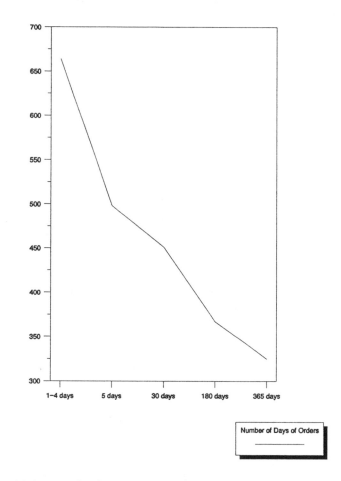

Figure 11.3. Length of 1990 209A Order

suggests that their continued abuse may not result so much from their inability to act as from the tenacity of their abusers to pursue them. In fact, in three of the cases studied, the victims revealed that they had fled other states and come to Massachusetts to escape their abusers—to no avail.

At least 42% of the women had children with their abusers, although this is probably underreported. The RO records show the presence of children only if the court orders the woman custody when the man is vacated from the home. If custody is not contested

TABLE 11.1 Dropped Versus Kept RO

	Dropped	*Kept*
1. NUMBER:	316	328
2. AGE:	32.66	32.8
3. WIFE:	50.64%	42.68%
EX-WIFE:	2.55%	4.88%
4. PRIOR RECORD:	77.46%	78.35%
# PRIOR:	13.20	12.53
AL/DRUG:	53.48%	54.57%
#AL/DRUG:	3.98	4.04
CRIMES AGAINST PERSONS:	42.4%	45.43%
# PERSONS CRIMES:	4.50	5.54
SEX OF VICTIMS: (males)	59.46%	68.29%
PROB/JAIL:	24.68%	23.17%
5. SIMULTANEOUS ARREST:	11.39%	10.06%
6. PRIOR 209A:	29.51%	37.85%*
7. INCIDENT (assault):	64.96%	62.63%
—AL/DRUG:	42.125%	35.29%
8. RE-ABUSED:	40.8%	44.8%

NOTE: *N = 305 for less than 365, and 325 for 365 or more; χ^2 = 4.8879; $p < .05$.

or if a superseding probate order regarding custody exists, the presence of children is not noted in the official records.

Criminal Justice System Intervention

The court issued temporary ROs in all cases and the 1-year order in the 75% of cases in which the victim returned to court to ask for it. In addition, in all cases, the court ordered the defendants not to abuse the victims. In all but two cases, the defendants were ordered to vacate the family household. And 41% of the men were ordered not to have any contact with their victims.

As mentioned, 10% of the abusers were also arrested for the incident that precipitated the request for the RO.

Re-Abuse

Almost half of the abusers (48.8%) re-abused their victims within 2 years of the 1990 RO. The percentage arrested for abuse was 34%, as broken down in Table 11.2. In addition, 95 of the abusers had new ROs taken out by their victims for new incidents of abuse.

Interestingly, another 146 of the abusers were arrested for new crimes that were not domestic in nature. In other words, the overall re-arrest rate was 56.4% for all new crimes.

Of those arrested for re-abusing their victims, most did so quickly. The hazard rates for the first three 30-day periods after issuance of the ROs were between .0012 and .0013. After the first 90 days, it dropped to .0009 for the fourth 30-day period and then fell to .0006. After the first 270 days, it fell to .0004. After the first year, it dropped to .0003 (see Figure 11.4).

Predicting Re-Abuse

The only statistically significant predictors for new abuse as measured by a new arrest were age, prior criminal history, and court-ordered "contact" provisions. Whether the abuser was also arrested at the time of the RO, whether the precipitating incident was violent or not, whether the victim had a prior RO or maintained the present RO, or any other independent variable did not predict re-abuse. A weak correlation was found between marital status and re-abuse, but if age is controlled for, age, not marital status, is the more powerful predictor.

For example, it made no difference what the presenting incident was, whether the abuse had been verbal or physical. The lack of difference may be because most of the women reported ongoing abuse, with many who came to court for threats reporting prior physical assaults. In addition, 33.9% of the victims had at least one prior RO against the same abuser either in Quincy or elsewhere.

It also made no difference whether the woman had previously divorced or physically separated from her abuser. Re-abuse rates were the same.

Age

Younger abusers re-abuse more than older abusers (see Figure 11.5). Younger abusers were also more likely not to be married to their victims and vice versa (see Table 11.3).

TABLE 11.2 Breakdown of Reabuse Arrests

Assault, Assault and Battery, With/ Without a Dangerous Weapon	49.19%
Abuse Prevention Act Violation (Violation of 209A)	40.54%
Sexual Offenses (Rape, Indecent Assault and Battery)	3.24%
Threats	3.78%
Other (Trespassing, Annoying Telephone Calls)	3.24%

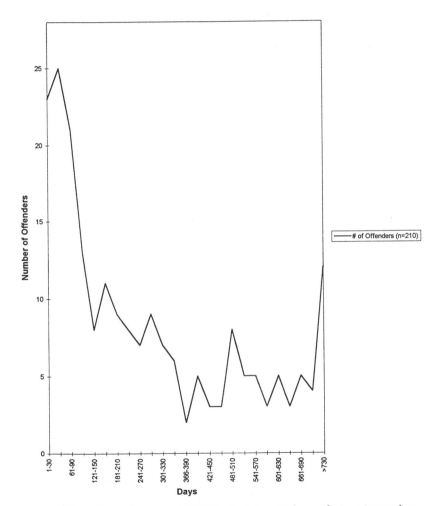

Figure 11.4. Days Between 1990 Restraining Order and New Arrest for Domestic Abuse

Criminal History

Those abusers without criminal histories or with inactive histories (last arrest more than 15 years ago) re-abused less than those with prior active criminal histories (arrest within 15 years). The majority of men with prior complaints re-abused; the majority of men without prior histories did not. In addition, those with more prior complaints re-abused more than those with lesser histories (see Figure 11.6).

The same pattern holds for abusers with prior histories of alcohol/drug crimes or crimes against persons. Those who had at least one prior complaint for either were more likely to re-abuse than those with no prior complaints for either type of crime. In addition, those with greater histories for each type of crime re-abused at greater rates (see Figures 11.7 and 11.8).

Court-Ordered Contact

If the court ordered "no contact," re-abuse was 35.7%. If contact was allowed, re-abuse was 27.3%. If the seriousness of the abusers' prior criminal history is controlled for, however, less difference is found between those with no-contact and contact orders. Only among offenders with no prior records do the two groups differ substantially in regard to re-abuse. In other words, abusers with longer prior criminal records re-abused regardless of differences in the specifics of the court RO provisions.

Major Findings and Conclusion

Male batterers brought to court for civil ROs are active criminals. It may be that most male abusers do not have criminal records, but the vast majority brought to court by their victims for ROs do. This is true in the current study among RO defendants not only in Quincy Court but also throughout Massachusetts (Commonwealth of Massachusetts, 1992, 1993). Court populations are generally found to be skewed to the poorer, more minority populations. It may be that a similar skewing is also true for females who use the courts to protect themselves from abusive spouses/partners. Spouses/partners of more middle- or upper-class abusers who do not have prior records may use alternative vehicles to court ROs to stop their

TABLE 11.3 Life Table: Survival Analysis Re-Abuse for Marital
Status and Age of Abuser

Age	Married (%)	Re-Abused (N)	Unmarried (%)	Re-Abused (N)
17-20	50	(4)	50	(12)
21-29	32.6	(83)	39.2	(166)
30-39	32.5	(151)	26.7	(105)
40-49	18.5	(65)	24.2	(29)
50 plus	4.8	(21)	28.6	(7)

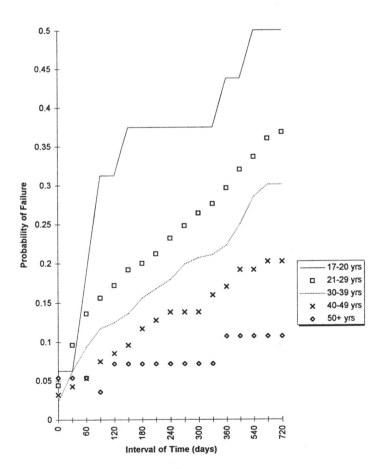

Figure 11.5. Survival Analysis for Age of Abuser

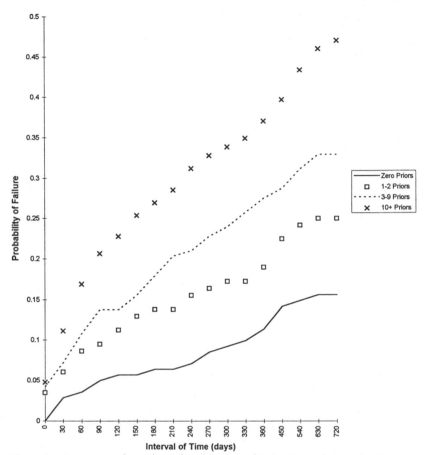

Figure 11.6. Survival Analysis for Number of Prior Complaints

abusers. Nevertheless, those males brought to court for ROs have extensive criminal histories; this is unrepresentative of males in the general population.

It is also true that studies of batterers arrested or brought to police attention reveal that most have prior histories of criminal records (e.g., see Dunford, Huizinga, & Elliot, 1990; Hirschel, Hutchison, & Dean, 1992; Sherman & Berk, 1984; Sherman, Schmidt, & Rogan, 1992).

Not only do abusers have prior active criminal histories, but also a third have prior RO histories (against the same victims). In

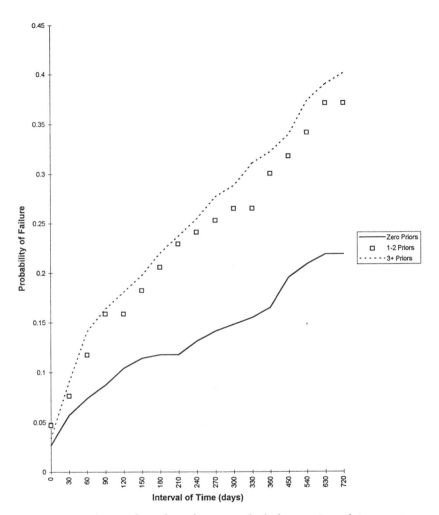

Figure 11.7. Survival Analysis for Prior Alcohol/Drug Complaints

addition to their prior criminal and civil records, the abuse that brings these men to court is, in the majority of cases, for a physical assault, behavior that is chargeable criminally.

Finally, not only do they have prior records like criminals and have abused their current spouses/partners like criminals, but they also re-abuse and reoffend at high rates, just like active criminals. In fact, the re-abuse rate of this population is equivalent to all men on probation in Massachusetts who are deemed to represent the

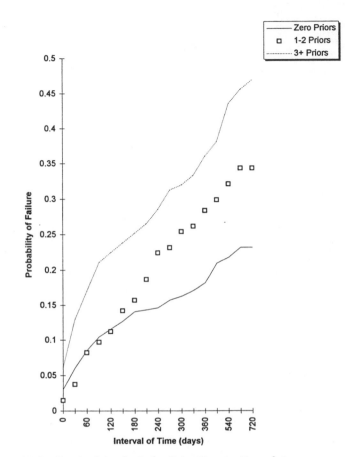

Figure 11.8. Survival Analysis for Prior Person Complaints

highest risk of recidivism by the Commissioner of Probation in Massachusetts (Pierce, McDevitt, Pattavina, & Miliano, 1991).[5]

Like probation recidivism in Massachusetts, re-abuse is also associated with substance abuse and length of prior record, as well as with instability of family relationships. Obviously, someone restrained from seeing his or her spouse/partner suffers from an instable family relationship by definition.

What makes male abusers even more dangerous than high-risk probationers is that so many have prior histories of violence, coupled with a ready access to their victims (Monahan, 1981). Even where the victim had sought to separate from her abuser, the Massachusetts probate courts, as elsewhere, routinely grant the abuser visitation, notwithstanding proven abuse of the mother.[6] This trend makes it impossible for women to hide from their abusers.

In short, male abusers brought to court for ROs look like criminals, act like criminals, and re-abuse like criminals. Recognition of this fact not only helps explain their behavior but also suggests countermeasures that might prove helpful in stopping it. Although brought into the court's civil door, these abusers should be treated at least as stringently as the highest-risk offenders released on probation. This is impossible to do, given the limited scope of civil ROs. Consequently, it behooves the criminal justice system to investigate these cases for criminal prosecution of the abusers and to increase protection for the victims.

Restraining orders do not adequately protect women from further abuse. Although the research does not reveal whether the use of ROs lessens the severity of continued abuse or the number of abuse incidents, it does reveal that the mere issuance of an RO fails to prevent future abuse against the same victim in almost half of the cases. Given the fact that re-abuse is most likely underreported in this study, it is probable that actual interviews with the victims would have revealed that most were actually re-abused, notwithstanding the court's civil intervention. Research of 500 ROs issued in Colorado, for example, found that the majority of women victims reported re-abuse despite a minimal arrest rate for new abuse and contempt rate for violation of existing orders (Harrell, Smith, & Newmark, 1993).

As reported, almost half of the women in this study dropped their ROs prior to the 1-year termination. As mentioned, the difference between those who dropped and those who maintained ROs was not statistically significant, except for whether or not they had prior ROs. Interestingly, the re-abuse rate was not different for those who dropped or those who kept their ROs. Unless significant, nonmeasured variables exist between those who dropped and those who maintained their ROs, it would appear that any utility of ROs that exists to stop abuse is in their issuance, not in their maintenance.

Although ROs may not prevent new abuse, those abusers who violated extant ROs were more likely to be arrested for new abuse. Those who re-abused their victims who did not have active ROs were less likely to be arrested; this put the onus on the victims to take out new ROs against their abusers. This difference is not remarkable, given that current law in Massachusetts mandates arrest for RO violations but not for domestic abuse itself (Mass. Gen. L. ch. 209A)

If one examines who these male batterers are, the fact that they routinely disobey court civil ROs is not surprising. Because most have had prior court criminal involvement, the issuance of civil ROs represents a lesser criminal justice response to their aberrant behavior. Moreover, prior arrests apparently did not deter them from continued criminal behavior, given the length of most of their records. Why should the mere issuance of civil orders deter them? As researchers concluded in their study of male batterer arrestees in North Carolina:

> Arrest as a preferred response tends to overlook the fact that many abusers have been arrested for battering and/or other crimes. It is naive to expect that arrest and incarceration will have a deterrent impact on many or most of them. (Hirschel et al., 1991, p. 68)

And they were talking about men who were arrested for domestic abuse, not simply issued ROs.

Even if abusers are impressed with civil ROs, their records indicate most have histories of substance abuse. It is likely that once under the influence, they forget about the ROs and the potential consequences for violating them. Victims in this study included in their affidavits that their abusers were drinking or using drugs in almost 40% of the incidents of abuse. Other abusers were also probably abusing drugs and alcohol, but their victims did not include the information in their affidavits.

Another reason why many abusers may not take ROs very seriously is that the criminal justice system does not appear to take them seriously either. Although the study was conducted in a jurisdiction nationally recognized for its programs to stop domestic violence, most re-abusers arrested for violating their ROs were not placed on probation, much less sentenced to jail.[7] Almost 33% of the cases were dismissed or *nol-prossed* outright; 10% were diverted without a finding of guilty; just over 25% were placed on probation; and 18% were jailed. Other studies in Massachusetts indicate that these dispositions were atypically strong. Most courts within the state historically have done even less (Curtis, 1991).

This study gave no indication that ROs provoke more abuse. Those who maintained orders were not abused more than those who dropped them. In addition, victims seem to believe that ROs are worthwhile—at least victims continue to come to court to take them out. A third of the victims in this study had taken out at least one previous RO, and 193 (30%) took out new orders after their 1990 order expired or was dropped. If the ROs provoked more new abuse than they obviously deterred, it is unlikely that so many victims would take them out more than once.

CONCLUSION

Even if ROs are better than no ROs in deterring some or the level of abuse, they are clearly not sufficient to protect women and children from continued abuse. If the goal of intervention is to end abuse for as many women as possible who ask for help, a primary reliance on civil ROs must be seriously questioned. A new intervention strategy must be developed that is based on the reality of who male abusers really are. Clearly, they are not, for the most part, "civil" men responsive to court civil orders. Not only are they, for the most part, active criminals, but they are also as high risk for repeat criminal behavior as any offenders generally allowed to be released to the community on probation. If they are allowed to remain in the community safely, they warrant the same intensity of supervision and scrutiny as the most hard-core offender currently under community-based supervision. To require such supervision, state intervention cannot be limited to the issuance of civil ROs. Whenever possible, the state must press forward with criminal prosecution against these men.

This means that arrest for domestic violence should be mandatory, whether an RO is in effect or not. Prosecutors should institute a "no-drop" policy and prosecute as many incidents of domestic violence as legally permissible. If convicted, male batterers should be sentenced accordingly. Sanctions should be mandatory, removing as much judicial discretion as necessary to eliminate the existing prejudices, knowledge gaps, and historical bias that currently prevent courts from treating domestic violence cases seriously.

When a women comes to court to seek an RO, in addition to issuing the RO if appropriate, the state must investigate the incident for possible prosecution. If the judge, ruling on the RO, hears probable cause that a crime has been committed and determines that the victim is in risk of further abuse, the judge should issue a criminal complaint accompanied by a warrant for the arrest of the alleged offender. This step not only will take the onus off the victim but also will preclude the victim's refusal to sign the complaint. The prosecutor must then work with the victim to encourage her to testify or otherwise assist the prosecution of the case. Often, particularly if the police do their job effectively, the prosecution can proceed without the victim's direct testimony.[8]

If the batterer is successfully prosecuted, the court can effect more control over him than it can simply through the issuance of an RO. If the batterer is placed on probation, for example, the court can mandate the batterer's treatment, abstinence from drugs and alcohol, intensive supervision, as well as incorporate the civil RO. The latter means that even if the victim is coerced into dropping the RO, the abuser must still contend with the court supervision. If the abuser exhibits dangerous behavior, the court can still bar the defendant from moving back in with the victim (Klein, 1994).

Mandatory arrest, prosecution, and sentencing of male batterers has been criticized by some as "disempowering" to women victims (Ford, 1991). To put it bluntly, it is more disempowering for the victim to be re-abused, even killed. As this study indicates, it is difficult for women to provide for their own protection, given the stalking behavior of many abusers. Further, women may not always accurately assess their own safety risks. Those women who took steps to end their ROs early were no safer than those who let the orders stand. Either these women were coerced to drop the orders or had a misplaced faith in their abusers' reformation. In addition, it is impossible for the police, the prosecutor, or the court to determine whether or not the victim's request to end the prosecution of her abuser is based on threats and fear. The Quincy study reveals that, in addition to reabusing their victims, these men are also committing a myriad of other crimes. They are violent to others, as well as to their partners and other family members.

Even if the abuser legitimately reconciles with his victim, his past criminal behavior should not be automatically erased. Imagine the reaction if charges against muggers and robbers were routinely dropped because the offenders promised not to do it again and/or reconciled with their victims.

Finally, any violation of an RO should bring certain punishment. One reason why ROs do not deter defendants is that their violation does not bring certain punishment. The law must establish a significant "going rate" for RO violation. The current criminal justice system simply fails to do as previously noted by Fagan (1988):

> The going rate for an offense is the sanction officials expect an offender to receive for specific offenses, and it is thought to be influenced by organizational factors independent of case specific variables. . . . The relatively short history of wife assault cases has not allowed for such a rate to be developed among the closed social network of court actors involved in plea negotiations. (p. 24, citations omitted)

In short, the study suggests that to rely on current strategies to combat spousal/partner abuse is to condemn a significant portion of, probably most, abused women who seek court assistance to stop further abuse. The development of ROs as a means to combat domestic violence was promoted by women's advocates who found the criminal justice system resistant to arresting, prosecuting, or sentencing abusers (Schechter, 1982). The civil RO allowed them to bypass the criminal justice system to get to court. ROs obviously were better than being totally ignored by largely hostile police, prosecutors, and criminal courts. Currently, although not as advanced or consistent as one might like, police, prosecutors, and criminal courts are beginning to open their doors to abused women. ROs no longer represent the only alternative to protecting abused women and their children. ROs have a significant role to play, but their optimal use may be in conjunction with vigorous prosecution and significant sanctioning of abusers, not standing alone (see Gelb, 1994).

NOTES

1. The state's criminal record file does not distinguish complaints based on the victim, so it is not possible to determine which of the total number of assaults were

domestic in nature. Statistics for ROs are contained in *Massachusetts Trial Court Interim Annual Report 1992* (1993), and for criminal cases in *Statewide All Offense Report 1992* (1993).

2. In fewer than a dozen cases, the defendant was a female and the petitioner a male. These cases were not included in the study. In slightly more than 100 cases, the defendant was the adult child of the petitioner. These cases were also not included, nor were gay or lesbian couples cases, miscellaneous relatives, roommates, and others qualified under the state's RO, Mass. Gen. L. ch. 209A, but outside the scope of this study.

3. Although a minority (19.7%) of abusers re-abused their spouses as determined by arrest record, the majority (60% to 80%) did, according to actual interviews with their victims.

4. Most victims were probably unaware that they could extend ROs after 1 year. As a result of this study, the court now routinely sends letters to victims after 1 year, advising them that if they are still in fear, they can have an order renewed; many victims now do so as a matter of course.

5. The re-abuse rate among abusers is almost 50% over 2 years and 56% for all arrests. The recidivism rate of probationers deemed to be highest risk (26% of all probationers) is 53% after 1 year. Although the period of recidivism is shorter in the latter study, the same study reveals that 80% of those who recidivate do so within the first year.

6. For this reason, the National Council of Juvenile and Family Court Judges Model Domestic Violence Code recommends that state law make it presumptively not in the best interest of the child to have visitation from a spouse deemed to have abused the child's other parent (National Council of Juvenile and Family Court Judges, 1992).

7. The Quincy Court Domestic Violence Program, for example, won the 1992 Ford Foundation Award for Innovations in State and Local Government and was designated a model program by the National Council of Family and Juvenile Court Judges (1992).

8. Such prosecutorial programs exist in Quincy, Massachusetts, and California (National Council of Juvenile and Family Court Judges, 1992, pp. 55-71). This study found that the Quincy prosecutors were able to successfully prosecute 70% of the re-abusers, whether or not the victim testified.

REFERENCES

Commonwealth of Massachusetts. (1992). *Over 8500 domestic restraining orders filed since September in Massachusetts.* Boston: Commissioner of Probation.

Commonwealth of Massachusetts. (1993). *Restraining order registry hits 51,000 in first year of operation.* Boston: Office of the Commissioner of Probation & Executive Office of Public Safety.

Curtis, S. (1991). *Criminal enforcement of restraining orders: A study of four district courts.* Cambridge, MA: Harvard Law School.

Dunford, F. W., Huizinga, D., & Elliot, D. S. (1990). The role of arrest in domestic assault: The Omaha Police Experiment. *Criminology, 28*(2), 183-206.

Fagan, J. (1988). *Contributions of family violence research to criminal justice policy on wife assault: Paradigms of science and social control.* New York: John Jay College of Criminal Justice.

Ford, D. (1991). Prosecution as a victim power resource: A note on empowering women in violent conjugal relationships. *Law & Society Review, 1*(2), 313-334.

Gelb, A. (1994). *Quincy Court Model Domestic Abuse Program manual.* Swampscott, MA: Productions Specialties.

Harrell, A., Smith, B., & Newmark, L. (1993). *Court processing and the effectiveness of restraining orders for domestic violence victims.* Washington, DC: Urban Institute.

Hirschel, J. D., Hutchison, I. W., & Dean, C. W. (1992). The failure of arrest to deter spousal abuse. *Journal of Research in Crime and Delinquency, 29*(1), 7-34.

Hirschel, J. D., Hutchison, I. W., Dean, C. W., Kelley, J. J., & Pesackis, C. E. (1991). *Charlotte Spouse Assault Replication Project: Final report.* Washington, DC: U.S. Department of Justice, National Institute of Justice.

Klein, A. (1994). *Spousal/partner assault: A protocol for the sentencing and supervision of offenders.* Swampscott, MA: Productions Specialties.

Kramer, R. (1989). *Alcohol and victimization factors in the histories of abused women who come to court: A retrospective case-control study.* Ann Arbor, MI: UMI Dissertation Service.

Massachusetts Trial Court Interim Annual Report 1992. (1993). Boston: Commonwealth of Massachusetts.

Monahan, J. (1981). *The clinical prediction of violent behavior.* Beverly Hills, CA: Sage.

National Council of Juvenile and Family Court Judges. (1992). *Family violence: State-of-the-art programs.* Reno, NV: State Justice Institute.

Pierce, G., McDevitt, J., Pattavina, A., & Miliano, R. (1991). *The classification of male and female offenders by the Massachusetts probation system.* Boston: Northeastern University, Center for Applied Social Research.

Schechter, S. (1982). *Women and male violence.* Boston: South End.

Sherman, L., & Berk, R. (1984). The specific effects of arrest for domestic assault. *American Sociological Review, 49,* 261-272.

Sherman, L., Schmidt, J. D., & Rogan, D. P. (1992). *Policing domestic violence: Experiments and dilemmas.* New York: Free Press.

Statewide All Offense Report 1992. (1993). Boston: Commonwealth of Massachusetts, Office of the Commissioner of Probation.

12

Effects of Restraining Orders on Domestic Violence Victims

ADELE HARRELL

BARBARA E. SMITH

THE PROMISE OF
CIVIL RESTRAINING ORDERS

Our research assessed the impact of restraining orders in domestic violence cases, with a focus on the extent to which restraining orders protected women from further abuse. The study is based on a sample of temporary restraining orders issued during the first 9 months of 1991 in two jurisdictions within a single state. The state statute provided restraining orders in cases of domestic abuse for married and unmarried parties who perceived they were exposed to continued danger.

AUTHORS' NOTE: This research was conducted under a cooperative agreement from the State Justice Institute. The points of view expressed are those of the authors and do not necessarily represent the official position or policies of the State Justice Institute.

The sample is limited to cases that involved abuse committed by a male on a female that met the statutory definition of an act or threatened act of violence committed by an actor on a person with whom (a) she lived in the same domicile, (b) she had lived in the same domicile, or (c) she was involved or had been involved in an intimate relationship with the abuser. Interviews were conducted with both the female complainants and the men named in the order 3 months after the initial order. The women were interviewed a second time 1 year after the order. Additional information on these cases was provided by the following court and police records: contents of the restraining orders; records of arrests for other incidents of domestic abuse or violations of the orders; and records on charges, dates, and dispositions of civil or criminal hearings for violations or domestic abuse in the year following the temporary order.

The Sample

Interviews were completed with 355 women who filed petitions for temporary restraining orders, alleging abuse by male partners (spouses, former spouses, or boyfriends) in two jurisdictions between January and September 1991. This number represents about 50% of the petitioners in 706 consecutive filings; 43% could not be located, and 7% refused to be interviewed. Interviews were conducted with 142 men named in 779 consecutive complaints.

In the sample, over half of the women were white, one third were Hispanic, over one tenth were black, and a small percentage were Native American or of another racial background. One third were unemployed, half were employed full-time, and nearly one fifth were employed part-time. The mean number of years of education was 12 (the national average), and the women's ages ranged from 16 to 60, with an average age of 32. The majority of these women (90%) had lived with the men named in the restraining orders at some time in the past, but half were not living with them at the time of the incidents that led the women to seek temporary restraining orders. Slightly more than half of the women had been married to the men at some point in time. Of these, the majority were married to them at the time of the incidents that led to the temporary restraining orders.

The Complaints

The forms completed by the women who received temporary restraining orders indicated multiple types of abusive behaviors. These have been grouped as follows:

- *Severe violence.* Includes eight acts of serious violence: kicked, bit, or punched her; choked or strangled her; beat her up; forced sex; used a weapon on her; tried to run her down with the car; threatened to kill her; threatened her with a weapon.
- *Other violent acts.* Includes seven acts that involved physical abuse: pushed, grabbed, or shoved her; slapped or spanked her; hit her; threw something at her; harmed or took the children; harmed or took pets; harmed others she cared about.
- *Threats of violence/property damage.* Includes nine acts: threatened to harm or take the children; threatened to hit her with an object; threatened to harm or take her pets; threatened others she cared about; destroyed property; threw or smashed an object; threatened her property; drove dangerously with her in the car; took money from her.
- *Psychological abuse.* Includes eight acts: made her stay in the house; shamed her in public; kept her from going to work; harassed her at work; tracked her around town; took her money; stopped her from using the car or telephone; swore, screamed at, or insulted her.

The specific acts of abuse in written petitions for restraining orders are described in Table 12.1.

Over half of the women (56%) sustained physical injuries during the incident that led them to seek temporary restraining orders. Two thirds of the injuries were cuts and bruises; facial injuries and internal injuries were less frequent. First aid, medical attention, or hospitalization was required by 39% of the injured women. If this sample is representative of women in other courts, the majority of women who seek temporary orders have serious complaints of abuse; women are not seeking relief because of trivial annoyances imposed on them.

The incident caused over one third of the women to leave their homes shortly after the incident. Most (80%) of the 114 women who left went to the home of a family member or friend, 7% went to a shelter, and the remaining 13% went elsewhere. On average, they stayed away from their homes for 30 days.

TABLE 12.1 Acts Listed on Complaint Forms Requesting Temporary Restraining Orders Reported by Percentage of Respondents ($N = 355$)

Severe Violence	
Punched her	28%
Choked or strangled her	11%
Beat her up	7%
Forced sex	4%
Used a weapon on her	3%
Ran her down with the car	2%
Threatened to kill her	31%
Other Violent Acts	
Grabbed or pushed her	32%
Harmed or took the children	13%
Slapped her	12%
Pulled her hair	6%
Hit her with an object	3%
Threw things at her	3%
Harmed or took her pets	1%
Harmed others she cared about	1%
Threats of Violence/Property Damage	
Threatened her with bodily harm	26%
Threatened to harm or take her children	17%
Destroyed property	16%
Threatened her with a weapon	8%
Threatened to hit her	6%
Threatened to harm or take her pets	4%
Threatened others she cared about	1%
Threw or smashed an object	8%
Drove dangerously with her in the car	< 0.5%
Psychological Abuse	
Made her stay in the house	50%
Shamed her in public	31%
Threatened to remove property from her house	7%
Kept her from going to work	5%
Removed property from her house	5%
Harassed her at work	3%
Tracked her around town	2%
Took her money	1%
Stopped her from using the car or telephone	1%

TEMPORARY RESTRAINING ORDER

In both study sites, each complainant had to complete a form by describing the act perpetrated by the respondent in order to obtain a temporary restraining order. At the initial hearing, the judge determined whether sufficient cause existed to issue a temporary restraining order. If a temporary order was issued, a permanent restraining order hearing date was set for 14 to 21 days later.

Many women thought the temporary restraining order was helpful in documenting that the abuse occurred: 86% said it was "very" or "somewhat" helpful in this regard; 79% said it was "very" or "somewhat" helpful in sending her partner a message that his actions were wrong; and 62% said the order was "very" or "somewhat" helpful in punishing her partner for abusing her ($N = 355$). Also, 88% credited the judge with "doing the right thing" for her and her children ($N = 355$). Combined, these findings strongly suggest that the women saw the restraining order as worthwhile in significant ways. Fewer than half of the women, however, thought the man believed that he had to obey the order.

We found that 30% of the women said they needed something they did not receive in the temporary order. What did they want? When the 118 women who wanted changes were asked,

25% said they wanted specifics about visitation of their partner with their shared children (some wanted *no* visits but visits were allowed, others wanted only *supervised* visits, and most wanted more details on how visitation would be arranged).

19% wanted more specifics in the order, such as provisions that the man not be allowed at her place of work, her parents' home, their vacation home, and so on, and more details on the distance he was to keep from her (e.g., not allowed within one quarter mile of her home).

11% wanted the temporary restraining order enforced.

10% wanted the police/courts to treat violations more seriously.

9% wanted child custody and/or child support.

8% wanted more guidance about how to obtain a permanent order.

8% wanted a permanent order but did not receive one.

7% wanted their property returned to them that was held by their partner.

3% wanted the abuse to stop.

PERMANENT RESTRAINING ORDER

At the permanent restraining order hearing, the person who requested the order had to appear and demonstrate proof that the plaintiff had been served with the temporary order. The plaintiff did not need to appear for the case to proceed. The judge held a brief hearing to determine whether the permanent order should be issued. One jurisdiction required proof of service of the permanent order as a condition of enforcement; the other did not. Permanent orders remained in effect until and/or unless the person who requested the order requested that it be vacated.

Of the women who obtained temporary restraining orders, 40% did not return to request that the order be made permanent. The women gave the following reasons for not seeking a permanent order ($n = 142$):

Order Not Needed
   Her partner stopped bothering her, at least temporarily (64%).
   She reconciled with her partner (27%).
   The man was no longer around (moved, deported, in jail) (10%).
Other Interventions
   The man went to counseling, other court order issued (25%).
   The man was arrested (9%).
Pressure From the Man
   The man talked her out of it (35%).
   Fear of retaliation (11%).
   Her partner threatened her (6%).
   The man forced his way back into the home (4%).
Unable to Have the Temporary Order Served
   The temporary order could not be served because the man could not
      be located (41%).
Inconvenience
   It was too much trouble (10%).
   It takes too much time (9%).
   Can't take time off work (8%).
   It costs too much (5%).
Lack of Information
   Did not realize that the first order was only *temporary* (7%).
   Forgot the date of the court hearing for the restraining order (6%).

Order Not Effective
> The temporary order did not work, so why bother getting a permanent order (10%).

Although most did not return because the abuser stopped bothering them, some women experienced problems related to court access. Under the law, the permanent order hearing could not be held until—and unless—the temporary order had been served by an adult other than the complainant. Problems getting the temporary order served were reported by 41% who did not return; this finding clearly indicates an issue that should be addressed by courts hearing these complaints. Other access problems, such as lack of time or money, were reported by relatively few. One of the most serious problems, reported by one third of the women, was pressure by the abuser to drop the complaint; and some reported fear of retaliation or threats if they persisted in the complaint.

An extensive analysis of personal characteristics and variables related to how the police and the courts handled the case revealed three additional factors that were significantly related to whether the woman returned to court to obtain a permanent order:

Age of the woman. The probability that a woman would return to court increased with age. Younger women were less likely to return to court; perhaps they were more likely to expect that the abuse would stop without further intervention by the courts.

Race/ethnicity of the woman. White and Hispanic women were slightly but significantly more likely to return to court to obtain a permanent order than were other women, most of whom were black: 57% of the women who listed their race/ethnicity as black (or other) returned, compared with 60% of the white women and 62% of the Hispanic women. The willingness of Hispanic women to return suggests that language was not a barrier to returning to court. Those who returned, however, had already overcome the language barrier to obtain a temporary order. We have no data on the extent to which Hispanic women were discouraged by language barriers from obtaining a temporary order. The lower rate of return to court among black women may indicate that these women are uncomfortable in the court setting or that they are able to resolve their problems without returning or, like younger women, that they hoped the abuse would stop.

Whether the woman gave a copy of the restraining order to the police. Women who personally took a copy of the temporary order to the police were significantly more likely to return to get a permanent order. Their initiative in giving a copy to the police may have been an indication of their desire for legal protection.

Factors that were not significantly related to the decision to return for a permanent order included the woman's education, employment status, presence of children in the home, whether she was living with the man at the time of the incident, length of her relationship with the man, duration of abuse in the relationship, and severity of the incident described in the complaint.

When a hearing for a permanent order was held, most men interviewed (85%) said they attended ($n = 142$). When men attended the hearings, their resistance was strong. According to the women, over three quarters of the men who attended the hearings denied the abuse or tried to persuade the judge not to issue the order. Although most of these men did not contest specific conditions contained in the orders, the most controversial conditions were giving "care and control" of the children to the woman (opposed by one in five) and the child visitation arrangements (opposed by over one third). One in ten attempted to gain control of the home.

VIOLATIONS OF RESTRAINING ORDERS

The majority of the men and women reported contact following a restraining order, with contacts with the other party during the first 3 months after a temporary order reported by 77% of the women ($n = 300$) and 71% of the men ($n = 142$). Having a permanent restraining order did not reduce the probability of a contact: 75% of the women with permanent orders reported some contact with the men named in the orders during the first year ($n = 300$). This was not significantly lower than the 80% of the women *without* permanent orders who reported some contact with the men during the year ($n = 300$).

In some cases, the contacts reflected reunion or reconciliation. During the first 3 months, 15% of the women said the men had moved back in, and 13% reported reconciliation (these categories were not mutually inclusive). For these women, postorder contacts were assumed to be of their own choosing. For the remainder, the postorder interaction may not have been voluntary. Although a similar proportion of men said they had moved back in (18%), they were twice as likely to say they had reconciled with their partners (28%, compared with 13%).

Unwanted contacts in the first 3 months after the first order were reported by over half of all the women who obtained temporary orders. These contacts involved unwanted telephone calls (reported by 52%); tracking or stalking (21%); and visits to the home (21%). Some of these violations occurred repeatedly. For example, when men came to the home between the time of the temporary and permanent orders ($n = 51$), over 80% came more than one time: 35% said it happened two to five times, 43% said it occurred five or more times, and 4% said they moved back in, compared with the 18% who said it happened once. Even after the permanent orders were issued, most men who came to their woman's home in violation of the order ($n = 42$) did so frequently: 25% came two to five times, and nearly half came five or more times, whereas 2% moved back in.

A similar pattern of unwanted contacts occurred during months 4 to 12. The most frequent type of contact was unwanted telephone calls, although this occurred at nearly half the rate as in the first 3 months. Stalking occurred at the same rate as in the earlier period, and coming to the home still occurred, but with somewhat less frequency.

PROBLEMS RELATED TO CHILDREN

One of the most important decisions a judge can make in issuing a restraining order involves care of the children. In our study, 92% ($n = 168$) of the cases in which the woman shared children in common with the man named in the order gave care and control of those children to the woman. In a few cases (3%), custody was being determined by another court. Only a small number of temporary orders (5%) made no provision for the minor children listed on the complaint form.

After care and control are decided, the next most important decision by the judge is whether the man may visit his children. In our conversations with judges, this was a particularly troubling issue for them (in fact, most judges said it was the *single* most troubling issue they had to grapple with). On the one hand, the judges wanted the children to be safe, but on the other hand, they did not want to wrongly deny the man access to his children (or the children access to him). Most judges said they err on the conservative side in issuing the temporary order, reasoning that a denial of visitation for a 2- to 3-week period would not unduly harm the man (or the children) and would help ensure the safety of the children. Their reasoning reverses, however, when considering visitation rights at the time of the permanent hearing. Most judges explained that they were extremely reluctant to deny the man visitation with his children for 120 days[1] without substantial proof that he would harm the children. Hence, the judges told us they often allow visitation in the permanent order, preferring to leave long-term custody and visitation considerations for the family court to decide. What the judges told us was borne out in our data. Visitation by the man named in the order with his children was allowed in only 5% ($n = 168$) of the temporary restraining orders, but such visitation was allowed in 61% of permanent orders in our sample ($n = 88$).

ABUSE DURING THE YEAR
AFTER A RESTRAINING ORDER

We asked about specific acts of abuse during the first 3 months and during months 4 through 12 ("since the last interview"): 60% of the women interviewed twice ($n = 300$) reported acts of abuse by the man named in the temporary restraining order. These acts were grouped into the four categories of abuse described earlier: severe violence, other violent acts, threats of violence/property damage, and psychological abuse.

Figure 12.1 illustrates the acts of severe violence reported by women. The bars show the percentage of women who reported each abusive act at any time. The divisions within the bars describe the percentage reporting this type of act: (a) during the first 3 months after the order, (b) during the 4 to 12 months after the first order, and (c) during both time periods. Threats to kill were reported by more than one fifth of the women. These threats did not appear to subside over time: 7% reported death threats only during the first 3

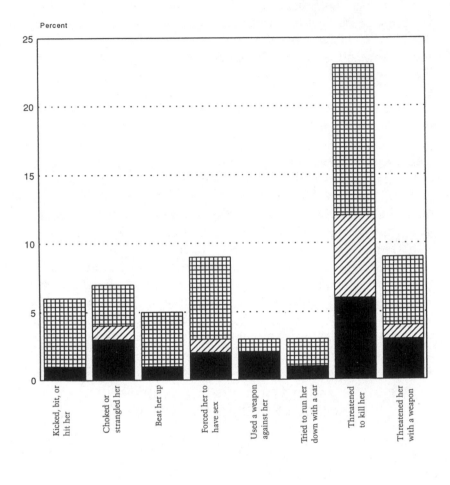

Percent

Figure 12.1. Extent of Severe Violence Reported by Women During the Year After a Temporary Restraining Order

months, whereas more than twice that number reported death threats that continued beyond 3 months or first began after 3 months. Other acts of severe violence—kicking, strangling, beating, forcing sex, and threatening with weapons—were reported by 5% to 9% of the women. Cumulatively, these acts of severe violence affected 29% of the women who got restraining orders.

The prevalence of other acts of violence is illustrated in Figure 12.2. Nearly one quarter (24%) of the women reported at least one of the violent acts in this category in the year following the initial order. One fifth were grabbed, pushed, or shoved by the man, and over one tenth said the man hit or tried to hit her. With the exception of harm to pets, these violent acts were as likely to first occur more than 3 months after the order; this finding indicates the persistent nature of abuse.

Threats of violence and acts of property damage meant to threaten or intimidate were reported by 43% of the women, most of whom reported more than one type of threat. The range of threats was diverse and undoubtedly included threats not listed in this scale. As Figure 12.3 shows, threats of harm to someone important to the woman (other than her children) were reported by 25% of all the women who received restraining orders. Threats to harm the children or pets occurred in fewer cases (under 10% and under 5%, respectively). Threatening to hit her, throw or smash things, threatening to damage her property, and actually damaging her property were all reported by more than 15% of the women and represented very aggressive efforts to frighten and control the women.

Psychological abuse was by far the most prevalent type of abuse in the year after a restraining order. More than half of the women (57%) reported one of the behaviors shown in Figure 12.4. A serious problem, now being addressed in new stalking legislation in some states, is that over 15% of all the women interviewed said the man followed or tracked her around town. This type of behavior suggested a potentially dangerous obsession with the woman's whereabouts. Aggressive acts to control her behavior were reported by more than 10% of the women and included making her stay in the home, harassing her at work, and keeping her from using the car or the telephone. The most frequent complaints reflected continuing conflict in the relationship. Over 40% reported said the man had sworn at, screamed at, or insulted them; 35% had been humiliated or shamed in front of others.

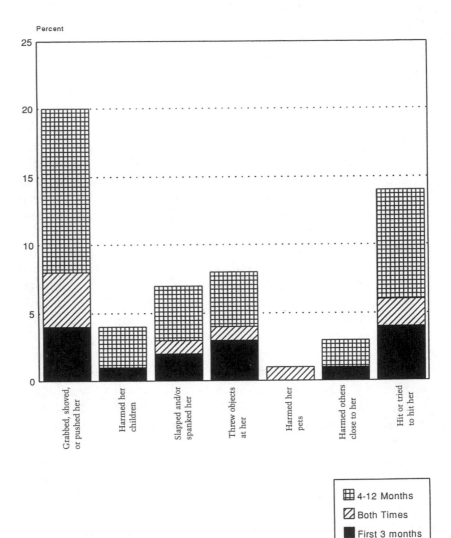

Figure 12.2. Extent of Other Violent Acts Reported by Women During the Year After a Temporary Restraining Order

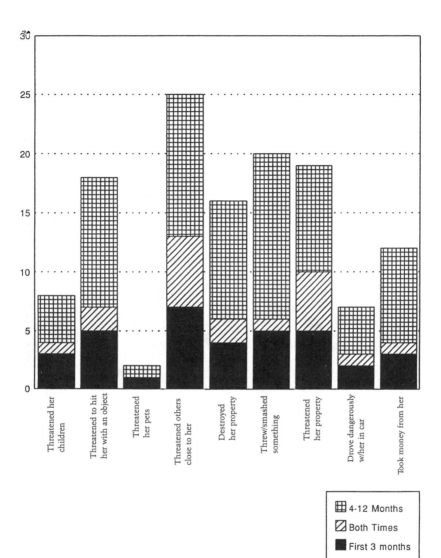

Figure 12.3. Extent of Threats of Violence/Property Damage Reported by Women During the Year After a Temporary Restraining Order

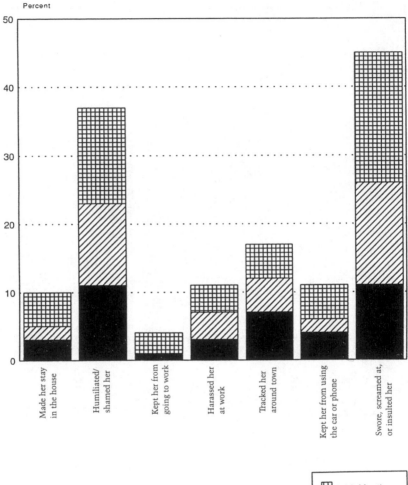

Figure 12.4. Extent of Psychological Abuse Reported by Women During the Year After a Temporary Restraining Order

IMPACT OF THE
PERMANENT ORDER

Having a permanent order did not appear to deter most types of abuse. Statistical tests showed no significant differences in the three most serious types of abuse—severe violence, other forms of physical violence, and threats or property damage—between the 212 women who had a permanent restraining order and the 143 women who did not have a permanent order. The existence of a permanent order did significantly reduce the likelihood of acts of psychological abuse. The women with permanent orders were just over half as likely to experience psychological abuse (odds ratio = .57, $p < .05$).

PREDICTORS OF
CONTINUED ABUSE

We examined several other factors that might be related to whether abuse occurred during the year following the first order. These included the severity of the incident that led to court and the history of abuse by the man; the personal characteristics of the woman and the man and their relationship; and the response of the justice system. Logistic regression was used to examine the likelihood of each type of abuse as a function of these factors. The models controlled for the level of that type of abuse during the year before the incident that led to court[2] to isolate those factors that independently affected compliance and the risk of continued abuse.

Severity of the Incident That Led to Court

We investigated the possibility that cases with more severe incidents described in the complaint forms would be more likely to have abuse continue after the order. Descriptions of the pattern of violence in battering relationships indicate that the frequency and severity of abuse often escalate over time; this suggests that the severity of the incident that led to court would predict the risk of continued abuse following the order. This did not prove to be the case.

Severity of the incident described in the complaint did not predict any abusive incidents or specific types of abuse—severe violence, other violent acts, threats of violence or property damage, or psychological abuse. Possibly, the incidents reported to the court represent merely "the straw that broke the camel's back" and occur at the point at which the women decide to seek protection, regardless of the severity of what happened.

History of Abuse

Patterns of violence and abuse did appear to recur when measured by the history of abuse during the year before the restraining order. The women seeking restraining orders had endured considerable abuse in the year before the temporary orders were issued. When asked whether they had experienced any of 31 different abusive acts by the men named in the restraining orders in the year *before* the temporary restraining orders had been issued, most women reported multiple types of abuse. Of the 31 abusive acts, 26 were reported by more than one fifth of the women, including very serious abuse such as strangling, forced sex, and beatings.

The most frequently abusive acts, experienced by more than half of those seeking relief, included reports that the man

swore, screamed at, or insulted her
pushed, grabbed, or shoved her
humiliated or shamed her
threatened to throw something at her
kept her from using the car or telephone
threatened to assault her
destroyed her property
threatened to destroy her property
bothered her while she was at her place of employment
restrained her from leaving the home

Between 20% and 50% of the women said the man named in the order had (in descending order of frequency)

attempted to hit her with some object
threatened to kill her
slapped or spanked her
kicked, bitten, or punched her
tracked her
taken money from her

thrown an object at her
forced sex
drove recklessly with her in the car
beat her up
threatened to harm others
choked or strangled her
threatened her with a weapon
threatened to harm her pets
harmed her pets
threatened to harm her children
restrained her from going to her job

Less common were harming her children, use of a weapon on the woman, harm imposed on others whom the woman cared about, and an attempt to run her down with an automobile.

The average number of abusive behaviors inflicted on the women in the year prior to the temporary restraining orders was 12.74 (out of a maximum of 31 behaviors; $N = 355$). Alternatively phrased, the average complainant had experienced *one out of every three* abusive acts included on this list (which is not by any means all-inclusive). In this sample, the duration of abuse (averaging verbal and physical abuse) ranged from a single incident to 31 years, with a median of 2.4 years. These statistics reveal that these women have had a very burdensome history of abuse with their partners and suggest that formal intervention through a petition to the court for relief is used, not as a form of early intervention, but rather as a signal of desperation following extensive problems.

The frequency of exposure of children to domestic violence is disturbing. According to the women, children under age 18 were in the home during the incident that led to court in 70% of all cases and were believed to have seen or heard the incident in almost half (47%) of the cases ($n = 300$).

The severity of prior abuse was significantly related to the severity of abuse in the year after a restraining order. Severe violence in the year before the order predicted severe violence in the year after the order ($p < .001$), and other violent behaviors in the prior year predicted other violent behaviors in the year after the order ($p < .01$). The same was true for threats of violence and property damage ($p < .05$) and psychological abuse ($p < .01$). The duration of abuse in the relationship, however, was not significantly related to the probability of any abuse or specific types of abuse following a restraining order.

The persistence in the pattern of violence, unlike the severity of the incident described in the complaint, was a predictor of risk of abuse following court action. This finding supported our interpretation that the incident that led a woman to seek a restraining order simply represented the point at which she decided to seek help and did not measure the general level of violence in the relationship. It also pointed to the utility of screening clients for a history of severe violence to assess for potential lethality and to work with women involved in the more serious types of abuse to develop safety plans. The fact that the risk of continued abuse was not related the duration of the abuse in the relationship indicates either variability in the point at which women are likely to request relief from the courts and/or variability in the time over which patterns of abuse recur and escalate.

Case Characteristics

Certain characteristics of the cases appearing in court were related to the probability of continued abuse. As noted earlier, most men attended the permanent order hearing, and many voiced their objections, either to the evidence of abuse presented by their partners or to proposed terms of the orders. Their resistance to the orders at the time of the hearings was measured on a scale of 0 to 5, based on the number of the following things he did: denied the abuse, tried to get the judge not to issue the order, tried to get care and control of the children, objected to the visitation arrangements, and tried to get the judge to let him stay in the home. The level of resistance at the time of the order significantly increased the probability of severe violence (odds ratio = 3.57, $p < .05$), threats and property damage (odds ratio = 2.87, $p < .10$), and psychological abuse (odds ratio = 4.12, $p < .01$). Although objection to the order is an important legal right and should not be limited in any way, it is important to note that strenuous objections voiced by the men should be treated seriously as a warning that abuse may continue. Efforts to address this risk could include firm and specific statements by the judge about the behavioral requirements of the order and the consequences of noncompliance. In addition, strenuous objections may indicate to women and their advocates the need for safety planning to minimize future exposure to risk.

Women who lived with the men at the time of the incidents that led to court were significantly less likely to experience any type of abuse after the order. Their risk of any abuse was about 60% of that of women who did not live with the men (odds ratio = .61, $p < .05$). Similar risk levels were observed for each type of abuse even after controlling for the level of this type of abuse in the year before the incident. This finding was consistent with reports that the period following a separation is particularly dangerous for abused women and underscores the danger of escalating violence in these cases.

Compared to women without children, women with children were 70% more likely to experience violent acts (odds ratio = 1.7, $p < .10$) and 50% more likely to experience threats or property damage (odds ratio = 1.5, $p < .10$), although overall their chances of any abusive act were not significantly higher. This might be reflected in the fact that these types of abuse occurred around visitation and might be indicative of a need for supervised visitation in some cases.

Content of the Order

Judges used the standard restraining order forms in the large majority of cases for both temporary and permanent orders. As a result, the inclusion of specifics, limited to a small number of cases, was not related to the probability of abuse in the next year. Similarly, the orders generally included specific instructions regarding child care and control and visitation. Thus, the exclusion of these conditions was relatively uncommon and not related to the probability of abuse. One indication of the need for additional specificity in orders, however, was provided by the women who said the orders did not contain all the provisions they wanted. Women who said they needed more in the orders were significantly more likely to report severe violence (odds ratio = 1.7, $p < .10$) and psychological abuse (odds ratio = 1.7, $p < .10$) than women who did not want additional conditions in the orders.

Personal Characteristics

Most personal characteristics did not affect the probability of renewed abuse after an order was issued. The woman's age, employment status (full-time, part-time, or not employed), and whether the man provided any financial support for her or her children after the order were not significantly related to any type of postorder abuse.

ENFORCEMENT

The response of the police and the courts to restraining order violations is crucial to their effectiveness. The police responded to the incident that led the woman to seek a temporary restraining order in 60% of the cases ($N = 212$). If the police arrested the man at the time of the incident that led to court, the likelihood of any severe violence during the next year was diminished. The odds of severe violence in cases in which an arrest had been made were less than half that of cases in which no arrest had been made, controlling for the level of severe violence in the prior year (odds ratio = .45, $p < .001$). The probability of other types of abusive acts was not reduced, however. This finding indicates that although men named in restraining orders continue their abuse, they are less likely to commit acts of serious violence when an arrest has been made. The implication is that aggressive arrest policies reduced the severity of future abuse, but not the likelihood that abuse would be reported.

The helpfulness of police intervention at the time of the initial incident, rated by the women as very helpful, somewhat helpful, and not helpful at all, was significantly related to reduced probability of severe violence following the restraining order (odds ratio = .60, $p < .05$). Again, this finding points to how important good police response can be in preventing violations to the orders.

During the first 3 months following their restraining order, 15% of the women called the police because the men bothered/assaulted them while the orders (temporary or permanent) were in effect. Many of these cases involved multiple problems, with an average of 2.7 police calls per case. The police had responded at least once to calls from half of the women, for a total of 147 responses to violations during this period.[3]

TABLE 12.2 Justice Agency Involvement in Abuse During the First 3 Months After Order (*N* = 355)

	Abuse Happened (%)	Police Responded (%)	Court Hearing (%)
Severe Violence			
Kicked, bit, or hit her with fist	1	*	0
Choked or strangled her	4	2	*
Beat her up	1	1	0
Forced sex	3	1	0
Used a weapon on her	2	1	0
Tried to run her down with the car	1	*	0
Threatened to kill	11	6	1
Other Violent Acts			
Grabbed, shoved, or pushed her	8	4	0
Harmed her children	0	0	0
Slapped or spanked her	2	1	0
Threw something at her	4	1	0
Harmed her pets	0	0	0
Harmed others she cared about	1	1	0
Hit or tried to hit her	6	3	0
Threats of Violence/Property Damage			
Threatened to harm her children	4	3	1
Threatened her with a weapon	4	3	*
Threatened to hit her with something	1	3	1
Threatened to harm her pets	0	0	0
Threatened to harm others she cared about	12	4	1
Destroyed property	5	3	1
Threw or smashed something	6	3	*
Threatened to ruin property	10	4	1
Psychological Abuse			
Made her stay in the house	5	1	0
Humiliated/shamed her	23	7	1
Kept her from going to work	1	1	0
Harassed her at work	11	4	*
Tracked her around town	12	5	0
Stopped her from using the car or telephone	5	2	*
Drove dangerously with her in the car	3	*	0
Took money from her	4	1	0
Swore at, screamed at, insulted her	25	7	2

NOTE: * = Less than 0.5%.

Table 12.2 presents descriptions of official handling of abuse that occurred during the first 3 months after the order. The first column shows the percentage of women to whom each type of abuse occurred. The second column shows the percentage of women who said the police responded at least once. The last column indicates the percentage of women who said the abuse resulted in a court hearing.

The incidents to which the police responded most frequently involved threats to kill, stalking, and/or acts of psychological abuse—swearing at her or humiliating her (more than one type of act occurred during most incidents).

Between the first and second interviews, 155 women reported further problems with the men named in the restraining orders. Just under half (46%) of these women called the police. Although women with permanent orders were not significantly more likely to ever call the police than women who had received only temporary orders (48% vs. 43%), those with permanent orders averaged 2.2 calls to the police (after excluding two cases that had more than 15 calls each), compared with 1.35 calls for women who did not have permanent orders.

Why did some women whose partners violated the orders elect not to call the police? Over 60% of these women ($N = 77$) were able to get the men to stop bothering them and did not think it was necessary to call the police. One quarter, however, were too afraid to call the police. Others were dissatisfied with the police protection they received, particularly those who had permanent orders. Of the 45 women with permanent orders who chose not to call the police for a violation, 30% said that calling the police would not do any good, and 24% cited lack of police response to prior violations. Women without permanent orders were more likely than those with permanent orders to abstain from calling the police because they thought they had insufficient evidence (47%, compared with 29%).

Although women with permanent orders may have been experiencing more problems with their abusers than those without permanent orders, it is also clear that they believed the order entitled them to police intervention and were more vocal in their disapproval of police responses. Satisfaction with the police response declined significantly from the first interview 3 months after the initial orders and the second interview 1 year after the orders. The percentage of women involved in postorder incidents to which the police responded who rated the police as "not at all helpful" increased from 25% at 3 months to 38% at the end of the year.

Only 14 women returned to civil court for violations at any time during the first year. Of the women reporting violations while orders were in place who gave reasons for not returning to court ($N = 133$), 47% were satisfied with the enforcement and nearly half were able to get their abusers to stop without returning to court. One fifth, however, were afraid to return to court, and one fifth thought going to court would not help.

SUMMARY AND DISCUSSION

Five conclusions and their implications for improving the response of courts and law enforcement to women issued orders of protection stand out.

1. The majority of women who received civil orders of protection presented to the court a profile of serious abuse by their partners.

By any measure, the majority of women requesting restraining orders who appeared in court had complaints of serious abuse; 40% of the women suffered physical injury during the incident that led to court. The most frequently reported violent acts included punching, kicking, or hitting (28%); grabbing, pushing, or shoving (32%); choking or strangling (11%); and slapping (12%). Many women were subject to extremely terrifying threats, such as threats to kill (31%); threats of bodily harm (26%); threats to take or harm the children (17%); and destruction of property (16%).

In many cases, the incident that led to court was the culmination of an extensive pattern of abuse. The average number of different acts of abuse these women experienced in the year before the orders was 13 (out of 31 acts listed). Overall, 77% of the petitioners reported at least one act of severe violence, 87% reported a less serious violent act, 89% reported threats or property damage, and 96% reported other psychologically abusive acts of manipulation or intimidation—all of which occurred prior to the incident that led to court. Also, 70% of the women said children had been in the home during at least one incident, and nearly half (47%) said children had witnessed abuse during the prior year.

Pattern of abuse has several implications for the courts. First, it is important to recognize the severity of the danger facing many of these women and to acknowledge the fact that restraining orders were not being used frivolously to gain advantages in other court actions. For judges to make thoughtful decisions about granting an order *and* the conditions in an order, they should be aware of the history of violence between the parties, the presence of children during the violence, and the full extent of the injuries sustained during the incident that led the woman to seek an order of protection. Considerable time and attention are warranted in cases fraught with physical abuse and injury.

2. The process of obtaining a temporary order of protection was easier in many respects for the women in our sample than was the process of obtaining a permanent order. Confusion about the content of both orders was evident from our research.

Receiving a permanent order proved difficult for many women for a variety of reasons. We found that 40% of those who obtained temporary orders did not return for permanent orders. The most frequently cited reason was that the men stopped bothering them (at least temporarily). Other reasons were of much greater concern for the courts. Over 40% of the women said the reason they did not return for permanent orders was because they were unable to get the temporary orders served on their partners. Few women seemed to understand that they could return to court and apply for an extension to get the temporary order served. Judges could take a leadership role in working with other agencies to help women get their temporary orders served. For example, they could educate sheriffs on the problems women have in serving the orders and encourage them to assist women who cannot find their partners to serve the papers. Sheriffs might be persuaded to make several attempts to locate the men and to be more resourceful in their tracking procedures. Judges might also work with the probation department to find men who cannot be served; many of these men might be on probation for the incidents that led to the orders (or for another offense), and probation departments might have records on their whereabouts.

Over one third of the women reported that pressure from the men or fear of retaliation caused them to drop the petition. This finding suggests that temporary orders should include explicit directions that coercion of the woman to drop the order is prohibited. Judges might spend time in the hearing reviewing steps the woman can take if she is being pressured by the man.

From our research, we conclude that judges took both the temporary and permanent order hearings seriously and acted in a way consistent with the women's requests. Judges generally relied on standard forms with standard conditions, however, and did not personalize the conditions of the orders. This lack caused confusion about the content of the orders and left orders that spelled out few specifics. Indeed, 30% of the women said there was something they needed but did not receive in their orders. Nearly a quarter of these women wanted specifics about visitation by their partners with their shared children. One fifth wanted more specifics in the orders, such as provisions that the man not be allowed at her place of work or her parents' home, and more detail on the distance he was to keep from her.

Over four fifths of the men claimed they obeyed all of the conditions of the temporary orders, yet nearly one fifth of the men said they tried to talk their partners out of obtaining permanent orders. If the temporary orders contain a clause stating there is to be no contact between the parties, how can they claim they obeyed the order yet report that they contacted their partners to "work things out"? Certainly, some men may simply have misrepresented the truth when they reported they obeyed all conditions of the orders. But from extraneous comments made to us during interviews with the men (and the women), it appears that some parties did not understand the *no-contact* clause and instead believed it meant the man should *not bother* the woman. Judges could do much to clarify this issue by explaining the conditions to the woman and handwriting conditions for the men so that they are not buried in standard clauses.

3. Calls to the police because of violations of restraining orders were high, but arrest was rare despite the law making violations a criminal offense. Use of courts to hear violations was low.

Many women called the police because their partners violated the restraining orders. There were 290 separate calls to which the police responded for the 355 women in our sample. According to law, the police are supposed to make an arrest if the man named in a restraining order is present when they arrive or if there is probable cause. In the 290 incidents reported to the police, only 59 arrests were made (20%). This number seems low in the light of the fact that women said the men remained at the scene in many incidents, the severity of the violations, and the fact that any violation was a criminal offense after June 1991. Law enforcement and the courts should reexamine the appropriateness of police response to violations and institute training and monitoring of enforcement of orders.

Very few women in our sample went back to court to seek a violation hearing. The number of calls to the police and their reports of violations during our interviews suggest a substantial underuse of the courts. Reasons included fear of retaliation by the man, believing that it would not help, and believing that the abuse would cease without court intervention. These are factors over which the court has little control. One reason why some women did not go back to court, however, was that they did not realize they could return to court. Judges could help by emphasizing during the temporary and permanent hearings that women can—and should—return to court to report violations.

4. Sixty percent of the women who received temporary orders of protection stated that their partners violated the order in the year following the order.

One year after the temporary order was issued, 60% of the women we interviewed told us their partners had violated the orders, a finding indicating that the orders or the contact with police and the courts may have deterred about 40% of the men. Permanent orders did not appear to increase the deterrence provided by the temporary orders. Women who had permanent orders were as likely as those without to report continued abuse. If these women were at greater risk than those without permanent orders, however, more of them might have been abused in the absence of the orders.

Although severity of the incident that led to court did not predict the risk of a violation, history of abuse in the prior year did. More serious prior abuse predicted more serious violations. This finding suggests that lethality assessments by advocates working with the courts at the time the first order is requested could provide a basis for assisting women at greatest risk and for identifying for the court those cases that need additional attention or specificity in the orders. A second powerful indicator was the man's resistance to the order during the hearing. The men who voiced objections to the orders were three to four times as likely to violate the order—with the risk increasing with the number of objections. This finding can serve as a cue to judges of which cases may pose continuing problems.

Women with children were also more likely to experience continued problems with the men. Violence and threats around visitation may be reduced by use of supervised visitation options in which neutral third parties agree to serve as intermediaries in the exchange; these have been developed in many jurisdictions. In supervised visitation programs, which may be operated by churches or other community groups, the party with the children delivers them and leaves prior to the time the other party is to pick them up.

5. Training and further research are needed to assist the courts in responding effectively to requests for restraining orders.

The complexities of these cases—and the serious level of violence associated with them—demand thoughtful consideration and continued training:

- Both parties in these cases need to be educated about what the order prescribes and proscribes, and women need to understand how violations can be reported to the court.
- Judges should be aware of these issues when hearing these cases. They could greatly benefit from training on the dynamics of domestic violence, the effects of civil orders of protection, and the types of conditions courts may impose in these cases.
- Law enforcement personnel, as well as judges, have training needs. The history of abuse commonly associated with these cases should be stressed to officers. Also, the frequency with which violations are reported—and the correct response of the police to violations—needs

consideration at law enforcement training sessions. Given the low number of arrests in cases in which women called the police in our sample, law enforcement policymakers need to reexamine arrest policies when violations of orders are reported.

Our findings also point to some new areas of inquiry. The hypothesis that the content of orders is critical and may be related to future violations received support from the study but could not be directly tested because specific conditions were so rarely included in the orders. Many women reported that the orders did not contain specific conditions they needed, especially in the area of child care and visitation. Others wanted more specifics on the distance their partners were to keep from them. Many men seem to think that contacting their partners to "work things out" did not violate no-contact orders. Handwritten details on the orders might help in this regard. A study of the impact of specifically tailored orders is an important area for further research.

The findings also indicated the need for additional research on the long-term impact on children who witness violence inflicted on their mothers and study of the correlation between spouse abuse and child abuse. Many women (43%) reported that their children witnessed the incidents that led them to seek restraining orders. Nearly 1 in 20 noted that their partners had actually harmed their children in the year prior to the orders. To what extent do men abuse both their intimate partners and their children? What is the level of violence? Who are most likely to commit this type of dual abuse?

NOTES

1. Child visitation conditions are only in effect for 120 days in the permanent order.

2. The general model specified the probability of abuse as the log of the odds of each independent variable and the level of abuse the prior year.

3. A review of official records generally confirmed the women's reports about the number of incidents to which police responded and the number of cases returning to court for violations.

13

Future Directions for Criminal Justice Policy on Domestic Violence

DAVID A. FORD

RUTH REICHARD

STEPHEN GOLDSMITH

MARY JEAN REGOLI

One can project the future course of criminal justice policy toward domestic violence[1] cases by examining the historical trends of the past three centuries. Many policies foreseen for the next century are already in place in jurisdictions around the United States, Canada, and elsewhere. Others will emerge with the growing awareness of violence as a problem to be addressed through law enforcement in concert with preventive, rehabilitative, and victim-assistance initiatives. The coordination of criminal justice and social service interventions is the guiding principle shaping policy for the year 2000 and beyond.

We first briefly trace the historical events most relevant to future policies. Then, we discuss the current state of criminal justice and domestic violence, especially as influenced by recent research

243

findings. In the remainder of the chapter, we sketch our thoughts on policies likely to be implemented by increasing numbers of police departments, prosecutors, criminal courts, and corrections agencies.

HISTORY

The U.S. criminal justice system's response to wife battering has shifted during the past 200 years from a victim-initiated system of dispute resolution to a formal, state-sponsored system dominated by police and prosecutors intervening on behalf of victim-witnesses. The change parallels a shift in society's stance toward women, morality, and violence. Three periods in U.S. history mark significant efforts to reform legal policies toward domestic violence.[2]

In the mid-17th century, the Massachusetts Bay and Plymouth colonies enacted laws prohibiting wife beating so as to preserve the peace and to uphold the sanctity of the family. There were no formal roles for police and prosecutors as we currently know them. Enforcement rested with community surveillance and complaints adjudicated by either church courts or secular magistrates. Few cases were prosecuted under colonial laws, and as the 17th century came to an end, state interest in family disharmony waned (Pleck, 1987).

Some 200 years later, the state's interest in violence against women rekindled with the growth of the 19th-century's women's rights movement. Although few states passed laws to protect women from violent husbands, the expanded domains of state prosecutors and police enabled the state to bring more men to justice. The efforts resulted in limited policy reforms.[3] But the combination of public attention, emerging feminist ideology, and attempted reforms contributed to a new level of awareness that, like the equal rights movement of the era, nurtured the dramatic changes of the 20th century.

Violence against women was rediscovered as a significant social concern in the 1970s. The role of the criminal justice system with respect to domestic violence shifted from maintaining social order and a family ideal to explicit protection for victims, with the recognition of women as entitled to legal redress despite traditional male dominance of American social institutions. During the past two decades, the criminal justice interest has focused on preventing repetitive violence, initially through a rehabilitative orientation and, more recently, through a control perspective. Wife battery has come to be recognized as a criminal offense deserving of prosecutorial and judicial attention.[4]

TODAY

Recent policy changes bearing on domestic violence have been guided, in part, by research demonstrating the effectiveness of criminal justice practices in preventing continuing violence by a man against his conjugal partner. The most influential of such research projects was the Minneapolis Domestic Violence Experiment (Sherman & Berk, 1984), funded by the National Institute of Justice (NIJ). The researchers found that when police arrested a suspected wife batterer, he was less likely than others to again batter the same partner within 6 months. This finding crowned advocacy for a more vigorous law enforcement reaction to wife battering,[5] and it reinforced two political movements calling for a punitive stance toward criminals. The "law and order" movement pushed for harsh sanctioning to control criminals in general. The feminist movement called for sanctioning wife battery to affirm its seriousness as a criminal offense.[6] Notwithstanding its limitations (e.g., see Binder & Meeker, 1988), the Minneapolis experiment's results instigated legislation and policy reforms throughout the United States and thus made arrest a preferred and, in some jurisdictions, mandated, police response to alleged wife battery (Sherman & Cohn, 1989).

Nonetheless, arrest is not universally effective. NIJ funded additional research projects, known collectively as SARP (Spouse Abuse Replication Program) experiments, designed to test the impact of warrantless arrests elsewhere. In Omaha, Dunford, Huizinga, and Elliott (1989) replicated the Minneapolis experiment and found no support for arrest as a uniquely effective intervention. Similarly, experiments in Charlotte (Hirschel, Hutchison, & Dean, 1992), Milwaukee (Sherman et al., 1992), and Colorado Springs (Berk, Campbell, Klap, & Western, 1992) found no significant reduction in the prevalence of new violence following on-scene arrest of offenders. Only in Dade County (Pate & Hamilton, 1992) did arrest have a significant deterrent impact, but only when measured by victim interview data, as opposed to official records.

Regardless of other limitations, an on-scene warrantless arrest cannot be effected if a suspect flees prior to police contact, as may occur in the majority of police runs on domestics. The Omaha study addressed this in an "offender absent" experiment (Dunford, 1990). When Omaha police officers initiated warrants for the arrest of suspected batterers, those arrested were significantly less likely to repeat their violence against the same victims over the next 12 months.

That any sort of police intervention, by itself, can deter violence is remarkable. But we usually expect judicial outcomes to prevent continuing crime. Prosecution can result in both punitive and rehabilitative sanctions specifically meant to reduce the chance of continuing violence. The Indianapolis Domestic Violence Prosecution Experiment found no evidence to suggest that rehabilitative outcomes are any more effective than other adjudicated outcomes in preventing repeat violence, regardless of whether a man was arrested by the police or identified by a victim-initiated complaint to the prosecutor's office (Ford, 1993; Ford & Regoli, 1992). In victim-complaint cases, however, if a victim is simply told that if she wants, she may have charges dropped following a suspect's arrest on a warrant, that man is significantly less likely to again batter the woman within 6 months of case settlement (Ford, 1993; Ford & Regoli, 1993).

CHANGING ATTITUDES TOWARD
WIFE BATTERING AND CRIMINAL JUSTICE

We do not foresee any weakening of the current trend toward recognizing wife battering as a criminal offense to be treated at least as vigorously as violence against others. Indeed, the 1994 Violence Against Women Act (VAWA) has stimulated considerable activity addressing domestic violence against women, including training and technical assistance, community-based interventions, and research.[7] Underlying the legal and policy changes are changes in social norms and values, reflected in the attitudes of criminal justice personnel, that will give certainty to a vigorous criminal justice response in the future. During the 1980s, several significant normative changes began to influence prosecutorial responses to domestic violence. In the future, the widespread acceptance of these changes will result in continuing progressive policy developments.

First, police officers, prosecutors, judges, and legislators have begun to discard gender stereotypes relating to domestic violence and are coming to recognize the rights of a woman in her home.[8] Greater numbers of women in criminal justice agencies and legislatures have accelerated this change. Second, there is a growing awareness that all domestic violence, even acts that do not leave the victim bloodied, is harmful because it subjugates women and instills in children a sense that violence is normal in conjugal relationships.

Third, and probably the least recognized of the normative changes, traditionally intransigent agencies are no longer reluctant to intervene in the family. In fact, this attitude has changed so much that the current new concern is over how multiple interventions, for various reasons, can be coordinated and controlled. Also, a strong base of applied research, begun with the recommendations of the Attorney General's Task Force on Family Violence and reinvigorated with the VAWA, will continue to cause thoughtful consideration of policy impacts.

Finally, more than in almost any other criminal justice area, officials have considerable information available on the scope, effectiveness, and potential for addressing a broad range of associated problems through domestic violence policy, as contrasted with the more simplistic view of prosecution as a simple case management response to police initiatives. In particular, limitations of prison capacity remove incapacitation as an easy answer and thus force more thoughtful intermediate sanctioning—this with the apparent possibility that results can be accomplished for many offenders and their victims even without significant incapacitation.

The simultaneous development of aggressive victim assistance units and individual advocates against domestic violence has accelerated. Currently, victims and their advocates are forcing criminal justice officials to pay attention to the problem and to possible solutions. Advocates will continue to use litigation on behalf of victimized women to compel changes in criminal justice policies. With society continuing to express its disapproval of wife battery, advocacy groups and victim's rights spokespersons will force attention to domestic violence in efforts to reform criminal justice interventions.

One problem with this generally optimistic picture of criminal justice concern for domestic violence is a conflict between the goal of protecting individual victims seeking help and the state's interest in sanctioning domestic violence as a crime against the state whereby the victim is treated as a mere witness, but one whose security could be compromised by aggressive state actions. For example, in some jurisdictions, police are mandated to arrest a suspected batterer if they find probable cause that a crime has been committed. Some officers elect to ignore a victim's right to defend herself and take injury to the perpetrator as evidence of "mutual combat" and arrest the victim as well as the criminal batterer. Another example occurs with prosecution. Some prosecutors adhere to a strict "no drop" policy to ensure that batterers are impressed by the state's resolve to prosecute, even when doing so may put the victim at greater risk (Ford, 1991, 1993; Ford & Regoli, 1993). Future reforms in policy will have to confront the potential harm of what seems appropriate in response to domestic violence.

BEYOND THE YEAR 2000

In the remainder of this chapter, we "predict" the state of criminal justice policy on domestic violence as the world moves into the next century. We see little in the future that has not already been implemented somewhere. Trends are evident not only in current practices but also in guidelines from such influential documents as the *Attorney General's Task Force on Family Violence Final Report* (U.S. Department of Justice, 1984) and the Violent Crime Control and Law Enforcement Act of 1994. What we describe here are policies likely to gain widespread acceptance as standards for criminal justice practice beyond the year 2000.

Law

We expect state legislatures to continue the trend, begun in the 1980s, of criminalizing wife battering as any other crime of violence. But policymakers, recognizing that domestic violence is a crime involving special and complicated relationships, will be forced to "customize" their interventions (Friedman & Shulman, 1990). We foresee a continuation of the proliferation of laws designed to protect victims, to increase the number of meaningful civil remedies for victims who are not participating in the criminal justice system, and to hold law enforcement officers accountable for their decisions—even if that means eliminating some of their historically unlimited discretion. More state legislatures and voters will consider adding what are known as "victims' bills of rights" to their state constitutions, thus giving victims of all crimes rights such as the right to be kept informed of the progress of a criminal case, the right to be notified of hearings, and the right to consult with the prosecutor concerning possible dispositions of the case.

New laws will enable the criminal and civil processes to operate more efficiently together. Legislators will increase the options for both battered women and officials by expanding the authority of civil courts to intervene and protect women. For example, lawmakers will criminalize the violation of traditional civil protections, such as orders of protection and restraining orders. State courts will also honor such orders even if they were issued by other jurisdictions; and federal prosecutors will opt to charge offenders who cross state lines while violating civil orders of protection.[9] "Federalization" of domestic violence crimes under VAWA will mean that, in certain instances, batterers may also face federal prosecution if they are subject to protective orders and exchange firearms.[10] State lawmakers will also adopt criminal laws designed to protect victims from "habitual batterers" in three primary areas. First, batterers will face a higher level of charges (and thus stiffer penalties) for their second battery on the same victim. Second, lawmakers will include the concept of "serial batterers" in the definition of *habitual battering* to account for new victims of one violent offender. Third, more states will enact legislation making stalking behavior a criminal offense.

State legislatures will endeavor to protect municipalities from equal protection litigation by enacting laws mandating training on domestic violence under a certified curriculum, by requiring police reports and data collection, and by mandating arrest for battery when probable cause exists under narrowly defined circumstances.[11] We further expect legislative action empowering police officers to initiate arrest warrants when suspected batterers are not on-scene when the officers respond, a practice found to have a preventive impact in the Omaha experiment (Dunford, 1990).

Finally, we foresee legislatures passing comprehensive "family violence prevention acts"[12] to expand the array of coordinated criminal and civil remedies available to victims of wife battering and their children and to consolidate statutes involving divorce, orders of protection, custody, visitation, and the like. Increasingly, public officials recognize that the difficult problems of reducing crime and poverty and of improving the health and well-being of families need solutions that stretch beyond popular rhetoric and quick fixes. Patchwork remedies often are ineffective because they are narrowly limited to addressing a specific event rather than the complex problem. The prevalence of habitual domestic violence demands interventions by more than criminal justice agencies. But too often, other relevant agencies are not incorporated as part of a coordinated response.

For example, a family may be involved with a number of separate governmental agencies in inconsistent ways. The wife may be receiving help with domestic violence and child support, the delinquent child may be involved with a probation worker, an abused sibling could be involved with the social welfare department, and the school may have assigned a social worker or truancy officer. Policies implemented by one professional may cause counterproductive results in another area. An understanding of applicable policy research will facilitate organized efforts to develop successful, integrated strategies. The VAWA provides for funded demonstrations and evaluation of coordinated, community-based interventions with representation of multiple community sectors, in addition to criminal justice.

Most notably, these functions will be adopted by specialized courts designed to replace the current "compartmentalized" approach under which in two or even three courts may issue separate orders with contradictory provisions regarding contact between victims, defendants, and their children. (Such "family courts" are described in the section "Judicial Policy in this chapter.)"

Police Policy

"To Protect and to Serve"

The next decade will see police departments across the United States implement policies acknowledging both their capacity and their responsibility to protect victims of domestic violence from continuing abuse. Research findings have shown that police intervention in domestic disturbances can reduce the chance of repeat violence, at least in the short term. These findings have reinforced public and political sentiment expecting more of the police in providing security for victims of domestic violence. During the 1980s, several celebrated lawsuits against police for failing to take action to protect victims have forced police departments to evaluate their policies for responding to violent domestic disturbances. We foresee the implementation of policies mandating a vigorous police response to domestic violence, including reporting, providing immediate assistance to victims (as in finding shelter or other protective services), giving victims information on legal remedies, making referrals to social service agencies, and making reports to document victim complaints. Departments will collect data for detecting violent relationships as they set up specialized investigative units to coordinate law enforcement with other agencies oriented toward assisting victims of domestic violence.

Probable Cause Arrest

Policies encouraging officers to arrest suspects will provide a continuing emphasis on the duty of police to provide immediate security to victims of interpersonal violence. Many departments now promote arrest as a decisive and preferred action to prevent the short-term recurrence of violence. We expect to see such policies adopted universally. But policy reforms will be less oriented toward mandating specific police practices than toward mandating action under guidelines favoring officer discretion in the interest of protecting victims. This emphasis on arrest and on the officer's own "judgment call" will entail new attention to training officers on the dynamics of domestic violence and the consequences of alternative actions.

Police officers will also be expected to act decisively in those disturbances where violence may not yet have occurred but where it is likely, as given a prior history of police intervention for alleged violence. When appropriate, arrest for such crimes as disorderly conduct, public intoxication, and criminal trespass will be expected to head off eventual violence. Alternatively, police will assist victims in securing shelter from their abusers.

Police-Initiated Arrest Warrants

Violent men seeking to avoid arrest do not remain at the scenes of their crimes to await the police. When offenders are absent, police officers may advise victims on how to protect themselves for the moment, as well as how to initiate charges with the prosecutor's office. The Omaha experiment demonstrates that officers can themselves take further action to protect victims by initiating warrants independent of the victim actions. Although the Omaha findings may not hold in all jurisdictions, just as on-scene arrest provides a discretionary tool for officers, police-initiated warrants will enhance an officer's capacity to prevent violence.

Specialized Domestic Violence Investigative Units

Future police participation in a coordinated system response to domestic violence will center on specialized investigative units working closely with social service agencies as well as other criminal justice agencies. Such units have several areas of responsibility. First, the unit oversees the implementation of departmental policies for domestic violence, including the investigation of reported violence. Second, it coordinates the service of warrants and orders of protection. Third, it joins with other agencies in detecting relationships at risk, including those involving children of violent adults. Finally, the unit collects data for analyzing domestic violence and for identifying "hot spots" for proactive intervention by either law enforcement or social service agencies.

Currently, police shoulder public expectations for criminal justice intervention to prevent recurring violence against women. In the future, however, the onus of protecting victims will shift to prosecutors and courts. Police patrol officers will act primarily as crisis intervenors with responsibility for immediate victim protection. Their actions will be judged on their effectiveness in removing suspects from violent settings and initiating judicial processes for long-term assistance to victims rather than short-term deterrence from arrest.

Prosecution Policy

Prosecution policy for the next century will be more attentive to the needs of battered women seeking relief from violence. Changing social norms and values, along with significant policy research, will challenge prosecutors to implement procedures acknowledging the public's ownership of the criminal justice system and checking prosecutorial discretion. Policies meant to support victims' individual efforts to find security will bolster those with direct preventive effects. Prosecutors will carefully calibrate their official responses to produce specific preventive outcomes. Here, we note some of the major changes signaling model policies for the future.

Central Role of the Victim

Breaking the victim's cycle of violence and responding to her needs will be central to future prosecutorial policy. Although this perspective seems obvious, the traditional system has not generally pivoted around the victim and what is best for her. A strong victim orientation will guide new policies.

In the previous few years, criminal justice initiatives for domestic violence victims emphasized on-scene arrests. But equally dramatic changes have not occurred for the woman who files her own complaint or does not present a legal request at all. Increasingly, prosecutorial responses will involve a range of services extending more aggressively to the point at which the battery occurs, regardless of police intervention. Prosecutors' citizen intake bureaus will become more open to filing charges against batterers based on complaints from abused women. At the same time, prosecutors will undertake a conscientious effort to fashion effective immediate sanctions comparable to those following an on-scene police arrest. Accused batterers will be arrested on warrants and ordered to stay away from the complaining victims. In essence, we foresee citizen complaint cases being treated more like outright arrests in terms of prosecutor response. The practice of prosecutors simply passing cases from the police to a court, without attending to victim needs at the time, will cease.

The victim orientation will result in an expressed effort to empower battered women. Officials will come to understand their responsibility to balance the differences in power between an aggressor and his female victim; this task involves both an awareness of the system's capacity for supporting victims' self-protective actions and an understanding that her actions may be ineffective if she is denied control over the process (Ford, 1991). Thus, whether the victim is allowed to "drop charges" or to participate in determining the case outcome, and how that information is communicated to the defendant, will be increasingly important.[13] A guiding principle for empowering battered women is that prosecutors stand in alliance with victims. The future impact of criminal justice will be gauged, in part, by the reliability of that alliance—what services it can mobilize for victims and how vigorously it responds to continuing abuse by a suspect.

Case Monitoring

Expanding technological advances for computer-assisted case management enable prosecutors to more closely supervise cases. Technology will facilitate the monitoring of defendants—detecting those with previous complaints by the same or another victim, supervising defendants who are diverted to counseling programs—and will aid in keeping readily available information on victims (e.g., names, addresses, complaints/affidavits, contacts and notifications, special interests or desired criminal justice outcomes).

Through computer tracking systems, especially those that integrate police and prosecutor databases, prosecutors' offices will be able to reach all victims known to the system, even without formal processing. These contacts may be in person—through advocate outreach, through hospital social workers in emergency rooms, in conjunction with shelters—or by letters from the prosecutor's office. Tracking information will enable officials to initiate multiple agency interventions to protect those at risk, especially where instances of repeated abuse occur.

A Wider and Integrated Range of Official Actions

The coordination of functions and the merging of sanctions is readily apparent in efforts to prevent contact between the abuser and his victim. We expect to see a fruition of those efforts, with civil courts having sweeping authority to grant protective orders denying the abuser contact with the victim and her family and excluding him from the victim's premises and nearby areas. Those orders will be centrally registered and their violation criminalized, so as to enable intervention even before a violent act is committed. Prosecutors will more frequently and routinely secure "no contact" orders at the preliminary hearings after a battery, affording similar protection as that offered by a civil order.

The debate about the efficacy of various sanctions will continue. We expect new research fashioned after the Indianapolis Prosecution Experiment; however, we do not expect new criminal justice research to be definitive or consistent from city to city. Effective prosecution policies will occur only after rigorous evaluations of rehabilitative interventions, such that effective treatment can be mandated under the threat of criminal sanctions. The uncertainty concerning the relative sanctions' effects on recidivism, coupled with pressure to avoid jail overcrowding, will result in prosecutors diverting increasing numbers of defendants out of the criminal justice system. Men who have been diverted will enter treatment under carefully negotiated contracts. And, as realistic criteria for treatment success are identified, prosecutors will use such rehabilitative counseling agreements as a strategy for assuaging victims who might otherwise not prosecute.

Judicial Policy

Judges have a greater role in the criminal justice system's response to wife battering than has been acknowledged in recent literature. They are involved at virtually all critical points in the process: They approve warrants and affirm probable cause for arrests; they set bond and issue protective orders; they approve pretrial diversion agreements; they adjudge guilt and sentence offenders; and ultimately they rule on violations of probation. Yet, judges have received little attention in discussions of wife battery and criminal justice. Perhaps this is because they hear only a small proportion of the cases identified by the police and prosecutors. Or perhaps they are sufficiently responsive to the plight of battered women that they are not associated with the insensitivity and recalcitrance noted in other agencies. In our experience, however, judges have generally been slow to recognize wife battering as a serious criminal issue that they might control.

Discretion and Judgments

Judges will become more responsive to the problem of battered women as society grows more disposed toward criminal justice solutions. Prodded by increasing numbers of women on the bench, by community sentiment, by legislative mandate, and by the demands of cases presented by police and prosecutors, judges will exercise their powers in ways consistent with ensuring victim safety while protecting the rights of the accused. Specifically, judges will routinely support police intervention by approving warrantless on-scene arrests for battery based on probable cause (rather than on the direct observation of a law enforcement officer). Judges will also approve warrants on charges initiated by victims and will see that they result in arrests.

As society comes to expect more concern on the part of the judiciary, judges will find themselves under greater scrutiny by victim advocates and, where relevant, by an intolerant electorate. Communities will hold judges accountable for pretrial release decisions, as well as for sentencing decisions. Legislation may serve to "regulate" judges by replacing some of their discretion with guidelines for pretrial release and postconviction sentencing in areas related to family violence. For example, statutes may specify certain factors to be weighted (and certain factors that should *not* be weighted) by judges when making release and sentencing decisions. Judges will receive training in adjudication oriented toward preventing domestic abuse at their continuing judicial education seminars, as encouraged by the VAWA.

Bail Decisions

Because of a growing recognition of the lethality of domestic violence, as well as the fact that it frequently escalates in severity, judges or court administrators will alter their bail policies in a number of ways. Some will include the imposition of a fixed "holding period" (e.g., 12 hours) for individuals arrested for crimes involving domestic violence, as a means of controlling those offenders who would otherwise be released and immediately commit new violence. Other policies will affect bail commissioners, requiring them to contact victims during the offenders' bail interviews in order to develop pretrial release plans that ensure the victims' safety after an initial police arrest or warrant arrest. Although most offenders will eventually be released pending trial, there are advantages to holding wife-battery offenders overnight at least until their initial hearing. This short pretrial incapacitation of a batterer provides an opportunity for the victim to safeguard her belongings and to seek shelter elsewhere. Criminal justice and social service agencies have the opportunity to contact the victim to provide information on what she can expect to happen and her options. If a batterer has not been immediately released, the prosecutor and the victim can provide important information to the judge to guide the decision whether release on recognizance should be granted, what bail should be set, and what conditions should be placed on this release, including protective orders.

State legislators and voters may also approve changes in state constitutions and statutes allowing judges to consider a defendant's dangerousness to both the individual victim and the public at large; this mirrors recent federal developments. Currently, judges in most states may consider only the likelihood a defendant will reappear for future court proceedings when making bail decisions.

Protection Orders

The process for obtaining orders of protection[14] will become more accessible than ever for victims. The procedures will be streamlined for victims who, often acting without legal counsel, need a user-friendly court system. Orders will be available on an emergency basis, even at times when courts are traditionally closed. Victims will also find it easier to proceed without paying any fees or court costs, as policymakers take a more realistic view of victims' economic dependence on their abusers. With legislative changes supporting a coordinated criminal and civil intervention process, victims will enjoy access to a wider array of remedies—remedies that were traditionally available only to married persons getting a divorce. For example, victims will be able to obtain evictions of their abusers, child support, and visitation, in addition to gaining the no-contact provisions historically available in orders of protection. Finally, with the criminalization of the violations of these orders, judges will be able to provide more effective sanctions.

Sentencing Alternatives

Domestic violence is one of the few crimes in which victim and offender share an intimate relationship, often living together. Many victims are understandably reticent about making sentencing recommendations when in the presence of their abusers. The advent of victims' bills of rights may pose a solution to the potential Sixth Amendment problem that is created if judges elect to obtain a recommendation from a victim outside the defendant's presence; many statutes allow judges to appoint "victim representatives" to speak on behalf of individual victims during the sentencing phase of a case.

Incarceration is the one sentence clearly conveying the seriousness of wife battering as a criminal offense. But, for a variety of reasons, including jail and prison overcrowding, the relative ineffectiveness of incarceration for preventing further violence, and victim reluctance to have their batterers incarcerated, judges will impose alternative sanctions, as described in the "Corrections" section below.

Judges will also endeavor to find rehabilitative alternatives for preventing continuing abuse of the original victim, as well as of women in future relationships. Thus, court-mandated treatment of batterers will increase, but the efficacy of the treatment may be influenced by three factors: First, new research on the relative effectiveness of treatment alternatives for different types of batterers will point to preferred options; second, judges or their staff must employ reliable assessment tools to match individual offenders with appropriate treatment programs; third, policymakers must make certain that the assessment tools screen for those individuals for whom treatment is *not* appropriate ("pathological" batterers).

Finally, judges will enforce conditions of probation and impose meaningful sanctions for violations of probation, in recognition of the importance of holding batterers accountable for their behavior. With prison overcrowding, probation violators may not be jailed for the full term of their original sentences. Instead, judges will impose incrementally longer sentences for each violation.

Specialized Courts

We foresee widespread development of courts empowered to hear both criminal and civil issues pertaining to couples in violent relationships. These family courts have jurisdiction over not only criminal family violence cases but also dissolutions of marriages, paternity establishment and child support enforcement actions, child protective services cases and some delinquency cases, and orders of protection. Such specialized courts provide a coordinated, holistic approach to ending family violence and to ensuring victim safety by facilitating information sharing and coordination among all of the different agencies that might encounter a particular family.

Specialized courts will support "vertical prosecution," whereby a single prosecutor manages a case from screening through adjudication and, when necessary, probation hearings. These courts will help prosecutors monitor each offender more closely and keep in contact with each victim, thus reducing victim attrition. Where comprehensive family courts are impractical for some jurisdictions because of a high volume of cases, policymakers in those areas may opt for specialized courts that hear criminal cases involving domestic violence only and mandate information sharing among all the relevant agencies and courts.

Corrections

Corrections agencies play a critical part in protecting a victim because they implement court-imposed sanctions. They will assume greater responsibility in the future for closer supervision of convicted batterers, for overseeing the effectiveness of counseling/rehabilitative agencies, for hearing victims' reports of probation/parole violations and acting on them, and for notifying victims of release or escape.

Incarceration

Jails and prisons are unlikely to play a major direct role in the future criminal justice response to wife battering, for reasons cited above. These institutions will be used selectively and in innovative ways as the final stages in a series of graduated sanctions to deal with wife batterers on the basis of seriousness and nature of the current charge and on the prior record and present circumstances of the offender. Incarceration will figure in future wife-battery policy primarily at the pretrial stage to protect victims, as a coercive trial outcome threatened to ensure other sanctions are fulfilled, and as a response to violations of other sanctions imposed.

Probation

After conviction, corrections will be used in a variety of ways to ensure the success of less intrusive sanctions. The most prevalent will be the use of suspended sentences in which prison terms are assessed but then suspended as long as the offender successfully completes other conditions, such as committing no further violence, paying fines and restitution to the victim, performing community service work, or completing a treatment program. Offenders with a prior record of violence or probation violations or who had trouble keeping conditions of pretrial release may be given split sentences involving a probation term preceded by a short term of incarceration to serve as a reminder to the offender of the consequences of not abiding by the conditions of probation. The incarceration term may be served all at once or intermittently, as on successive weekends, evenings, or vacations. In the future, this short jail term may be served at halfway houses for batterers where group or individual counseling can be combined with incapacitation.

Future policy will also employ corrections within the community in "intensive supervision probation" programs. Intensive supervision will provide more stringent control than usually experienced by men on probation. It allows offenders to maintain employment to pay child support and victim restitution, but still provides a substantial degree of security for the victim. Current programs usually involve some form of curfew or house arrest, with offenders being allowed to leave their homes for such purposes as work, school, community service work, probation and counseling sessions, and religious services. Future restraints on the offender's movements will be enforced by frequent contact with a probation officer and may be enhanced by some type of passive or active electronic monitoring device.

Probation will also be used to force participation in rehabilitative programs. As discussed above, currently there is no conclusive evidence that batterer treatment programs are effective in rehabilitating violent men. But we expect to see considerable research on rehabilitation programs in the near future. The need for evaluation research is obvious. For one, courts currently are sentencing men to unproven rehabilitative programs. At some point, the programs will be held accountable if they cannot demonstrate success. Also, continuing research on batterers will enable programs to tailor their treatments to more refined classifications of batterers for more general use in shaping coordinated services.

Home Detention

The improvement and expansion of electronic monitoring technology may provide the greatest security short of incarceration for victims who face continual threats of violence after separating from their offenders. A central computer stores information on the restrictions to movement for each offender. "Passive" electronic devices do not provide constant monitoring, but rather the computer generates random calls to offenders who must verify their presence through voice identification, via a video image, or by inserting a wristlet into a verification box attached to the telephone. "Active" electronic devices involve placing a transmitter on the ankle, waist, wrist, or neck of the offender. If the offender is not within a 150-foot radius of a receiving device in the home at scheduled times, the probation office is notified (Ball, Huff, & Lilly, 1988; Morris & Tonry, 1990). These technologies will be replaced by continuous-monitoring, satellite tracking systems so that victims can be equipped with portable receivers to detect the presence of a transmitter worn by the batterer anywhere. Victims would be instructed on appropriate measures to take if the signal indicated the batterer was within a certain distance. If necessary, the alarm will not only alert police but also locate the victim and offender anyplace in the nation. This sort of sophisticated electronic monitoring of domestic violence offenders will become commonplace with reduced costs, with the proliferation of antistalking laws,[15] and with the shortage of prison space.

Straight prison terms will be reserved for felony battery cases and more serious misdemeanor charges, especially those involving repeat offenders. Special prison programs for violent offenders, including wife batterers, will be developed as effective rehabilitative strategies are identified. These would be therapeutic communities within the prison but with ties to outside social services and perhaps using former batterers as peer counselors.[16]

CONCLUSION

As we presume to look into the future, we are reminded how ethereal policy can be. The best of extant policies may be lost to fiscal cuts or political whim. The best of anticipated policies may never be implemented because of a host of constraints and hindrances—for example, value conflicts, financial crises, officials' recalcitrance, jail overcrowding, and fear of litigation.

Indeed, rapidly changing social conditions and criminal problems will force policy adaptations. The mounting press of cases and workloads, the complicating challenge of drugs in communities, the impotence of the expected social control functions of schools and families, and the failure of law enforcement in other areas cause fundamental shifts in operating styles and strategies of criminal justice agencies.

With respect to family violence, whether it is committed against children, spouses, or elders, criminal justice practitioners sit at a pivotal point in deciding what intervention from arrest, to prosecution, to counseling is most appropriate. Increasingly, urban families face multiple problems with limited resources. The risks to their well-being will force a cooperative and coordinated response by social service agencies, along with police, prosecutors, judges, advocates, and correction officials; for example, court-mandated batterers' groups may be combined with substance abuse programs or drug testing. And child abuse investigators will more frequently make inquiries concerning spousal abuse that result in more frequent and broader based and coordinated interventions involving multiple family members. This will lead not only to more effective criminal case dispositions but also to results that treat underlying problems in a more holistic manner. Informed by important practical research, unburdened by traditional gender stereotypes, and concerned about the deleterious effects of spousal violence, the criminal justice system will join other community institutions in combating abuse through more comprehensive, though more individually tailored, programs.

NOTES

1. The term *domestic violence* is used here as a generic descriptor of violence against women by their conjugal partners. Elsewhere in the chapter, we use *wife*

battery, a synonym meant to more precisely convey the criminality of such violence. The violence may range from simple misdemeanor assault and battery through the most serious of felony assaults. Our discussion centers on misdemeanor battery, the crime charged in the vast majority of cases.

2. This historical summary is based principally on Elizabeth Pleck's *Domestic Tyranny* (1987). The general changes in the domains of criminal justice roles are discussed in William McDonald's "The Prosecutor's Domain" (1979).

3. Pleck (1987) reports that antebellum feminists were primarily interested in seeking reforms in divorce laws to protect women from drunken and cruel husbands. Wife beating, however, became a law-and-order issue in the late 19th century as legislatures considered harsh punishments, including especially whipping posts, as means of deterring violent men. Only Maryland passed a whipping-post law for wife beating during that period.

4. Domestic violence was so certified with issuance of the final report of the Attorney General's Task Force on Family Violence in 1984 (U.S. Department of Justice, 1984). Currently, however, in some major urban jurisdictions, criminal justice agencies, especially district attorneys' offices and courts, are still unwilling to act on complaints of domestic violence.

5. See, for example, the U.S. Department of Justice (1984).

6. Mederer and Gelles (1989) argue that at least five factors led to the adoption of current control strategies: (a) the feminist movement's concern over criminal justice indifference to violence against women, (b) the findings of the Minneapolis experiment, (c) the publication of the Attorney General's Task Force report, (d) the threat of litigation on the heels of a $2.3 million judgment against the police in *Thurman v. City of Torrington,* and (e) the "control atmosphere" accompanying an era of political conservatism.

7. The Violence Against Women Act (VAWA) is Title IV of the Violent Crime Control and Law Enforcement Act of 1994.

8. The VAWA includes the Civil Rights Remedies for Gender-Motivated Violence Act, which in Section 40302 amends 42 U.S.C. Section 13981 to provide for a new civil right: the right to be free from crimes of violence motivated by gender. Although this language is gender neutral, it is expected that most of the litigation commenced under this new section will involve domestic violence allegations. Of course, favorable judgments, monetary damages, and attorneys' fees may be merely symbolic in nature, depending on the abuser's financial situation. One assumes that it will not be cost efficient for victims to bring lawsuits under this section unless the abusers are wealthy.

9. The VAWA also contains a subsection entitled the "Safe Homes for Women Act of 1994," which amends the United States Code to mandate that state courts honor and enforce protective orders issued by courts of different states (the constitutional term for this is "full faith and credit"). This section of the VAWA also creates federal crimes for violating protective orders when the offender crosses state lines to do so.

10. Title XI of the 1994 Violent Crime Control and Law Enforcement Act contains language prohibiting domestic abusers from receiving and/or disposing of firearms. This legislation is codified in Title 18 of the United States Code.

11. Although mandatory arrest laws have been enacted in response to litigation against the police, we do not think many jurisdictions that do not now mandate arrest will do so in the future without qualification. Contradictory findings on the effectiveness of arrest as a deterrent (Fagan & Garner, 1995) and failures in implementing mandatory policies (Ferraro, 1989) currently favor discretionary arrest powers except in life-threatening circumstances. Through its grants program, however, the VAWA

calls for implementation of mandatory or proarrest policies for responding to domestic violence. It remains to be seen which policy orientation is favored in grants.

12. For examples of such acts, see Lerman's "A Model State Act: Remedies for Domestic Abuse" (1984) or the newer, more comprehensive "Family Violence: A Model State Code" (1994), published by the National Council of Juvenile and Family Court Judges. The adoption of such model laws, along with the proliferation of federal laws concerning domestic violence, should help promote much-needed interstate uniformity and eliminate the current situation in which a victim in one state may enjoy greater protection from domestic abuse than her neighbor in the next state.

13. The one prosecution policy found to protect battered women in Indianapolis is to give a woman permission to have charges dismissed, following an initial hearing, while assuring her of continuing support no matter what she decides (Ford, 1993; Ford & Regoli, 1993). Because a woman is least likely to be battered anew if she "follows through" with prosecution, however, the prosecutor's office discourages dropping and grants her a say in the decision to offer a defendant pretrial diversion to counseling or to prosecute him with alternative sentencing options.

14. Orders of protection include what are variously called restraining orders, no-contact orders, stay-away orders, and protective orders.

15. The VAWA contains a "National Stalker and Domestic Violence Reduction" section, which encourages states to forward data about stalkers and domestic violence offenders who violate orders of protection to the National Crime Information Center (NCIC), which is the same national database used by the FBI to track an offender's criminal history on a national scale. State jurisdictions also use the NCIC's records to determine whether an individual has engaged in criminal activity elsewhere in the United States. As the number of states with antistalking laws increases, prosecutors will become more creative with charging decisions and will begin to charge domestic abusers with stalking (in addition to other, more traditional crimes) when they are able to detect clear patterns of intentional harassment, threats, and actual harm.

16. Such a "community" might be modeled after the therapeutic drug treatment programs currently found in prisons (e.g., Wexler, Falkin, & Lipton, 1990).

REFERENCES

Ball, R. A., Huff, C. R., & Lilly, J. R. (1988). *House arrest and correctional policy: Doing time at home.* Newbury Park, CA: Sage.

Berk, R. A., Campbell, A., Klap, R., & Western, B. (1992). A Bayesian analysis of the Colorado Springs Spouse Abuse Experiment. *Journal of Criminal Law and Criminology, 83*(1), 170-200.

Binder, A., & Meeker, J. (1988). Experiments as reforms. *Journal of Criminal Justice, 16,* 347-358.

Dunford, F. W. (1990). System-initiated warrants for suspects of misdemeanor domestic assault: A pilot study. *Justice Quarterly, 7,* 631-653.

Dunford, F. W., Huizinga, D., & Elliott, D. S. (1989). *The Omaha Domestic Violence Police Experiment: Final report.* Washington, DC: National Institute of Justice.

Fagan, J., & Garner, J. (1995). Published results of the NIJ Spouse Assault Replication Program: A critical review. *Journal of Quantitative Criminology, 8,* 1-29.

Ferraro, K. J. (1989). Policing woman battering. *Social Problems, 36,* 61-74.

Ford, D. A. (1991). Prosecution as a victim power resource: A note on empowering women in violent conjugal relationships. *Law & Society Review, 25,* 313-334.

Ford, D. A. (1993). *The Indianapolis Domestic Violence Prosecution Experiment: Final report.* Washington, DC: National Institute of Justice.

Ford, D. A., & Regoli, M. J. (1992). The preventive impacts of policies for prosecuting wife batterers. In E. S. Buzawa & C. G. Buzawa (Eds.), *Domestic violence: The criminal justice response.* Westport, CT: Auburn House.

Ford, D. A., & Regoli, M. J. (1993). The criminal prosecution of wife assaulters: Process, problems, and effects. In N. Z. Hilton (Ed.), *Legal responses to wife assault: Current trends and evaluation.* Newbury Park, CA: Sage.

Friedman, L. N., & Shulman, M. (1990). Domestic violence: The criminal justice response. In A. J. Lurigio, W. G. Skogan, & R. C. Davis (Eds.), *Victims of crime: Problems, policies, and programs.* Newbury Park, CA: Sage.

Hirschel, J. D., Hutchison, I. W., & Dean, C. W. (1992). The failure of arrest to deter spouse abuse. *Journal of Research in Crime and Delinquency, 29*(1), 7-33.

Lerman, L. G. (1984). A model state act: Remedies for domestic abuse. *Harvard Journal on Legislation, 21,* 61-69.

McDonald, W. F. (1979). The prosecutor's domain. In W. F. McDonald (Ed.), *The prosecutor.* Beverly Hills, CA: Sage.

Mederer, H. J., & Gelles, R. J. (1989). Compassion or control: Intervention in cases of wife abuse. *Journal of Interpersonal Violence, 4,* 25-43.

Morris, N., & Tonry, M. (1990). *Between prison and probation.* New York: Oxford University Press.

National Council of Juvenile and Family Court Judges. (1994). *Family violence: A model state code.* Reno, NV: State Justice Institute.

Pate, A. M., & Hamilton, E. E. (1992). Formal and informal deterrents to domestic violence: The Dade County Spouse Assault Experiment. *American Sociological Review, 57,* 691-697.

Pleck, E. (1987). *Domestic tyranny.* New York: Oxford University Press.

Sherman, L. W., & Berk, R. A. (1984). The specific deterrent effects of arrest for domestic assault. *American Sociological Review, 49,* 261-272.

Sherman, L. W., & Cohn, E. G. (1989). The impact of research on legal policy: The Minneapolis Domestic Violence Experiment. *Law & Society Review, 23,* 117-144.

Sherman, L. W., Schmidt, J. D., Rogan, D. P., Smith, D. A., Gartin, P. R., Cohn, E. G., Collins, D. J., & Bacich, A. R. (1992). The variable effects of arrest on criminal careers: The Milwaukee Domestic Violence Experiment. *Journal of Criminal Law and Criminology, 83,* 137-169.

Thurman v. City of Torrington, 595 F. Supp. 1521 (1985).

U.S. Department of Justice. (1984). *Attorney General's Task Force on Family Violence: Final report.* Washington, DC: Author.

Wexler, H. K., Falkin, G. P., & Lipton, D. S. (1990). Outcome evaluation of a prison therapeutic community for substance abuse treatment. *Criminal Justice and Behavior, 17,* 71-92.

Author Index

Subject Index

misdemeanor vs. felony, 58, 102,
154, 159, 179-180, 182, 187
pathological vs. criminal behavior,
123-124, 139
policy recommendations, 51-53
predictors of, 136-139, 229-234,
242 (n2)
private vs. public issue, 49, 52,
92-93, 133, 153
substance abuse and, 65-66, 81
(n3), 187, 194, 202, 205
(figure), 208
unreported incidents, 63, 72, 79,
89, 142, 236
victim-blaming in, 101
See also Battered women;
Offenders; Recidivism
Drugs. *See* Substance abuse
Duluth, MN, arrest research project,
38, 40, 144

Education:
programs for victims, 106-109, 188
See also Counseling
Elderly, domestic violence and, 18, 129
Electronic monitoring technology, 261
Employment status:
of offenders, 46-49, 47 (table), 51,
64-65, 69-70, 125-126, 131-132
of victims, 215
Entrapment:
defined, 122, 147 (n4)
loss of autonomy from, 132, 143
Ex parte orders, 168

Families:
abuse within vs. battering, 129,
134-135
coordinated response for, 250,
258-259, 264 (n12)
crime control issues within, 15-16,
22-24, 134-136
See also Children
Family courts, 250, 258-259, 264 (n12)
Family therapy. *See* Counseling
Family therapy model, intervention
strategy of, 23-24
FBI domestic violence data, 2-3
Fear:
chronic, 123, 147 (n5)

of retaliation, 64, 99-101, 219-220,
236-237, 239
Feminism:
criticism of replication studies, 179
domestic violence activisim, 31-33,
119-120, 127, 130, 244-245,
263 (n3)
inequality and violence, 22-24,
119-124, 134-136, 147, (n3-7)
Florida replication study, 45-48, 47
(table), 245

Georgia, replication study, 45-46

Harrell-Smith restraining order study:
complaints in, 216, 217 (table)
conclusions, 237-242
enforcement in, 234-237, 235
(table), 239-240
permanent restraining orders in,
219-221, 229
recidivism in, 223-225, 224
(figure), 226-228 (figures),
229-234, 242 (n2)
sample, 215
victim assessment in, 218-220
violations in, 221-222, 239-241
High-risk offender, defined, 23
High-risk violence:
intervention strategies for, 22-24
measurement instrument for,
20-22, 21 (table)
Home detention, future use of, 261
Homicides:
by battered women, 20, 137
of battered women, 34, 100-101
statistics on, 2-3
threats, 216, 217 (table), 223-225,
224 (figure), 230, 235 (table),
236-237

Incarceration:
as deterrent, 14-15, 45, 110-111,
247, 258
future role of, 259-261
of victim, 109
recidivism after, 112-113
restraining order violation and,
208-209

About the Authors

Thomas L. Austin, Ph.D., is Professor of Criminal Justice at Shippensburg University, Shippensburg, Pennsylvania. He received his Ph.D. from the School of Criminal Justice at Michigan State University. He is working on an evaluation project for the Pennsylvania Department of Welfare. He is the author of numerous articles on criminal sentencing and independent living programs for foster children.

Carl G. Buzawa, J.D., is Adjunct Professor of Criminal Justice at the University of Massachusetts at Lowell and an attorney in private practice. He received his B.A. from the University of Rochester, his M.A. from the University of Michigan, and his J.D. from Harvard Law School. He is a coauthor of two books and numerous chapters and articles on the criminal justice response to domestic violence.

Eve S. Buzawa, Ph.D., is Professor of Criminal Justice at the University of Massachusetts at Lowell. She is a coauthor of two books on the criminal justice response to domestic violence and numerous chapters and articles. She is a Past President of the Northeast Association of Criminal Justice Sciences and a current board member for the Academy of Criminal Justice Sciences. She is the editor of a forthcoming series with Sage Publications on *Gender and Crime*, for which she is writing the volume *Women as Victims*.

David A. Ford, Ph.D., is Associate Professor and Chair of the Department of Sociology at Indiana University at Indianapolis. He was Principal Investigator for the Indianapolis Domestic Violence Prosecution Experiment and is a member of the National Research Council Panel on Research on Violence Against Women. He is active in community efforts to prevent family violence as Chair of the Indianapolis Mayor's Commission on Family Violence and as Director of the Training Project on Family Violence for Indiana Law Enforcement Officers.

Richard J. Gelles, Ph. D., is Professor of Sociology and Psychology and the Director of the Family Violence Research Program at the University of Rhode Island. He is the author or coauthor of 19 books and more than 100 articles and chapters on family violence. His most recent books are *Intimate Violence* (1989), *Physical Violence in American Families: Risk Factors and Adaptations in 8,145 Families* (1990), *Intimate Violence in Families* (Sage, 1990), and *Sociology: An Introduction* (1993), now in its fifth edition.

Stephen Goldsmith is Mayor of Indianapolis, Indiana. He previously held office as the Prosecuting Attorney of Marion County, Indiana. He is a Fellow in Criminal Justice at the John F. Kennedy School of Government at Harvard University and teaches part-time at Indiana University.

Adele Harrell, Ph.D., Director of the Program on Law and Behavior at the Urban Institute, has studied the justice system response to domestic violence for the past decade. Her research includes a quasi-experimental evaluation of the impact of court-ordered treatment for domestic violence offenders, an assessment of court-related practices in restraining orders for domestic violence victims, an analysis of violence and victim empowerment in custody and visitation disputes, and an evaluation of the Bureau of Justice Assistance 8-Site Family Violence Demonstration programs. Her *Guide to Research on Family Violence* was prepared for the National

Conference on Family Violence and the Courts, conducted by the National Council of Juvenile and Family Court Judges and the Urban Institute. She evaluated the police training provided under the Family Violence Prevention and Services Act. She received her Ph.D. in sociology from George Washington University in 1983.

Barbara Hart is Legal Director of the Pennsylvania Coalition Against Domestic Violence and is Associate Director of the Battered Women's Justice Project, a national resource center on law and practice. She is a coauthor of *Confronting Domestic Violence: Effective Police Response* and *Seeking Justice: Coordinated Justice System Intervention Against Domestic Violence*, and author of *Safety for Women: Monitoring Batterers' Programs, Accountability: Program Standards for Batterer Intervention Services*, and *Battering and Addiction: Consciousness Raising for Battered Women and Advocates*. In her private consultation and training practice, she provides assistance to lawmakers, business leaders, battered women's coalitions, and treatment programs for battering men.

J. David Hirschel, Ph.D., is Professor of Criminal Justice at the University of North Carolina at Charlotte. He earned his B.A. in law from Corpus Christi College, Cambridge University, and holds a Ph.D. in criminal justice from State University of New York at Albany. His publications and professional interests include spousal abuse, victims and the criminal justice system, drugs and crime, and comparative criminal justice.

Ira W. Hutchison, Ph.D., is Associate Professor of Sociology in the Department of Sociology, Anthropology, and Social Work at the University of North Carolina at Charlotte. He completed his M.A. and Ph.D. in sociology at the University of Notre Dame. His teaching and research interests are in the general area of family violence and social change.

Andrew R. Klein, Ph.D., has served as Chief Probation Officer of the Quincy District Court in Massachusetts since 1977. In 1985, his department was recognized by the American Probation and Parole Association for its model restitution program. In 1992, the court's Domestic Violence Program received the Ford Foundation's Innovations in State and Local Government Award. In 1994, he won the Sam Houston State University Award for publishing in corrections. He is a graduate of Harvard College and received his Ph.D. from Northeastern University's Law, Policy, and Society Program in 1994. He is also author of *Alternative Sentencing*, a legal text (1988). He teaches part-time at the University of Massachusetts at Lowell Graduate Program in Criminal Justice.

Peter K. Manning, Ph. D., is Professor of Sociology and Criminal Justice at Michigan State University. He is the author of many articles and chapters in scientific publications and has written 13 books, including *Semiotics and Fieldwork* (1987), *Symbolic Communication* (1988), and *Organizational Communication* (1992). His general research interests are in occupations and organizations and criminology, with special interest in fieldwork, semiotics, and qualitative methods.

Donald J. Rebovich, Ph.D., is Director of Research for the American Prosecutors Research Institute (APRI) in Alexandria, Virginia. In that role, he directs a number of national research programs dedicated to the study of the prosecution of environmental crime, organized crime, domestic violence, and drug-related offenses. He led APRI's national study of the prosecution of domestic violence offenses, focusing on the use of prosecution "no-drop" policies. Before coming to APRI, he served for 10 years with the Office of the New Jersey Attorney General. During that time, he conducted statewide evaluations of the effectiveness of victim assistance programs, drug courts, and speedy trial programs and studied characteristics of police physical activities and the use of reasonable force by local police. He received his B.S. in criminal justice and psychology from Trenton State College, and his M.A. and Ph.D. in criminal justice from Rutgers University.

Mary Jean Regoli is Research Coordinator for the Pediatric Psychology Laboratory of Indiana University at Bloomington. She also assists Bloomington's domestic violence and rape crisis center, Middle Way House, Inc., in evaluating prosecution of family violence cases in Monroe County, Indiana. She is investigating the impacts of alternative criminal justice policies on domestic violence in rural counties.

Ruth Reichard is a Municipal Court Judge in Marion County, Indiana. Her court is dedicated to cases of domestic violence. Previously, she was a Deputy Prosecutor in Marion County. She organized and was head of the prosecutor's Domestic Violence Unit. She frequently trains judges and other criminal justice officials on legal responses to family violence.

Janell D. Schmidt, M.S., is a supervisor of Child Protective Services in Milwaukee County, Wisconsin, and was formerly Director of the Milwaukee office of the Crime Control Institute. She served as the Site Manager of the Milwaukee Domestic Violence Experiment from 1987 to 1989 and is a contributing author of several publications and a book describing the experiment's results. She is managing community-oriented crime analysis efforts with the Milwaukee Police Department.

Lawrence W. Sherman, Ph.D., is Professor of Criminology at the University of Maryland and the President of the Crime Control Institute in Washington, D.C. He is an experimental criminologist whose best-known work is the Minneapolis Domestic Violence Experiment. He has directed 15 field experiments with close to $8 million in federal funds, obtained primarily under peer review competitions. The author of more than 80 books and professional journal articles, he earned his Ph.D. in sociology at Yale University.

Barbara E. Smith has been a consultant for the American Bar Association for more than 12 years. She has served as the Project Director or Principal Investigator for numerous federal projects for the National Institute of Justice, the State Justice Institute, the Office of Juvenile Justice and Delinquency Prevention, and the Bureau of Justice Assistance. She has worked in the victims field for nearly 20 years and has conducted research on family violence issues including the prosecution of child abuse cases, the effectiveness of restraining orders in domestic violence cases, the impact of a specialized domestic violence court, and the court processing of nonstranger violence cases. She has published widely on criminal justice topics and has directed many research and evaluation studies. She is coauthor (with A. Harrell and L. Newmark) of *Court Processing and the Effects of Restraining Orders for Domestic Violence Victims* (1993).

Evan Stark, M.S.W., Ph.D., is Associate Professor of Public Administration and Social Work at Rutgers University, Newark, New Jersey, and Codirector of the Domestic Violence Training Project, an award-winning program in New Haven, Connecticut. A founder of one of the nation's first battered women's shelters, he collaborated with Anne Flitcraft on pathbreaking research identifying domestic violence as the leading cause of female injury. He is a consultant on domestic violence to the National Institute of Justice, the Centers for Disease Control and Prevention, and other federal agencies and the recipient of numerous awards for his research and program development. He has testified on behalf of battered women and their children in more than 50 criminal and civil cases.

Murray A. Straus, Ph.D., is Professor of Sociology and Codirector of the Family Research Laboratory at the University of New Hampshire at Durham. He was the President of the National Council on Family Relations (1972-1973), Society for the Study of Social Problems (1988-1989), and Eastern Sociological Society (1990-1991). He received the American Sociological Society Award for contributions to undergraduate teaching (1979) and the Ernest W. Burgess Award of the National Council of Family Relations for outstanding research on the family (1977). He is the author or coauthor of 15 books and more than 200 articles, including *Family Measurement Techniques* (3rd ed., 1990), *Handbook of Intimate Violence* (1988), *Four Theories of Rape in the American Society* (1989), *Physical Violence in the American Families* (1990); and *Beating the Devil Out of Them: Corporal Punishment in American Families* (1994).